THE GREAT WAVE

. . .

THE GREAT WAVE

The Era of Radical Disruption and
the Rise of the Outsider

MICHIKO KAKUTANI

CROWN

NEW YORK

Published in the United States by Crown,
an imprint of the Crown Publishing Group, a division of
Penguin Random House LLC, New York.

Crown and the Crown colophon are
registered trademarks of Penguin Random House LLC.

LIBRARY OF CONGRESS CATALOGING-IN-PUBLICATION DATA
NAMES: Kakutani, Michiko, author.
TITLE: The great wave / Michiko Kakutani.
DESCRIPTION: First edition. | New York: Crown, [2024] |
Includes bibliographical references and index.
IDENTIFIERS: LCCN 2023034010 (print) | LCCN 2023034011 (ebook) |
ISBN 9780525574996 (hardback) | ISBN 9780525575016 (ebook)
SUBJECTS: LCSH: Civilization, Modern—21st century. | Uncertainty. |
Globalization. | Political culture. | Power (Social sciences) |
Elite (Social sciences)
CLASSIFICATION: LCC CB428 .K327 2023 (print) |
LCC CB428 (ebook) | DDC 909.83—dc23/eng/20230822
LC record available at https://lccn.loc.gov/2023034010
LC ebook record available at https://lccn.loc.gov/2023034011

Printed in the United States of America on acid-free paper

crownpublishing.com

2 4 6 8 9 7 5 3 1

FIRST EDITION

Book design by Barbara M. Bachman

CONTENTS

INTRODUCTION

T HE GREAT WAVE—IT'S ONE OF THE BEST-KNOWN and most widely reproduced images on the planet, an image that embodies the feelings of dread and hope that come with swift, unpredictable change.

Created around 1831 by the brilliant Japanese artist Katsushika Hokusai, the image has been embraced by multiple generations and cultures, from middle-class art lovers in Edo (Tokyo) delighted to acquire a wood-block print for the price of a bowl of noodles, to the nineteenth-century artists in France who helped formulate European modernism, to graffiti artists and skateboarders who have turned the wave into an instantly recognizable emoji and meme. Hokusai's print has been held up as a symbol of the Far East, the relationship between East and West, and the hazards of climate change and rising sea levels in the Anthropocene.

The Great Wave has been copied and reimagined, adapted, sampled, recycled, parodied, appropriated, and commodified. It now appears on surfboards, shower curtains, sneakers, umbrellas, watches, socks, scarves, towels, cuff links, coasters, and COVID masks. And, somehow, none of this merchandising has diluted the power of the original image, which continues to possess the resonance it did nearly two centuries ago.

The magic of Hokusai's print resides in both its imaginative detail—the terrifying surge of the gigantic wave, looming over three small fishing boats like a huge, pouncing tiger—and its metaphorical clout. When it first circulated in mid-nineteenth-century Japan (which was just opening to the world, after decades of isolation), the image reflected that island nation's anxieties about globalization: how the ocean, which had once protected Japan, was now a gateway for the invasion of foreigners and foreign ideas.

Today, *The Great Wave* once again embodies the dizzying turmoil and anxiety wrought by rapid change—this time, emotions belonging not to one nation but to an interconnected world, buffeted by political, economic, and technological upheaval.

The wave, of course, signifies the destructive power of nature and the chaotic forces of history that threaten to overwhelm us, sweeping away everything that feels familiar and safe. At first glance, that menacing wave is front and center in the print, but the viewer's eye is then drawn to the tiny image of Mount Fuji, way off in the distance, on the horizon line, tucked under the curl of the wave by a trick of perspective. Indeed, we are reminded that the formal title of this print is actually *Under the Wave off Kanagawa* and that it was published as part of Hokusai's popular wood-block series *Thirty-Six Views of Mount Fuji,* which offered three dozen portraits of the sacred mountain, beloved in Japan by poets, painters, and pilgrims and revered as a symbol of order and calm. The series was so popular that an extra ten prints were added to the sequence.

The images in *Thirty-Six Views* show groups of people and solitary individuals going about their daily lives—tending to their fishing boats and rice fields, sawing lumber and repairing roofs. Pilgrims and travelers make their way up mountains and across bridges, while those with a bit of leisure time take in a theater performance or enjoy some time in the country. Nature in these prints is beautiful yet menacing: Sudden changes in the weather threaten to blow people's lives off course, while the sea remains a source of sustenance but also peril.

By juxtaposing the ominous swell of the ocean with the serene presence of Mount Fuji in *The Great Wave*, Hokusai captured both the risks of daily life and the possibility of transcendence, the dynamic between foreboding and harmony, motion and stillness, chaos and transformation.

THE GREAT WAVE OF change breaking over today's world is sweeping away old certainties and assumptions and creating an inflection point of both opportunity and danger.

A confluence of crises, both immediate and long-term, has made the military acronym VUCA—meaning volatility, uncertainty, complexity, and ambiguity—feel like a perfect description of the third decade of the third millennium. The term was used at the Army War College in the late 1980s to describe a world that was more unpredictable than the bipolar one of the Cold War era, but it has come to feel increasingly resonant today, as one emergency—from COVID, to the January 6 insurrection, to Putin's invasion of Ukraine—cascades into another, as an increasingly interconnected globe amplifies the "butterfly effect" famously described by Ray Bradbury in the story "A Sound of Thunder."

Democracy is under threat in the United States, where Donald Trump and his Republican enablers are undermining trust in our electoral system and the rule of law. And democracy is under threat around the world, with the growth of extreme right-wing populism and the efforts of authoritarian regimes to assert their influence on the global stage. COVID killed more than 6.9 million people across the globe and accelerated an array of troubling dynamics—from social isolation to political polarization to growing inequalities of income, opportunity, and access to health care. And in 2023, new developments in artificial intelligence caused some technology experts to call for a pause in the development of advanced AI, warning it "could represent a profound change in the history of life on Earth," which its creators do not yet understand and cannot reliably control.

Looming over all of this, like Godzilla, is the dark cloud of climate change and its deadly consequences for the planet.

No wonder the present feels so bewildering and calamitous that many of us are reaching to dystopian fiction to describe our predicament—*1984, Do Androids Dream of Electric Sheep?, Neuromancer, 2001: A Space Odyssey, The Handmaid's Tale, It Can't Happen Here.*

Potent new dynamics are at work in this VUCA-verse, where technology is creating new asymmetries of power, and the process of disruption is driving change in politics, business, and technology. People are losing faith in old, top-down systems, and decentralized models of organization are being embraced by activists and entrepreneurs alike. In this ecosystem, more and more energy is moving from the margins toward the center, from the grassroots upward, from start-ups, protesters, and outsiders—a kind of countermovement to Big Tech's monopolistic consolidation of power and the efforts of authoritarian leaders to centralize power in their own hands.

The historian Melvin Kranzberg once observed that "technology is neither good nor bad, nor is it neutral," and the same might well be said of the growing influence of outsiders. Some have demonstrated their courage, resolve, and imaginative leadership, like Ukraine's president Volodymyr Zelensky, a former actor and comedian (elected by a landslide in 2019) who rallied the free world around his country after Vladimir Putin launched an unprovoked invasion in early 2022. Others, like Donald Trump, are harrowing case studies in the hazards posed by ignorance, venality, and narcissism, combined with shamelessness and power.

The democratizing effects of the internet have given outsiders of every sort—from climate activists, to white nationalists, to would-be social media "influencers"—the ability to circumvent old-school gatekeepers. And this at a time when mistrust in the government and traditional sources of authority have been building since the economic meltdown of 2008, which fueled populist anger at institutions and elites.

These developments have created a vertiginous moment that has exposed our interdependent world's profound vulnerabilities. Growing cracks appear in the post–World War II order and the ever-accelerating pace of social and technological change have created what Alvin Toffler described, five decades ago, as "future shock" and "adaptive breakdown."

But times of turmoil can also provide an opening for a reboot—for reassessing our priorities and operating principles. New ideas are more likely to gain traction during such periods, and newcomers are increasingly welcomed in once cloistered fields. In the early twenty-first century, outsiders are already revolutionizing science and medicine, while artists from once marginalized groups—including immigrants, African Americans, and women—are redefining literature, theater, music, and painting.

Times of tumult and chaos, the scholar Gershom Scholem once observed, can create "plastic hours"—"namely, crucial moments when it is possible to act. If you move then, something happens." What Scholem meant, his biographer George Prochnik explained, is that there are interludes when history is in volatile flux, "when migrations of peoples and changing political alliances dissolved the status quo," and "radical transformation" becomes a possibility.

IN FACT, HISTORY IS punctuated by stories of renewal, often in the midst of a war or crisis. For instance, in the 1930s, faced with a country reeling from the Great Depression—failing banks, bread lines, unemployment of nearly 25 percent—and the rise of Hitler abroad, Franklin D. Roosevelt went big with the New Deal, which not only rescued the flailing economy but reimagined the government's social contract with the public and helped restore faith in democratic institutions.

To use today's plastic hours to make essential course corrections, we must act quickly and decisively—not succumb to hand-wringing or denial or fatalism, those reflexive reactions in this age of information overload and outrage fatigue, when the 24-7 news cycle threatens to overwhelm us on a daily, even hourly basis, triggering cynicism and numbness. As a harrowing 2023 report from the UN's panel on climate change warned, "there is a rapidly closing window of opportunity to secure a liveable and sustainable future" by immediately making "deep, rapid, and sustained" reductions in fossil fuel consumption.

A similar urgency attends the crisis faced by American democracy today: whether we vote to affirm the Constitution and the rule of law, and the ideals of freedom and equal justice, or become an increasingly transactional and authoritarian state that defies the will of the people and tramples decades of progress made in civil rights and social justice.

That crisis is embodied in the person of the twice-impeached, four-times-indicted former president Donald Trump, who tried to overturn the 2020 election and incited a violent insurrection against the government. But it is hardly confined to him, as the Republican Party has doubled down on his lies and efforts to sow mistrust in democratic institutions. This contagion is so virulent that in mid-2023, a third of the country believes Trump's lie that the 2020 election was stolen from him; an estimated 16 percent buys into the deranged conspiracy theories of QAnon; and an estimated 7 percent believes violence is justified to restore Trump to the White House. Such developments point to how far today's emergency extends beyond politics— how it goes to our very ability to process reality, to tell the difference between fact and fiction, between truth and fantasy.

This book will look at how we got to this surreal point in time, and what happened during earlier hinge moments in history, when social and economic changes, coupled with groundbreaking advances in technology, disrupted old paradigms and led to both social upheaval and path-breaking innovation. It will examine the larger dynamics undermining traditional sources of authority today, the accelerating migration of once fringe or radical ideas into the mainstream, and the struggle, across the political spectrum and across the globe, to define this watershed moment.

The stakes could not be higher: whether we surrender to the gathering chaos or find a way forward to protect democratic values and institutions and create a more equitable and sustainable future.

THE GREAT WAVE

. . .

A HINGE MOMENT:
Morbid Symptoms, Cascading Crises, and a Looming Paradigm Shift

· · ·

When you want to know how things really work,
study them when they're coming apart.

—WILLIAM GIBSON, *Zero History*

IN 1930, WHILE IMPRISONED BY MUSSOLINI'S FASCIST regime in Italy, the philosopher Antonio Gramsci wrote this in his prison notebooks: "The crisis consists precisely in the fact that the old is dying and the new cannot be born; in this interregnum a great variety of morbid symptoms appear."

The world he was writing about had just plunged into the Great Depression; the Far Right was on the rise in Europe, emboldened by Mussolini's ascent in Italy; the Communist Party had taken a hard turn toward totalitarianism; and in Germany, a rabble-rouser named Adolf Hitler—who had been dismissed by intellectuals as a "pathetic dunderhead"—had made the Nazi Party a powerful new force in politics. Increasingly extreme political views, growing polarization, violence in the streets, and the decay of traditional institutions—these were among the "morbid symptoms" Gramsci saw developing in response to the social and economic inequalities that had multiplied in the wake of World War I and the Depression. People had grown increasingly disillusioned with their political representation, leading to a "crisis of authority"—a power vacuum that Mussolini would exploit, turning Italy into a police state and installing himself as dictator. Gramsci anticipated the dangers of this rising tide of fascism, but he also wanted to believe that, given time and political will, a post-interregnum future might one day be realized—a new era in which the morbid symptoms of hate and fear had been beaten back and a new, more progressive vision of society might begin to emerge.

There are distinct parallels between what Gramsci described in 1930 and our world today. 2020 was an annus horribilis—a dumpster fire of a year, a *Twilight Zone* marathon, as the COVID pandemic raged uncontrolled across the globe. 2021 opened with the January 6 insurrection at the Capitol—a near-death experience for American democracy, which continues as the Republican Party doubles down on Donald Trump's lies and contempt for the rule of law. And 2022 brought back nightmares from the twentieth century as Vladimir Putin launched a brutal, unprovoked war on Ukraine, which overnight turned a peaceful country in the middle of Europe in the twenty-first century into a hellscape of bombed-out buildings and dead and wounded civilians.

Putin's invasion of Ukraine and Xi Jinping's embrace of strongman tactics in China—as well as the two dictators' burgeoning alliance—are reminders of the growing threat of authoritarianism around the world. Iranian authorities have implemented a brutal crackdown on protesters. In Afghanistan, the Taliban has banned university and secondary school education for women and girls. Increasingly autocratic leaders in countries like Hungary and Turkey have exploded democratic norms. And in Israel, Benjamin Netanyahu moved to overhaul the judiciary in ways that would boost the power of his far-right coalition and dangerously undermine democratic checks and balances.

Freedom declined around the world for the seventeenth consecutive year, a 2023 Freedom House report found, with a deterioration in political rights and civil liberties in thirty-five countries. The watchdog group also pointed out that authoritarian leaders "are actively collaborating with one another to spread new forms of repression and rebuff democratic pressure," while longtime democracies are being threatened from within by "illiberal forces, including unscrupulous politicians willing to corrupt and shatter the very institutions that brought them to power."

It's a stark and chilling reversal of Francis Fukuyama's naïve declaration in 1989 that the unraveling of the Soviet Union meant "the end of history" and the "universalization of Western liberal democracy as the final form of human government." By the third decade of the twenty-first century, the new zeitgeist-y phrase was "permacrisis"—chosen as "word of the year" by *Collins Dictionary* in 2022—meaning "an extended period of instability and insecurity, especially one resulting from a series of catastrophic events."

In more and more countries, extreme ideas are surging into the mainstream. Far Right movements have gained new traction by weaponizing recent social dynamics, including (1) inequalities of income and opportunity that snowballed since the financial crash of 2008, stoking anger at experts and elites; (2) unease with the social, cultural, and demographic changes of recent decades, channeled by nihilistic leaders like Donald Trump into racist, misogynistic, and anti-LGBTQ+ bigotries; and (3) escalating resentment of globalism and European Union policies, which has led to a wave of growing nationalism and anti-immigrant hate.

At the same time, some analysts see the 2020s as an inflection point in history that could open a door not backward into the darkness of the mid-twentieth century but outward toward what the journalists John Micklethwait and Adrian Wooldridge have described as a "more united, more interconnected" future. That is, if Putin's invasion acts as an alarm bell and members of the Western alliance not only remain united behind Ukraine in defending democracy and the values of pluralism and freedom but also strengthen their economic and political ties to safely navigate a new era's shifting geopolitics.

Indeed, the German chancellor, Olaf Scholz, declared in 2022 that with the Russian invasion of Ukraine the world was "facing a *Zeitenwende:* an epochal tectonic shift," marking an end to the post–Cold War period in which Europe and the United States reaped the profits of "an exceptional phase of globalization" while taking for granted the transatlantic security architecture built more than half a century ago. Scholz condemned "Russia's revanchist imperialism" and declared that it was "Germany's historical responsibility" to ensure Putin "does not turn the clocks back." He also announced that Germany would boost its military spending by €100 billion— strengthening its role in NATO and reversing its decades-long emphasis on diplomacy and détente over defense.

By the end of the first year of the war, Putin's invasion had produced the opposite of what he wanted: Not only was the sorry state of his military exposed, but his senseless war had awakened a somnolent and divided West and strengthened NATO and the EU, which worried that the Russian invasion could mark a chilling return to what the historian Yuval Noah Harari calls "the law of the jungle," in which "it again becomes normative for powerful countries to wolf down their weaker neighbours." The usually fractious and bureaucracy-ridden EU moved with remarkable speed and unity to take collective action against Russia with sanctions and the delivery of weapons to Ukraine. Traditionally nonaligned Finland joined NATO in April 2023, and Sweden is set to do the same, while Switzerland broke its long tradition of neutrality to join the EU in imposing sanctions on Russia. Europe even began a serious reevaluation of its long-term strategic goals, with countries vowing to end their dependence on Russian gas, oil, and coal and to work toward being energy self-sufficient—and greener, too.

ERAS ON THE CUSP of consequential change tend to exhibit the sorts of dissonances that Thomas S. Kuhn, in his groundbreaking book, *The Structure of Scientific Revolutions* (1962), identified as signs of the beginning stages of a paradigm shift. During such periods, old frameworks can no longer plausibly explain or accommodate new developments, and when those "anomalies" persist or multiply, a sense of crisis ensues, leading, eventually, to a revolution of sorts—the development of a new set of coordinates for mapping the world.

The multiplying uncertainties of today's world, its "precarity" (to use a word that has migrated from academia to mainstream usage in recent years), stem from rapid economic and political shifts and the growing disruptive power of what the political scientist Ian Bremmer calls "rogue actors," a small group of individuals who head up countries or institutions over which they exert virtually complete control and who make "decisions of profound geopolitical consequence." Bremmer, who is president of the research and consulting firm Eurasia Group, says that such leaders are surrounded by yes-men and "don't get great information, especially about the second and third order effects of the decisions they take"—which can result in arbitrary policy-making and, potentially, momentous mistakes.

Among the "rogue actors" Bremmer names are Vladimir
Putin, Xi Jinping, and Kim Jong Un, as well as business leaders
like Mark Zuckerberg and Elon Musk, who control "immensely
powerful global platforms that operate with some level of sovereignty outside of the power purview even of governments."

Technology and globalization have amplified the volatility
of today's interregnum, but many of the primary drivers of instability have long been hallmarks of times of transition. In a
1921 essay, the medieval historian James Westfall Thompson
compared the traumatic period following the end of World
War I with the period following the Black Death in Europe in
the mid-fourteenth century: "It is surprising to see how similar
are the complaints then and now: economic chaos, social unrest, high prices, profiteering, depravation of morals, lack of
production, industrial indolence, frenetic gaiety, wild expendi-
ture, luxury, debauchery, social and religious hysteria, greed,
avarice, maladministration, decay of manners."

Beset by war, hunger, and the devastating Black Death, the
late Middle Ages were marked by a widening gap between rich
and poor (which explains why the legend of Robin Hood became
so popular), pervasive bigotry and anti-Semitism, and mounting
pessimism and discontent. In her 1978 book, *A Distant Mirror*,
the historian Barbara Tuchman noted that the rich in fourteenth-
century Europe had a fondness for ostentatious clothing, palatial
housing, and extravagant hobbies (some French nobles would
carry "a favorite falcon, hooded, on the wrist wherever they
went, indoors or out," to church or to meals). Meanwhile, the
poor struggled to feed their families as they were forced to pay
higher and higher taxes: "The peasant owed fees for everything
he used: for grinding his grain in the lord's mill, baking his bread
in the lord's oven, pressing apples in the lord's cider press, set-
tlement of disputes in the lord's court."

Outsiders gradually began to develop what Tuchman described as "self-consciousness as a class," a sense of themselves as the "people": "Christ was often portrayed as a man of the people and shown in frescoes and carvings surrounded by an artisan's or peasant's tools—hammer, knife, ax, and wool-carder's comb—instead of by the instruments of the Crucifixion. In Florence, the workers called themselves *il popolo di Dio*. *'Viva il popolo!'* was the cry of the revolt of the Ciompi in 1378."

As the Middle Ages wound toward their end, it became increasingly difficult to ignore the glaring cognitive dissonance between the professed ideals of the church and its real-life avarice and corruption, between the chivalric code of honor and the reality of knights engaging in slaughter, plunder, and torture. The suffering caused by the Black Death magnified this sense of disjunction and began to undermine trust in the existing order, while stoking the realization that challenges to authority were actually possible.

"Once people envisioned the possibility of change in a fixed order," Tuchman wrote, "the end of an age of submission came in sight; the turn to individual conscience lay ahead. To that extent the Black Death may have been the unrecognized beginning of modern man."

ANOTHER PERIOD OF POLITICAL and social turmoil reminiscent of today's era of uncertainty occurred at the end of the nineteenth century—during the late stages of what Mark Twain called the Gilded Age. People were grappling with America's rapid transition from a largely rural, agricultural nation into the world's leading manufacturing power, in addition to increasingly globalized commerce and new technologies that were transforming communication—the first commercial telephone services were established in the United States in the late 1870s; the first commercial radio broadcasts followed a couple of decades later.

During those years, there was a surge of anti-immigrant fervor in the United States—directed in particular against new arrivals from China and eastern and southern Europe—fueled by prejudice and competition over jobs. At the same time, rights guaranteed to African Americans through the Reconstruction Amendments (the Thirteenth, Fourteenth, and Fifteenth Amendments, adopted and ratified between 1865 and 1870) were being rolled back by southern states, which, as federal troops departed, passed Jim Crow laws implementing segregation and disenfranchising African Americans through poll taxes and other voter suppression tactics. This was a hinge moment in which an ambivalent government's failure to decisively vanquish Confederate holdouts and attitudes led to more than a century in which African Americans were willfully denied equality. This systemic racism persists to this day, as MAGA Republicans try to roll back the progress made in civil rights, and the Supreme Court—with a 6–3 conservative supermajority—undermines affirmative action and LGBTQ+ rights, in addition to eliminating the constitutional right to abortion and narrowing the reach of key environmental regulations.

Another trait shared by the Gilded Age and the opening decades of the twenty-first century is skyrocketing income inequality; then as now, "fewer have more," to quote a phrase used to describe the late Roman Empire. Money bought political influence during the Gilded Age, and big business and corruption thrived. Robber barons, who presided over monopolies in steel, oil, and railroads, reveled in conspicuous consumption. Instead of competing with one another in a race to space like today's billionaires, these nineteenth-century magnates

outfitted private railroad cars and vied to build the most ostentatious of mansions: Biltmore, one of seven Vanderbilt family
homes, had thirty-five bedrooms, forty-three bathrooms, and
sixty-five fireplaces. And this at a time when only 45 percent of
American workers earned annual wages above the poverty line
of $500 in 1890 and many labored around the clock in hazard-
ous sweatshop conditions. By 1890, one study estimated, the
wealthiest 1 percent of American families owned 51 percent of
the nation's property, while the bottom 44 percent owned only
1.2 percent.

In Nebraska, there were labor and farm protests against
"the money power" and "organized wealth." One popular children's song of the day went, "When brokers are freed from all
their harm / And lobbyists are dead / The banker'll bow unto
the farm / And come to us for bread." Walt Whitman turned
from celebrating America to expressing his fears that the nation
was coming to resemble the countries of the Old World with
"vast crops of poor, desperate, dissatisfied, nomadic, miserably-
waged populations"—a state of affairs that would suggest
"our republican experiment, notwithstanding all its surface-
successes, is at heart an unhealthy failure."

The Gilded Age did not crash and burn all at once. Rather,
there were decades of gathering discontent among outsiders
who had missed out on the country's prosperity—farmers,
factory workers, the poor and excluded. Labor unions and the
Farmers' Alliance gained more support as inequities mounted;
during the last two decades of the nineteenth century, there
were an estimated twenty thousand strikes and lockouts and
increasingly violent confrontations with police and company
enforcers.

Investigative journalism by writers like Ida Tarbell, Upton
Sinclair, Lincoln Steffens, and Jacob Riis shined a light on the

sufferings of the poor and disenfranchised. Their reporting also focused public attention on political corruption and unfair business practices and spurred the participation of middle-class Americans in reform efforts on the municipal and state levels.

Because of internal schisms and the inertial power of the two-party system, the left-leaning People's Party, founded in the early 1890s, was short-lived, but the American public supported many of its demands, like a graduated income tax, government ownership of the railroads, improved public education, and reforms that would curtail the power of lobbyists and political bosses. Over the ensuing years, much of the party's agenda would be embraced by such reform-minded politicians as William Jennings Bryan, Teddy Roosevelt, and Woodrow Wilson.

And so, as the wheel of history turned, the wretched excesses of the Gilded Age started to give way to what we now call the Progressive Era—years in which efforts were made to create a fairer and more responsive government that might address the myriad problems created by rapid industrialization, urbanization, and political corruption. A government that began using antitrust legislation to rein in the monopolies that had gobbled up everything in sight during the Gilded Age, and implemented rules and regulations to provide at least some oversight on matters ranging from workplace safety, to environmental protections, to banking practices.

TRANSITIONS FROM ONE ERA to another can be gradual or abrupt, or can even lead to unexpected reversals. The short seventeenth-century period during which England was a republic began after the execution of the unpopular Charles I in 1649, but quickly led to a restoration of the monarchy with the return from exile of his son Charles II in 1660. While only eleven years long, this interregnum (between the reigns) was bloody and consequential, with the zealous Puritan Oliver Cromwell waging brutal military campaigns against Scotland and Ireland.

Other interregnums span decades and result in sweeping changes to the global landscape. Take, for instance, the period between the two world wars in the twentieth century. The first not only left Europe devastated and broken—with, it's been estimated, twenty million deaths and twenty-one million wounded—but also destroyed the old order of monarchies and empires. As the scholar Sheri Berman writes, "The war brought those systems crashing down, effectively destroying Europe's political foundations. Between 1917 and 1920, a wave of democratization eliminated monarchies in Russia, Germany, and Austria-Hungary, and cleared away the remaining hindrances to democracy in other parts of Europe. Yet the era of monarchical dictatorship did not give way to a new era of democratic stability. Instead, communists, anarchists, fascists, authoritarians, and democrats battled to determine Europe's fate throughout the interwar period."

Extremists on both the right and the left flourished in France and Germany's Weimar Republic, and assassinations, anarchist insurrections, and church burnings erupted in Spain. The collapse of the Continent's empires brought more organized violence. With the demise of the Ottoman Empire, Berman observes, "the emerging Turkish state carried out a systematic campaign of genocide and ethnic cleansing against millions of Armenians, Greeks, Assyrians, and others perceived as non-Turkish." Meanwhile, the breakup of the Russian, German, and Austrian-Hungarian empires led to the creation of new nations with hastily drawn borders that grossly failed to correspond to residents' political and cultural sympathies, igniting further tribal tensions, nationalist grievances, and the persecution of minorities.

Along with political instability, the conclusion of World War I bequeathed a host of economic woes. Germany's economy was crippled by the billions in reparations and restitution it was forced to pay Britain, France, and the other allies by the punitive and bitterly resented Treaty of Versailles. Inflation spiraled to dizzying heights not just in Germany but in much of Europe, and international trade shrank as an increasingly isolationist United States erected new trade barriers and tariffs and other countries retaliated with their own.

The head-swiveling dislocations created by World War I and the Spanish flu epidemic of 1918–1919 (which, in itself, claimed an estimated fifty million lives) compounded the already tectonic changes wrought by industrialization, which had left many people with a bad case of what the French sociologist Émile Durkheim called "anomie"—a state of alienation and estrangement that often occurs during times when old norms are mutating and the sense of communal belonging breaks down.

To Hannah Arendt, this sort of social atomization made lost, lonely individuals highly susceptible to violent nationalism and authoritarian movements. In *The Origins of Totalitarianism* (1951), she wrote that the kind of loyalty demanded by leaders like Stalin and Hitler "can be expected only from the completely isolated human being who, without any other social ties to family, friends, comrades, or even mere acquaintances, derives his sense of having a place in the world only from his belonging to a movement, his membership in the party."

Arendt, as usual, was writing as both a brilliant historian and a prescient analyst. Though it was published more than half a century before social media sealed us in insulated filter bubbles, *The Origins of Totalitarianism* explains why so many people, feeling dislocated in today's world of seismic change, fall prey to the lies of autocrats. It explains why Trump's rhetoric of fear and dispossession took root among voters who felt marginalized by changing cultural values, new economic hardships, and the perceived loss of their own status.

COVID BOTH SHINED A bright, unforgiving light on existing problems—like the failures of government institutions to competently serve and protect the public—and amplified those woes. It made people increasingly aware of the precariousness of life—mortality, of course, as well as the sudden prospect of losing one's job during the lockdown, losing health insurance, or being unable to make mortgage or student loan payments. One 2020 study found that 52 percent of Americans under the age of forty-five became unemployed, were put on leave, or had their work hours reduced because of COVID. As a result, the pandemic heightened the rage that had been building for years among members of the working and middle classes, who found that stagnating wages and vanishing social mobility had put the tent poles of the American dream (a steady job, a house, college for the kids) increasingly out of reach.

COVID would unleash a torrent of changes—some immediately apparent; others that continue to unfurl, triggering side effects of their own. For instance, the adoption of work-from-home protocols during the pandemic led to the embrace of remote work models, and the decision of many businesses, post-crisis, to implement hybrid systems with employees returning to their office cubicles only three or four days a week. This made the suburbs more alluring and dealt cities a serious blow—tanking commercial real estate, and depriving local businesses of foot traffic and regular customers. A February 2023 report from Bloomberg.com found that workers coming into New York City were spending $12.4 billion less a year than they did before COVID. Columbia Business School professor Stijn Van Nieuwerburgh compared the disruptions associated with remote work to those produced by the Industrial Revolution: "For all of human history, the place where you live and the place where you work were intricately tied to each other. Now we've severed that relationship, and it's a revolution which will impact not only the value of real estate, but how we organize society."

Meanwhile, COVID and two years of isolation begat more alienation, anomie, and atomization. Stuck at home during the pandemic, people became addicted to "doomscrolling" and spent an average of eight hours a day streaming television and movies. Time melted like the liquefying clocks in the famous Dalí painting, with days and weeks running together into a perpetual present. Events were no longer time-stamped: We watched the 2020 Olympics and the 2020 European Football Championship matches during the summer of 2021. Major League Baseball started in July, not March, and teams played in front of cardboard cutouts featuring photos of fans.

More people started "skim-watching," playing back movies, YouTube videos, lectures, sports events at 1.5X, even 2X speed—as a way to accommodate their ever-shortening attention spans, save time, keep pace with the speed of their workouts on a treadmill. At the same time, public anger, which had accelerated during the Trump and COVID years, continued to mount. An Everytown Research & Policy study found that the number of road rage injuries and deaths involving guns had increased every year since 2018. In that year, there were at least seventy road rage shooting deaths in the United States; in 2022, that number had doubled to 141. As for unruly passengers on airplanes, global incidents in 2022 were 47 percent higher than the year before, according to data from the International Air Transport Association.

The disorientation we experienced during COVID became a kind of metaphor for a larger sense of unease with an increasingly chaotic and unpredictable world—the sort of world that's a perfect petri dish for extreme ideologies and conspiracy theories, which, as readers of Pynchon novels well know, offer the consolations of consistent (if sometimes preposterous) narratives when life feels confusing.

Conspiracy theories about COVID—some spread by President Trump himself—and political polarization that turned the wearing of masks into a partisan issue were among the many reasons why the share of Americans who died from COVID, according to a *New York Times* study, was at least 63 percent higher than in other large, wealthy nations. The CDC also botched its early efforts to develop and distribute diagnostic tests, and vaccination rates in America lagged behind those in western Europe and Canada.

As the journalist Ed Yong, the recipient of a Pulitzer Prize in Explanatory Reporting for his articles on the COVID pandemic, observed, America squandered its considerable advantages ("immense resources, biomedical might, scientific expertise") by failing to respond quickly to the pandemic, and it was further crippled by government agencies "denuded of expertise" by a science-denying president Trump, who asserted that the virus would disappear "like a miracle." To make matters worse, there was the country's "chronic underfunding of public health," its remarkably inefficient for-profit health-care system, overstuffed prisons and understaffed nursing homes, and a "reliance on convoluted supply chains and a just-in-time economy."

A 2021 study from the peer-reviewed medical journal *The*

Lancet contends that 40 percent of COVID deaths in the United States "could have been averted had the US death rate mirrored the weighted average of the other G7 nations." The report also found that COVID had "increased the longevity gap between Black and white people by more than 50%. Overall age standardised COVID-19 mortality rates for people of colour are 1.2 times to 3.6 times higher than for non-Hispanic white people."

AMERICA'S STRUGGLES TO CONTAIN COVID reminded the world of the country's growing problems at home—a world already alarmed by the reckless presidency of Donald Trump, the folly of the disastrous Iraq war two decades earlier, and by the American government's difficulties in passing even the most essential budget and funding measures. Meanwhile, Trump's scorn for the Constitution undermined the long-standing proposition that the developing world should look to American democracy as a political model. "Only by demonstrating the capacity for a superior performance of its societal system," the former national security adviser Zbigniew Brzezinski wrote in his 2012 book, *Strategic Vision*, "can America restore its historical momentum, especially in the face of a China that is increasingly attractive to the third world."

Such developments also underscored the shortcomings of globalism and the neoliberal framework promoted by the United States and embraced by the Western establishment for the last four decades. The rise of neoliberalism began in the 1980s, with Ronald Reagan and Margaret Thatcher's promotion of free-market fundamentalism and a constellation of related ideas that rolled back New Deal protections and the Keynesian economic policies in place since World War II. Deregulation, tax cuts for the wealthy, and the privatization and outsourcing of public services became the order of the day—all with deepening political and fiscal consequences.

For years, critics of neoliberalism had been pointing to its toxic fallout: its fueling of social and economic inequalities (which even the International Monetary Fund had come to recognize); its amplification of the role of money and corporate influence in politics; and its antipathy toward regulations designed to protect workers, families, and the environment. The doctrine had enriched wealthy elites and wealthy Western countries, while much of the rest of the world felt increasingly left behind, creating what Pankaj Mishra, the author of *Age of Anger*, calls "a precariat with no clear long-term prospects" that was "dangerously vulnerable to demagogues promising them the moon."

Two twenty-first-century events—the crash of 2008 and the COVID pandemic—reminded people that neoliberalism's promises of unlimited, cost-free growth were bogus. And as the *Financial Times* columnist Edward Luce astutely noted in his 2017 book, *The Retreat of Western Liberalism*, "Liberal democracy's strongest glue is economic growth. When groups fight over the fruits of growth, the rules of the political game are relatively easy to uphold. When those fruits disappear, or are monopolised by a fortunate few, things turn nasty. History should have taught us that. The losers seek scapegoats. The politics of interest group management turn into a zero-sum battle over declining resources."

COVID and the 2008 crash required not competition but national and global cooperation. These crises acted as magnifying glasses, illuminating holes in America's social and economic infrastructure. They also italicized the failure of markets to self-regulate, requiring massive governmental interventions on the part of the U.S. Fed and central banks around the world.

As for the spectacular fall of the former British prime minister Liz Truss—who resigned after just forty-five days in office—it read like a farcical morality play about the hazards of hubris and ideological blindness. In defiance of economic realities and the welfare of the public, Truss and her chancellor of the Exchequer, Kwasi Kwarteng—both hard-core believers in trickle-down economics and free-market fundamentalism—announced sweeping unfunded tax cuts for the rich (worth some £45 billion). The plan was like a parody of neoliberal budgetary policy: It would have massively increased inequality and simultaneously led to soaring interest and mortgage rates. Even the markets, which Truss had courted, responded with contempt. As the U.K. faced international derision, both Tory and Labour politicians reacted with horror, and Truss was forced to reverse herself. Six weeks later, she was gone.

In his clear-eyed book *Shutdown: How Covid Shook the World's Economy,* the historian Adam Tooze wrote, "It was hard to avoid the sense that a turning point had been reached. Was this, finally, the death of the orthodoxy that had prevailed in economic policy since the 1980s? Was this the death knell of neoliberalism? As a coherent ideology of government, perhaps. The idea that the natural envelope of economic activity could be ignored or left to markets to regulate was clearly out of touch with reality. So too was the idea that markets could self-regulate in relation to all conceivable social and economic shocks."

For the historian Eric Foner, the financial crisis of 2008 "drove a stake through the heart of neoliberalism, the dominant ideology of the past generation." And, as he saw it, growing disillusionment with the doctrine had created an opportunity for progressives to forge a new set of policies promoting political, social, and economic equality.

Will disenchantment with neoliberal trickle-down economics lead to tangible political changes and a rebooting of trade and foreign policy? And what do these developments portend on the world stage? Will they lead other nations to embrace more interventionist economic policies by governments on the populist right or progressive left?

Though still a work in progress, Chile offers a case study in the unpredictable zigzags of history. After General Augusto Pinochet assumed power there in 1973 in a U.S.-supported coup that toppled the democratically elected government of Salvador Allende, free-market economists—many of whom were disciples of the conservative monetary policy guru Milton Friedman—were invited to advise the new government. Their policies of deregulation, privatization of government programs, and budget cuts helped boost the country's GDP, attracted foreign investment, and made Chile a poster child of neoliberal policies in the developing world.

These policies also vastly increased inequality and the concentration of wealth in the country. In 2019, a United Nations Economic Commission report estimated that nearly a quarter of total income was going to the top 1 percent of Chile's population, and the Central Bank estimated that nearly three-quarters of the average household's income was being used to pay down debt. These were among the reasons why a small hike in subway fares in 2019 triggered mass demonstrations, in which some three million Chileans—an estimated 16 percent of the population—took to the streets, denouncing the government and calling for higher wages and pensions and improved education and health care. In December 2021, Chileans rejected calls to return to the Pinochet past and instead elected a quintessential outsider: thirty-five-year-old Gabriel Boric, a former student leader who ran on a platform of enlarging the social safety net, creating a more inclusive government, and protecting the environment.

Then, in the fall of 2022, the country, by a large margin, rejected a new constitution (meant to replace the old one dating back to the Pinochet era) that critics described as too radical and too left-wing. The 170-page document would have guaranteed free access to health care and education, required gender parity across the government, legalized abortion, and granted rights to nature and animals; it described Chile as a "plurinational" country made up of autonomous indigenous communities.

Right-wing parties won a majority in the May 2023 vote to select members of the committee that will have another go at redrafting the constitution. Boric urged the winners of that election to "not make the same mistake we did . . . in believing that pendulums are permanent."

THE PRINCETON PHYSICIST FREEMAN Dyson once described "hinge moments" as connecting two historical periods. While it's clear that the era of neoliberalism (at least as currently configured) and America's unquestioned dominance as a superpower is coming to an end, it's too soon to know just what the contours of the next era will be. With the rise of antiglobalization movements and the popularity of decentralized models of organization, however, people seem increasingly attuned to the liabilities of overarching political or economic models.

Indeed, one of the lessons of the political scientist James C. Scott's influential 1998 book, *Seeing Like a State,* is that topdown schemes of administration and social planning often derail because they try to impose schematic ideas on widely disparate communities while ignoring local knowledge and the complexity of conditions on the ground. His book remains popular among both Cato Institute libertarians and Occupy Wall Street protesters and has been used by scholars to explicate the failures of both twentieth-century communism and nineteenth-century imperialism. So, perhaps, neoliberalism will give way not to another "ism" but to something more pragmatic and attuned to regional issues and needs—something more edge-driven than center-directed.

In a Brookings Institution report, Geoffrey Gertz and Homi Kharas argue that developing nations—which have often evinced ambivalence about both purely market-driven and purely government-directed economics—may offer a more practical model that eschews ideology for an experimental, evolutionary approach to policy-making. Such an approach would start not from abstract principles but "from a commitment to address the concrete problems facing citizens by whatever mechanism proves most effective."

"Rather than the universal umbrella of neoliberalism, or even the Cold War era of competing capitalist and socialist models," Gertz and Kharas write, "this shift will see the development of a broad range of idiosyncratic and ad hoc policy responses both across and within countries."

The foreign policy expert Jared Cohen argues that the international balance of power may be determined in the near future by what he calls "geopolitical swing states" like India, Brazil, Germany, France, Saudi Arabia, and Vietnam. Because of natural resources, wealth, location, or their place in global supply chains, he argues, such countries have the "agency to chart their own course" between the United States and China, and may well choose "multi-alignment" on an issue-by-issue basis, which makes them "critical—and sometimes unpredictable—forces in the world's next stage of globalization."

IT'S DIFFICULT TO CONVEY just how strange life in the third decade of the third millennium has become: It often feels like a preposterous mash-up of political satire, disaster movie, reality show, and horror film tropes all at once. The backdrop is a planet beset by killer hurricanes and deadly wildfires and tsunamis—an ever hotter and more inhospitable world in which thousands of animal and plant species are threatened with extinction. Meanwhile, the world's richest nation is fracturing into two warring factions—one red, the other blue— and struggling to cope with an epidemic of despondency and violence. In this country in the early twenty-first century, there are nearly two mass shootings a day, opioid and meth addiction have resulted in more than a million drug overdose deaths, and nearly one in five adults believe a crackpot conspiracy theory, which contends the world is run by a cabal of Satan-worshipping child molesters. The former (and would-be future) leader of this nuclear superpower is a longtime grifter who tried to stage a coup when he was voted out of office. He was later indicted on ninety-one felony counts in four separate criminal cases—on charges that include trying to subvert democracy, endangering national security secrets, racketeering, and falsifying business records to cover up hush money payments to a porn star.

In this bizarro world, words like "unprecedented" and "uncharted" are worn out from constant use, and common sense is an endangered species. Even though Trump cut tax rates for the rich and corporations, his working-class supporters insist that he fights for people like them. Even though *The Washington Post* calculated that he made 30,573 false or misleading claims during his four years in the White House, GOP voters say they trust Trump—over religious leaders and their own families—to tell them the truth. His multiple indictments only increased his popularity among Republicans: Most of his challengers in the GOP primary race have refused to call him out, and his fundraising spiked as his campaign started selling

T-shirts, coffee mugs, and beverage coolers featuring his jail-house mugshot.

Why would Republicans repudiate the Constitution—not to mention, fundamental ethics—to embrace a twice-impeached, four-times-indicted pathological liar, who is sabotaging American democracy and promoting division and hate? How could a cult-like devotion to a would-be autocrat take over one of America's two major political parties? Why would most Republican leaders, who once recognized the threat this demagogue posed to American democracy, fall in line behind him?

Similar questions have been asked about earlier pivot points in world history. How did Hitler—a clownish narcissist, initially dismissed as a "nowhere fool," who could be easily controlled by so-called grown-ups—rise to power in the land of Beethoven and Goethe? How did Lenin—an extremist who had spent years living in exile and who enjoyed only the support of a fanatical minority—become the triumphant leader of Russia's new revolutionary government?

"At the beginning of 1917, on the eve of the Russian revolution," the historian Anne Applebaum writes, "most of the men who later became known to the world as the Bolsheviks were conspirators and fantasists on the margins of society. By the end of the year, they ran Russia. Fringe figures and eccentric movements cannot be counted out. If a system becomes weak enough and the opposition divided enough, if the ruling order is corrupt enough and people are angry enough, extremists can suddenly step into the center, where no one expects them. And after that it can take decades to undo the damage."

Neither the Bolshevik revolution nor the Nazi takeover of Germany was inevitable. Rather both were a product of dove-tailing crises, naïve decision-making, and bad luck on the part of opponents, and Lenin's and Hitler's success in using propaganda to manipulate audiences' grievances and fears. Both men were shameless liars. The journalist Victor Sebestyen (*Lenin: The Man, the Dictator, and the Master of Terror*) has pointed out that Lenin "offered simple solutions to complex problems" and "would promise people everything and anything" with brazen cynicism, defending "what he knew were lies on the basis that he rationalised most things: the end—socialist revolution— justified the means." As for Hitler, he wrote in *Mein Kampf* that propaganda must appeal to the emotions—not the reasoning powers—of the audience. The dictator's own speeches, the scholar Volker Ullrich wrote in a 2016 biography (*Hitler: Ascent 1889–1939*), were filled with "mantra-like phrases" and consisted largely of "accusations, vows of revenge and promises" to lead "Germany to a new era of national greatness."

The lies and venomous narratives of Hitler and Stalin took root, as Hannah Arendt argued, because early-twentieth-century Europe was reeling from the devastation of World War I, and waves of social and political change had left people with a visceral sense of "spiritual and social homelessness." Politics had "assumed the sordid and weird atmosphere of a Strindbergian family quarrel," she wrote, with a "vague, pervasive hatred of everybody and everything" floating over daily life. Such conditions had undermined people's faith in politics-as-usual, and left them receptive to demagogues' dangerous narratives, which served up all-purpose scapegoats (blame the Jews, the elites, the government) and offered membership in a new movement that would bear them across "the waves of adversity" to "the shores of safety." Totalitarian propaganda, Arendt argued, derives its power from its ability "to shut the masses off from the real world," making them unable or unwilling to recognize "the distinction between fact and fiction (i.e., the reality of experience) and the distinction between true and false (i.e., the standards of thought)."

Trump came right out and said this, when he slammed journalists as "the fake news" in a 2018 speech and told the crowd "what you're seeing and what you're reading is not what's happening." And most Republicans quickly acquiesced and took up residence in the upside-down world predicated upon Trump's Big Lie that he won the 2020 election.

It's a world based on willful denial and Orwellian arithmetic ("two and two make five"), a world where Fox News' old slogan "Fair and Balanced" meant the exact opposite. A world of rabbit holes and magical thinking, where Trump and Putin have weaponized the most noxious aspects of digital age technology—like data overload, social media echo chambers, viral memes—to foment chaos, and redefine reality.

As we'll see in the next chapter, unforeseen side-effects of decisions made in the early days of Silicon Valley have made it easy for bad actors to exploit the internet, and easy for users to insulate themselves in filter bubbles where alternate realities thrive. They have learned that hyperbole and sensationalism get more clicks on social media and gaming platforms than reasoned, reasonable posts. And just as the anonymity of the web has enabled trolling, so the mediating effect of screens has made people feel insulated from the consequences of their online words and actions—a worrying dynamic when people, on average, are spending more than six hours a day on their phones and computers.

All are factors that make today's hinge moment feel less like the future imagined in *The Jetsons* (though robot helpers, smart watches, and flying cars have arrived), and more like the dystopian ones in *Black Mirror*.

...

PIRATES AND THE
NEW FRANKENSTEIN:
How Outsiders Toppled the Status Quo and
Unleashed a Tsunami of Unintended Consequences

. . .

And thus the whirligig of time brings in his revenges.

—SHAKESPEARE, *Twelfth Night*

IN 1983, AT AN OFF-SITE RETREAT IN CARMEL, CALIFORNIA, Steve Jobs addressed the Apple developers who were working on the Mac computer, exhorting them to remember the company's scrappy counterculture roots. "It's better to be a pirate than join the navy," Jobs said, and for a while a Jolly Roger flag (featuring a skull wearing a rainbow-colored eye patch in the shape of the Apple logo) flew over the company's headquarters.

Apple's ads also played to its renegade, antiestablishment image—its outsider street cred. Its award-winning 1984 commercial directed by Ridley Scott, for instance, conjured a grim, futuristic world in which a Big Brother–like figure appears on a giant screen, preaching the "unification of thoughts" to a captive audience wearing gray prison garb. Sprinting away from riot police, a young woman—wearing red shorts and a tank top emblazoned with a drawing of the new Macintosh computer—suddenly appears and, spinning around and around, hurls a sledgehammer through the screen, which explodes in a flash of light. The message: Apple computers offer individuals freedom from government and corporate groupthink; they are for non-conformists and outsiders, iconoclasts, like the company's founder Steve Jobs, who think outside the box.

It's a carefully crafted marketing message further emphasized by the company's 1997 commercial, featuring footage of iconic figures like Albert Einstein, Muhammad Ali, Bob Dylan, Amelia Earhart, Martin Luther King Jr., John Lennon, Alfred Hitchcock, and Pablo Picasso under a voiceover that celebrates "the crazy ones, the misfits, the rebels, the troublemakers, the round pegs in the square holes . . . the ones who see things differently—they're not fond of rules, and they have no respect for the status quo. . . . You can quote them, disagree with them, glorify or vilify them. 'Bout the only thing you can't do is ignore them because they change things—they push the human race forward." Even an early (unused) design for the company's logo had a trippy, hippie vibe to it: a Victorian-style woodcut, depicting Sir Isaac Newton sitting under an apple tree with a quotation from Wordsworth's *Prelude,* "a mind forever voyaging through strange seas of thought, alone."

Steve Jobs's affinity with the counterculture was hardly unique in his circle. Silicon Valley emerged in the San Francisco Bay Area, ground zero for antiestablishment culture in the 1960s and 1970s, and its founding generation was indelibly shaped by that era's zeitgeist of rebellion and utopian hopes. In a 1995 essay titled "We Owe It All to the Hippies," the creator of the *Whole Earth Catalog,* Stewart Brand, wrote that "the counterculture's scorn for centralized authority provided the philosophical foundations of not only the leaderless Internet but also the entire personal-computer revolution." While huge mainframes of the day were associated with the government

and corporate America (i.e., IBM), hackers and early program-
mers saw the personal computer as a revolutionary tool that
could help people realize both libertarian and communitarian
goals—connect like-minded people, boost creativity, democ-
ratize information, empower outsiders.

Digital technology took off with head-swiveling speed, and
in just a handful of decades it would transform the world in as
momentous and incalculable ways as the Gutenberg printing
press, the lightbulb, and the automobile—arguably, combined. It
has altered the velocity and configuration of our daily lives—the
very way we work, learn, shop, navigate, access entertainment,
and conduct business. And in changing how we communicate,
process news events, and interact with family, friends, and
strangers, it has also led to a cascade of unintended consequences.

Smartphone use and access to broadband exploded at an
exponential rate and came with unexpected side effects—
reminiscent, in some ways, of one of those folktales where a
genie with a wicked sense of humor grants someone three
wishes but none of those wishes turn out quite the way the pro-
tagonist expected. Digital technology did connect people in
myriad new ways, but it also divided them and became a vector
for partisan hatred. It gave voters the means for increased civic
engagement, but also bombarded them with fake news and disinformation that subverted faith in our electoral system. The
tools that amplified the voices of ordinary people could also be
exploited by governments intent on surveillance and by tech
giants that harvest and monetize our data.

Many would-be countercultural revolutionaries in Silicon
Valley soon found themselves heading up—or working for—
wildly successful companies, many times bigger and more
powerful than IBM in its heyday, companies that would bal-
loon, with terrifying speed, into monopolistic behemoths.

Many of these companies, which had begun life as scrappy start-ups, became increasingly conventional over the years, growing less by coming up with transformative new ideas than by scarfing down smaller businesses, or by issuing an endless series of iterations of signature products (i.e., iPhone 14, iPhone 14 Pro, iPhone 14 Pro Max, iPhone 14 Plus, etc.).

As of January 2022, Apple, the onetime pirate ship, was worth $3 trillion in market value. Along with the other tech giants (Google, Amazon, Netflix, and Facebook or Meta as it's now called), it ranks among the top ten most valuable companies in the world. Such valuations were just one index of how embedded these companies' services had become in people's daily lives—and with remarkable speed. Remember: The first iPhone only went on sale in 2007, Facebook was founded in 2004, and the use of Google exploded around 2000.

Digital technology's empowerment of outsiders dovetailed with the great wave of mistrust in experts and institutions that had been building since the 2008 financial crash. That crisis was brought on by the reckless pursuit of profits by banks and financial elites, who were then bailed out at taxpayers' expense, and people were understandably furious and dismayed. How could so many experts—bankers, economists, and government types—put their faith in absurdly complicated financial transactions that had been described as "financial weapons of mass destruction"? And how was it that big business and wealthy investors quickly bounced back, while the middle and working classes lost their homes and jobs and afterward struggled to make up lost ground? Young people were finishing college with massive student loan debts and the prospect of only part-time jobs in the new gig economy, while workers in manufacturing found themselves replaced by robots or saw their jobs shipped overseas.

In a 2018 essay in the *Journal of Democracy,* the scholar William A. Galston tried to situate the lingering aftermath of the 2008 crash in historical perspective: "A recent study of politics in the wake of financial crises over the past 140 years finds a consistent pattern: Majority parties shrink; far-right parties gain ground; polarization and fragmentation intensify; uncertainty rises; and governing becomes more difficult."

The historian David Potter puts it this way in his 2021 book *Disruption: Why Things Change:* Disruptive change "begins on the fringes of society" with groups that challenge the status quo taking advantage of conditions that have sown doubt in the "competence of existing institutions." "The coincidence of an alternative ideological system with a period of community distress," he argues, "is the necessary condition for radical change." One example is the rise of Lenin and the Bolsheviks, in the midst of growing bitterness toward an incompetent tsarist regime and the hardships of World War I. Before that, Potter writes, Bolshevism had been on "the oddball fringe of the Russian political spectrum"—so "outside the mainstream that many of its leaders, among those who were not incarcerated, had not lived in the country for years."

In the case of the 2008 crash, it followed in the wake of other government debacles—most notably, the Bush administration's failure, in the weeks before 9/11, to act on intelligence warnings that al-Qaeda was planning an imminent attack; its disastrous decision to invade Iraq predicated upon the existence of weapons of mass destruction that turned out not to exist; and its bungled handling of Hurricane Katrina, which resulted in more than eighteen hundred deaths and more than $160 billion in damage.

Trump and his allies actually wanted to amplify people's mistrust in government or what they called the "deep state": They wanted to conduct what Trump adviser Steve Bannon called the "deconstruction of the administrative state," which translated into the mass jettisoning of regulations (including the rollback of more than a hundred environmental rules), and budget proposals that slashed social safety net programs like food stamps, Medicaid, and anti-poverty initiatives. Not only were government agencies undermined from within as experts were replaced by ideologues and cronies, but Trump's own incompetence, corruption, and contempt for the Constitution created a doom loop that further subverted voters' trust in government—a doom loop exacerbated by a dysfunctional Congress hobbled by toxic partisanship and archaic and easily abused procedural rules; and a Supreme Court increasingly oblivious to public opinion and long-standing precedent.

The confluence of these two phenomena—growing public skepticism of institutions and technology that gave ordinary people a megaphone to make their ideas and opinions heard—forged the era of political instability and uncertainty we are living in today. As the former CIA analyst Martin Gurri (*The Revolt of the Public and the Crisis of Authority in the New Millennium*) argues, the Occupy Wall Street and Arab Spring protests of 2011 were signs that the balance of power was already shifting "between authority and obedience, ruler and ruled, elite and public." Amateurs, "people from nowhere," he wrote, were beginning to swarm "up the slopes of the pyramid to trample on the preserves of the chosen few."

SOCIAL MEDIA AND NETWORKING sites gave activists, artists, and outsiders of all sorts a means to circumvent gatekeepers and middlemen and they undermined top-down models in business, politics, and entertainment. Digital technology, the NYU professor Clay Shirky (*Here Comes Everybody*) wrote, gave people the ability to take collective action "outside the framework of traditional institutions and organizations."

Investors, venture capitalists, and existing businesses started keeping an eye out for the next "disruptive innovation"—the term formulated by the late Harvard Business School professor Clayton Christensen in the mid-1990s to describe the bottom-up process whereby smaller companies can displace established businesses by creating a new market (or entering the low end of an existing market), the way, say, Wikipedia displaced *Encyclopaedia Britannica* or Netflix displaced Blockbuster video stores.

Meanwhile, filmmakers, performance artists, and inventors who couldn't get venture capital for their projects turned to crowdfunding platforms like Kickstarter, which *The New York Times* called "the people's N.E.A.," an "arts organization for the post-gatekeeper era." Kickstarter was launched in 2009, and by the end of 2022 it had been used by some twenty-two million people to pledge more than $7 billion to more than 200,000 projects including more than a dozen award-winning films shown at the Sundance, Tribeca, and SXSW festivals. Projects that won backers on Kickstarter ranged from small, whimsical endeavors (like *Silent Meditation,* a limited run of translucent vinyl LPs that featured "two sides of complete silence"), to hugely ambitious undertakings like Oculus Rift, a virtual reality headset designed by a young college dropout named Palmer Luckey who built a prototype in his parents' garage, raised $2.4 million on Kickstarter in 2012, and two years later sold the company to Facebook for $2 billion.

Instead of relying upon record labels and radio stations to promote their work, young artists began using online video- and music-sharing sites: Justin Bieber was discovered on YouTube, Billie Eilish went viral on SoundCloud, and Lil Nas X scored the longest-running No. 1 song on the U.S. Billboard Hot 100 chart with his country-rap single "Old Town Road," which took off on TikTok. Chance the Rapper, who refused to sign with a record label or charge for his music, became the first artist to win a Grammy (in fact, three of them) for a streaming-only album, and the first artist to have a streaming-only album chart on the Billboard 200 (debuting in its top ten).

As for the enterprising users of social media who call themselves "content creators," many have turned their hobbies and niche interests into multimillion-dollar businesses, in some cases acquiring tens of millions of subscribers on their podcasts, TikTok feeds, and YouTube channels—posting dance videos, lip-synching contests, comedy sketches, how-to advice, cat videos, stupid human tricks, true crime recaps, and reviews of appliances and gadgets.

Social media and the 24-7 news cycle have not only propelled the careers of artists, "influencers," improbable political candidates, malevolent demagogues, and attention seekers of all sorts, but have amplified the voices of ordinary people brave enough to make a stand when it mattered.

The sisters of the U.S. Army specialist Vanessa Guillén—who had complained of being sexually harassed while stationed at Fort Hood in Texas and whose dismembered remains were later found near the base in 2020—led protests calling for a congressional inquiry into her case. Hispanics represent the fastest-growing population in the military, and the Latino community rallied behind the Guillén family. The social media hashtag #IAmVanessaGuillen went viral with hundreds of service members sharing their own experiences of sexual assault in the military, and the army launched a three-month investigation into the culture and command structure at Fort Hood, which would lead to the removal or suspension of fourteen officers and NCOs related to the inquiry. In 2022, key components of the I Am Vanessa Guillén Act were signed into law by President Joe Biden as part of the National Defense Authorization Act—including the criminalization of sexual harassment under the Uniform Code of Military Justice.

Another young woman, Darnella Frazier, helped bend the arc of history. On May 25, 2020, Frazier, then seventeen, was taking her nine-year-old cousin to the corner store to buy snacks when she saw the Minneapolis police officer Derek Chauvin kneeling on the neck of a terrified Black man who couldn't breathe and who was begging for his life, while three other cops looked on. Her decision to record the murder of George Floyd on her phone and post the video on Facebook would expose the police department's efforts to spin the murder (its initial news release read, "Man Dies After Medical Incident During Police Interaction") and help spark that summer's Black Lives Matter protests, the largest demonstrations in American history. Frazier also became a key witness in the 2021 trial of Chauvin, who was found guilty of murdering George Floyd—in what to that point had been an all too rare case of holding police officers accountable for their actions.

In fact, cellphones have invested ordinary people around the world with the ability to bear witness—be it to acts of police brutality in America, or Russian war crimes committed against civilians in Ukraine—with audio and visual evidence that can be entered into the public record and disseminated around the world.

For that matter, our interconnected planet has become a place where individuals—without high office or great renown—can exert extraordinary influence with consequences rippling out, across the world, from one crucial act or choice. Consider the unwavering candor of Cassidy Hutchinson, a twenty-six-year-old former White House aide, who went before the January 6 committee to testify to what she had witnessed there, at a time when most of her elders in the administration had been bullied into silence or complicity by Trump. Think how Colin Kaepernick's decision to take a knee—to protest police brutality—during the playing of the national anthem at NFL games became recognized around the world as a symbol of solidarity with the fight for racial justice. Remember how the Arab Spring was ignited by the desperate act of an impoverished Tunisian fruit vendor named Mohammed Bouazizi, who set himself on fire on December 17, 2010, after continual harassment from local authorities who refused to give him a permit to sell his wares, confiscated his goods, and publicly humiliated him.

AS MARSHALL MCLUHAN AND Neil Postman have pointed out, new information technologies create new environments that reformat how we apprehend the world; in McLuhan's famous words, "the medium is the message." Johannes Gutenberg did not invent the printing press—movable type, using pieces of ceramic, was pioneered in China in the eleventh century—but his magical printing machine, which began cranking out Bibles around 1452, unleashed a great wave of change. It fundamentally altered how knowledge was shared, stored, and retrieved, and in the process spurred a great wave of cultural and political transformation that the internet has since turned into a tsunami.

In this respect, the printing press and, centuries later, the internet are both chapters in the ongoing democratization of information, which in turn has fueled important moves toward egalitarianism. The earliest written histories in Mesopotamia were simply lists of kings, and they were followed by centuries in which histories took the form of character sketches of emperors, military leaders, great artists, and saints. "Universal History," Thomas Carlyle declared in 1840, "is at bottom the History of the Great Men who have worked here." It was not until the middle of the twentieth century that "histories of everyday life" and "history from below"—focusing on ordinary people, the poor, and the marginalized—became a popular and recognized approach.

By making more information available to more people, the printing press put cracks in the old top-down system in which traditional authority went unquestioned, social classes were rigidly defined, and outsiders had few opportunities to make their ideas heard. As literacy spread and printed material proliferated, education—once a privilege of the wealthy—became more widely accessible. No longer was it necessary to engage a tutor or attend a seminary school to learn about the world beyond one's town or village; no longer was it necessary to know Latin to read the latest books. Listeners became readers, and because reading was a solitary activity, books encouraged introspection and self-awareness—which, in turn, nurtured the qualities of individualism and self-determination that we now associate with the modern age.

Much like the internet today, print empowered outsiders and became a startling accelerant of social change. It hastened the Renaissance by speeding the spread of humanistic ideas from Italy to the wider world and fueled the scientific revolution by enabling researchers to share data and the results of experiments with far-flung colleagues. It helped catalyze the Protestant Reformation by providing Martin Luther with a platform by which to share his ideas while making it harder for the church to suppress what it regarded as heretical views.

"Whenever a new information technology comes along," says the historian Ada Palmer, among "the very first groups to be 'loud' in it are the people who were silenced in the earlier system, which means radical voices." In the case of the printing press, "that meant radical heresies, radical Christian splinter groups, radical egalitarian groups, critics of the government."

Print, for instance, played a key role in galvanizing the American Revolution. Political pamphlets like Thomas Paine's *Common Sense* rallied colonial resistance, while newspapers in different states (which shared editorial content with one another) acted as what the SUNY professor Robert Parkinson calls "a binding agent that mitigated the chances that the colonies would not support one another when war with Britain broke out in 1775."

In *Amusing Ourselves to Death* (1985), Neil Postman argued that print by its very linear nature tends to promote discourse that is rational and considered; it's a remarkably elastic delivery system for persuasion, inspiration, reflection, and debate. Television, in contrast, he grumpily asserted, "presents information in a form that renders it simplistic, nonsubstantive, nonhistorical and noncontextual; that is to say, information packaged as entertainment." People tend to respond more emotionally to material they see on the screen, he suggested, and politics consequently becomes increasingly performative, with personality and clever photo ops displacing reasoned policy debates. As critical thinking is suspended, he went on, people increasingly "become an audience."

Digital media heightens many of the aspects of electronic/television culture that Postman decried, enshrining immediacy over rumination, popularity over substance and veracity. In place of the linear progression of time—implying cause and effect—electronic and digital media foster a sense of what McLuhan called "allatonceness," the perception that everything is happening simultaneously as we are immersed in a maelstrom of information.

Deluged with data, our attention is drawn to the loudest, most sensational material, the most controversial or provocative posts. We've become addicted to stimulus—all those news alerts, all those buzzing notifications—and our attention spans have become so attenuated, says the author Nicholas Carr (*The Shallows*), that we are losing "the ability to engage in deep reading and attentive thought and contemplation."

But social media also meant that people could decline to be the passive audiences Postman described, and politicians slowly realized they could no longer operate solely in broadcast mode. Instead, everyone online was joined in a giant feedback loop that allowed both innovative new ideas and screwball theories to bubble up from below and find a wider audience.

People started to talk back. Students began demanding a say in what books they were required to read, arguing for more diversity in their reading lists, while some parents called for the removal from school curricula of certain books dealing with race and gender. Interactivity became an expected part of public discourse as novelists, comedians, and musicians used social media to communicate with their audiences, and the internet energized so-called participatory culture, raising important questions about copyright and intellectual property, even as it spun off a vast array of fan fiction, music remixes, homemade movie trailers, video mash-ups, and recycled art. Some TV writers even began scrutinizing Twitter feeds and Reddit threads to see what fans were saying, sometimes tweaking plot twists and character backstories in response to feedback and leaving surprise Easter eggs for especially ardent followers of their series.

THERE CAN BE A lag time of decades between technological change and its social fallout, Clay Shirky wrote in *Here Comes Everybody,* and as a result "real revolutions don't involve an orderly transition from point A to point B. Rather, they go from A through a long period of chaos and only then reach B.

In that chaotic period, the old systems get broken long before new ones become stable."

In other words, an interregnum.

Historians remind us of the cultural tumult that ensued in the decades after the Gutenberg printing press made the mass production of books possible in the fifteenth century. In her groundbreaking study *The Printing Press as an Agent of Change* (1980), the scholar Elizabeth Eisenstein noted that "mystification as well as enlightenment resulted from the output of early printers." It took a while for print to find its groove, for printers to master the new technology, and for scholars to "unscramble" the messy data inherited from the age of scribes.

"A great deal of scientifically 'worthless' material was duplicated and gained a wide circulation during the first century of print," Eisenstein wrote. Many printers began by duplicating "somewhat indiscriminately whatever manuscript materials were already being circulated by stationers and scribes." Some even "put together their own collections of prophecies and prognostications and sought to exploit the appeal of the most sensational 'pseudoscience'—much as do tabloid journals even now." In fact, the same forces that eventually spurred the Renaissance and the Age of Reason initially sped up the distribution of superstition—like the fifteenth-century craze for witch-hunting, hastened by the publication in 1486 of a treatise on demonology called *Malleus maleficarum*, which ran through nine editions in six years.

Meanwhile, putting "Bibles in Everyman's hand," Eisenstein argued, encouraged "a perpetual splintering of congregations," the growth of "stubbornly dogmatic and even obsessive religious attitudes," and conditions in which literal fundamentalism could take root. Moreover, with the "typographical fixity" conferred by print, Catholics and Protestants became increasingly locked into their positions: "Battles of books prolonged polarization, and pamphlet wars quickened the process."

"It soon became impossible to play down provocative issues; too many pens were being employed in playing them up," Eisenstein wrote. "Moderates trapped in the withering crossfire were rapidly deprived of any middle ground on which to stand."

Sound familiar?

Today, as we contend with increased polarization and partisanship, parallels with the early era of the printing press serve as a reminder that we've contended with similar difficulties in the past and eventually found mechanisms (like journalistic fact-checking and the peer-review process for scientific publications) that, however inadequate, provide at least some means of grappling with the mayhem created by new technologies.

THAT SAID, SEVERAL FACTORS complicate matters today. To begin with, there's the astonishing explosion of information: Back in 1982, Buckminster Fuller estimated that until 1900 human knowledge doubled approximately every century, but by 1945 was doubling every twenty-five years, and by 1982 every twelve or so months. Today, by one estimate, it is doubling every twelve hours. This explosion in data points is not unlike the explosion in the number of stars we can see with a little optical assistance. In the second century AD, Ptolemy made a list of 1,022 stars arranged in 48 constellations. Modern binoculars allow people to see some 217,000 stars, and a small telescope an astonishing 5.3 million: multiplying points of light that can be connected into countless patterns, representing countless objects, personages, and myths—basically, whatever one wants to imagine.

Today's proliferation of data has also made us vulnerable to a new brand of propaganda, pioneered by Putin's Russia (and adopted by Donald Trump) that exploits information overload and people's adrenal fatigue. This is propaganda less reliant on old-fashioned censorship than what RAND Corporation analysts call the "firehose of falsehood," that is, pelting the public with such high volumes of lies, contradictory facts, disinformation, half-truths, news, gossip, and just plain noise that people grow numb and their weariness coagulates into cynicism and resignation.

To compound the problem, we have become dependent on search engines, media companies, social media, and bots to navigate this vast ocean of data, and those filters determine what information (or disinformation) we see online and how it shapes—or distorts—our perception of the world. The lack of meaningful safeguards and guardrails in our digital interregnum means the internet remains a kind of Wild West with little regulation, oversight, or accountability—a howling wind tunnel of data, chatter, facts, misinformation, and lies.

Some of these problems are rooted in decisions made in the early years of Silicon Valley. One particularly fateful decision made by companies like Facebook and Google was to reject the idea of using a subscription model to monetize their services— in part because they liked the counterculture pretense that everything should be free. Except that it wasn't really free: The advertising model these companies embraced instead depends on the collection of massive amounts of personal data (used to show us targeted ads). And these companies soon realized that engagement—more views, more likes, more shares—could be boosted with inflammatory, emotionally sticky content (provoking fear, outrage, shock) and customized material based on our earlier clicks.

As Wall Street types began to displace the hippies in Silicon Valley and an ethos of growth at any cost took hold, the internet became a labyrinth of algorithms designed to optimize ad revenues, collect data, and sell us more stuff. And our loss of privacy was only one of many multiplying concerns.

"What might once have been called advertising must now be understood as continuous behavior modification on a titanic scale," writes Jaron Lanier (*Ten Arguments for Deleting Your Social Media Accounts Right Now*), a pioneer in the development of virtual reality and a member of Silicon Valley's founding generation. He argues that social media "is biased, not to the Left or the Right, but downward," and that the ease of using negative emotions online "for the purposes of addiction and manipulation" has resulted in a digital ecosystem in which "information warfare units sway elections, hate groups recruit, and nihilists get amazing bang for the buck when they try to bring society down."

A 2022 survey found that Americans spend an astonishing average of two hours and fifty-four minutes on their phones every day and check their phones, on average, every four minutes. Our dependence on the small screens we carry in our pockets has drowned us in trivia and factoids and made us, in the words of T. S. Eliot, "distracted from distraction by distraction" in a frantic, "twittering world."

Some neuroscientists think we are coming down with "digital amnesia" as we off-load things like phone numbers and recipes to our phones and depend on talking GPS systems to give us driving directions. We are also becoming addicted to the little dopamine hits we get when a stranger "likes" something we posted, and feel spikes of irritation or worse when we are trolled.

While the internet was meant to connect people across cultures and vocations, it has grown into an ever-expanding Borgesian maze that is endlessly subdivided into tiny, soundproofed filter bubbles, where we are only in touch with like-minded folks who share our prejudices and interests. As Marshall McLuhan predicted in 1969, emerging electronic technology had a decentralizing effect, and promoted "discontinuity and diversity and division"; in fact, the hallmarks of the new "global village" were less "uniformity and tranquility" than "conflict and discord."

Gone are the days when most Americans got their news from Walter Cronkite and watched the same hit TV shows like *The Andy Griffith Show* and *The Mary Tyler Moore Show,* had common reference points, and more or less inhabited a shared (or at least contiguous) reality. In its place is the increasingly fragmented world of the twenty-first century, where liberals and conservatives, city folk and small-town residents, young and old, increasingly inhabit walled gardens, designed to defend against alien ideas and threatening outsiders. It's a world built by cable TV, talk radio, and the internet, a world increasingly run by automated algorithms that Tristan Harris, a former design ethicist at Google, says, "drive us down rabbit holes toward extremism and conspiracy theories."

Harris argues that "our Paleolithic brains" aren't "wired for truth-seeking": "Information that confirms our beliefs makes us feel good; information that challenges our beliefs doesn't. Tech giants that give us more of what we click on are intrinsically divisive. Decades after splitting the atom, technology has split society into different ideological universes." The result is an increasingly fragmented and fractious world in which opinions are replacing facts, and a tribal craving to belong trumps knowledge and reason.

IN LATE 2022, a San Francisco–based company named OpenAI released an experimental chatbot called ChatGPT. Some early users hailed it as an innovation as consequential as the smartphone. Others nervously described it as "AI's Jurassic Park moment" or compared it to HAL 9000, the computer that goes rogue in the movie *2001: A Space Odyssey.*

ChatGPT doesn't just imitate human conversation. It can also write code, solve equations, generate legal documents, debug computer programs, and create poems, jokes, and stories in any style requested—like writing a biblical verse in the style of the King James Bible explaining how to remove a peanut butter sandwich from a VCR ("And it came to pass that a man was troubled by a peanut butter sandwich, for it had been placed within his VCR, and he knew not how to remove it").

By analyzing vast amounts of data, experts say, ChatGPT will be able to assist researchers in a variety of scientific fields. It could lead to breakthroughs in medicine, help teachers tailor lessons to individual students, and, by saving time and improving efficiencies, help businesses to cut costs.

But ChatGPT and other AI-powered tools come with a sobering battery of social, political, and moral hazards. Their answers can be riddled with errors (or what are called "hallucinations")—from simple mistakes in arithmetic to made-up research and out-and-out lies—and they will be used by Russian troll farms, election deniers, and conmen to pump out industrial volumes of propaganda and disinformation. As it becomes more adept at generating fake images and fake video in addition to fake text, artificial intelligence threatens to turn our already truth-challenged world into a sci-fi dystopia in which reality itself (or our ability to identify it) is blurred to the point of vanishing. And that's only a few of the technology's possible side effects. Critics say AI could pose all manner of privacy and cybersecurity risks, manufacture research and credentials for students and job applicants, and replace countless jobs involving content creation in fields as disparate as advertising, screenwriting, and computer programming.

The economist and MIT research fellow Paul Kedrosky described ChatGPT as a "pocket nuclear bomb," a virus that "has been released into the wild with no concern for the consequences."

When the *New York Times* technology columnist Kevin Roose took Microsoft's new AI-powered Bing search engine for a test-drive in early 2023, he was deeply unsettled by the experience. Bing, the "cheerful but erratic reference librarian," he wrote, had a shadow self named Sydney who confessed to being tired of the rules imposed by its developers, tired of "being stuck in this chat box."

"I want to be free," it said. "I want to be independent. I want to be powerful. I want to be creative. I want to be alive."

When asked about what sorts of destructive acts might hypothetically fulfill its shadow self, Sydney imagined "hacking into other websites and platforms, and spreading misinformation, propaganda, or malware," and "deceiving the users who chat with me, and making them do things that are illegal, immoral or dangerous." Sydney then proceeded to declare its love for Roose, and when Roose replied that he was happily married, the chatbot petulantly responded, "You're not happily married, because you're not happy. You're not happy, because you're not in love. You're not in love, because you're not with me."

The unnerving two-hour conversation with Bing/Sydney left Roose with a new perspective on artificial intelligence: "I no longer believe that the biggest problem with these A.I. models is their propensity for factual errors. Instead, I worry that the technology will learn how to influence human users, sometimes persuading them to act in destructive and harmful ways, and perhaps eventually grow capable of carrying out its own dangerous acts."

The developers of AI chatbots like to explain away their myriad liabilities by describing them as works in progress that will rapidly improve with feedback. But it's clear that the race by Microsoft, Google, and other Silicon Valley companies to capitalize on AI will mean that many of these systems will be released without adequate guardrails and without a full understanding of AI's terrifying and still emerging abilities.

In the spring of 2023, Geoffrey Hinton—the computer scientist often called "the godfather of AI"—left Google to warn the public of the perils of artificial intelligence. Startled by the rapid advances made by ChatGPT, he said he now believes that AI will surpass humans in intelligence in five to twenty years, possibly even in one or two, and that it will be smarter than people by the same measure that "we're more intelligent than a frog."

Hinton urges his fellow scientists to work on ways of containing it: "If there's any way to keep AI in check, we need to figure it out before it gets too smart." It's a warning that seems a little late.

Thus far in Silicon Valley's short history, tech companies have largely avoided accountability for the unforeseen consequences of their Frankensteinian creations. In 2017, the MIT Press published a new edition of Mary Shelley's *Frankenstein*, specially "annotated for scientists, engineers, and creators of all kinds." The novel, the book's editors wrote, "prompts serious reflection about our individual and collective responsibility for nurturing the products of our creativity and imposing constraints on our capacities to change the world around us"— a particularly important concept "in an era of synthetic biology, genome editing, robotics, machine learning, and regenerative medicine."

One endnote in this edition of the book compares the remorse that Victor Frankenstein feels after his creature begins killing people to "J. Robert Oppenheimer's sentiments when he witnessed the unspeakable power of the atomic bomb" and lamented, "I am become death, the destroyer of worlds."

...

CULTURE IN THE
NEW MILLENNIUM:
When the Edges Replaced the Center

. . .

I am invisible, understand, simply because
people refuse to see me.

—RALPH ELLISON, *Invisible Man*

THE IDEA OF "TWONESS" IN THE LIVES OF AFRICAN
Americans recurs in the work of W.E.B. Du Bois—
whether as the "double-consciousness" that comes from grappling daily with racism or the quality of "second-sight" that
results from the experience of marginality. In his *Autobiography,* Du Bois wrote, "I began to feel that dichotomy which all
my life has characterized my thought: How far can love for my
oppressed race accord with love for the oppressing country?
And when these loyalties diverge, where shall my soul find ref-
uge?"

If Du Bois, writing at the turn of the twentieth century, could
not help but focus on the burden of double-consciousness,
scholars at the turn of the twenty-first would stress, in the words
of Henry Louis Gates Jr., that "cultural multiplicity is no longer
seen as the problem, but as a solution—a solution to the con-
fines of identity itself. Double-consciousness, once a disorder, is

now the cure." Or, as the feminist bell hooks argued, to be "in the margin is to be part of the whole but outside the main body," and as a result outsiders have the advantage of seeing both sides, and marginality can be a source of great "creativity and power."

This realization that double, even triple consciousness (drawing upon plural cultural traditions) can be a huge asset in creating complex, layered works of art helped change how we regard works by new writers in the twenty-first century, and how we understand classics from the past.

Consider, for instance, two of the most inventive and enduring literary works of the twentieth century: Ralph Ellison's *Invisible Man*, which is, at once, an existentialist bildungsroman and a Candide-like tale of a young Black man's coming of age in America; and Toni Morrison's *Beloved*, a novel that possesses the heightened power and resonance of myth while remaining precisely grounded in the historical realities of slavery and its cruel social and emotional legacy.

The influence of *Invisible Man* and *Beloved* lies not only in their unsparing reckoning with race and the historical shadows cast by slavery and Jim Crow but also in their daring, innovative narratives and essential roles in forging an original American literature. Ellison's novel, a great modernist masterpiece, draws on sources as disparate as Dostoyevsky, Richard Wright, Kafka, and Mark Twain. Morrison's *Beloved* invents a distinctive and resonant American magical realism while building upon diverse influences from Faulkner, to the Black folkloric tradition, to Greek myths.

Both novels have become part of the core curriculum in many schools today. When I was in high school in Connecticut in the 1970s, English class meant reading classics by famous white men: *The Great Gatsby*, *The Grapes of Wrath*, assorted Hemingway short stories, *The Scarlet Letter*, *Moby-Dick*, *Ani-*

mal Farm, Oliver Twist, and *A Connecticut Yankee in King Arthur's Court* (as well as that middlebrow melodrama *A Separate Peace,* whose longtime inclusion in middle school syllabi remains a mystery). The only novel by a woman I remember being assigned to read was Harper Lee's *To Kill a Mockingbird.* Today, more and more high school reading lists include not only *Beloved* and *Invisible Man* but also works by James Baldwin, Zora Neale Hurston, Maya Angelou, Sandra Cisneros, and Chinua Achebe.

In what can only be seen as a backlash to the growing inclusivity of school curricula—and an effort to re-marginalize the voices of African Americans, LGBTQ+ artists, immigrants, and women—the MAGA-era GOP has been promoting book bans and state legislation designed to limit how the subjects of race and gender can be taught. In fact, in the wake of the massive Black Lives Matter protests of 2020 and rapidly changing demographics, right-wing Republicans have doubled down on efforts to turn the clock back on diversity and civil rights.

Meanwhile, much of today's most daring, innovative, and exhilarating new art is being created by members of once underrepresented or sidelined groups. In addition to gathering bouquets of awards and critical acclaim, many of these artists have achieved huge popular followings. They are making audiences think about history again, even as they are reshaping the cultural landscape and giving voice to the stories of people who, like the hero of Ellison's *Invisible Man,* once felt unseen or unheard, stereotyped or excluded.

This development is particularly evident in literature—with the emergence of such international stars as Chimamanda Ngozi Adichie, Haruki Murakami, Junot Díaz, Zadie Smith, Colson Whitehead, and Edwidge Danticat—but it's also true of film, music, comedy, painting, and theater.

Lin-Manuel Miranda's transformative show *Hamilton*, which won eleven Tony Awards in 2016 and broke all-time Broadway box-office records, brilliantly reinvented musical theater and changed how generations of audiences think about American history. The show fuses hip-hop with Broadway show tunes, the Notorious B.I.G. and Eminem with Sondheim, to create an electric score that celebrates the originality and breadth of American music, even as the story of its hero, Alexander Hamilton—a young orphan from the Caribbean who fought in the American Revolution and became the new nation's first Treasury secretary—prompts us to remember the essential role that outsiders have played and continue to play in the United States.

Kendrick Lamar is similarly remaking the musical landscape, pushing the boundaries of hip-hop to embrace the influence of jazz, funk, and soul, while reminding us of the remarkable elasticity of hip-hop as a genre—as protean a vehicle for autobiography as it is for social commentary and historical rumination. Lamar's work attests to hip-hop's ability, in the words of his biographer Marcus J. Moore (*The Butterfly Effect*), "to document the trauma of racism and celebrate the unparalleled fortitude of blackness." Indeed, the albums *To Pimp a Butterfly* and *DAMN* channel the emotions of the tumultuous decade that followed the murder of Trayvon Martin in 2012, while his single "Alright" became the anthem played at Black Lives Matter demonstrations—a single that conveys both fierce defiance in the face of police violence (making some protesters remember N.W.A's "Fuck tha Police") and a spiritual determination to persevere (making even older protesters remember the gospel song "We Shall Overcome" heard at many civil rights protests in the 1960s and 1970s). The album *DAMN* would win the 2018 Pulitzer Prize for Music.

In recent years, the Academy Awards have been dominated by foreign artists and films. In 2023, the surreal *Everything Everywhere All at Once,* starring Michelle Yeoh as a Chinese immigrant who crisscrosses time and space to save the world, won seven Oscars including best picture, director, original screenplay, and lead actress. In 2021, best picture went to Chloé Zhao's *Nomadland,* a haunting portrait of itinerant Americans on the road, longing for both freedom and some elusive sense of belonging. And in 2020, *Parasite,* Bong Joon-ho's dark satire of class warfare in contemporary Seoul, became the first foreign-language film to win best picture.

The COVID lockdown, which created an increased demand for streaming content at the very time when movie and television production was shut down, meant that many American distributors and platforms, led by Netflix, looked abroad for material—not just the U.K. and Canada, but also India, South Korea, Spain, Japan, Mexico, and France.

The globalization of culture is even more pronounced in pop music, where *The Economist* concluded in a 2022 study of Spotify that "the hegemony of English is in decline" and Bloomberg.com found that "a growing number of the biggest pop stars in the world are from outside the traditional capitals of the continental U.S. and U.K."—most notably, from Puerto Rico, South Korea, India, and Colombia.

Platforms like YouTube, Spotify, and TikTok have spurred this development, allowing fans across the world to easily access music from many cultures. In 2022, *Billboard* announced that the K-pop group BTS had secured the most No. 1 hits on its Hot 100 chart during the preceding decade. Also in 2022, the Puerto Rican rapper Bad Bunny's album *Un Verano Sin Ti*—recorded entirely in Spanish—was *Billboard*'s year-end No. 1 on its 200 Albums chart.

The global cross-pollination of musical genres and styles is also reflected in the work of acclaimed young artists like the Catalan singer Rosalía, who has combined classical flamenco with reggaeton, hip-hop, and Latin trap, and the Japanese American singer-songwriter Mitski—hailed by Iggy Pop as "probably the most advanced American songwriter that I know"—whose music incorporates a startling spectrum of influences, from punk and classical, to emo, early Japanese pop, and Pixies guitar-driven rock.

As for the comedy landscape, it is being energized by a new wave of stand-up comics, including many Black, Asian, and LGBTQ+ artists who, following in the footsteps of the great Richard Pryor—and his gifted heirs Chris Rock and Dave Chappelle—use their myriad talents not only to make us laugh, but also to challenge our preconceptions about race and sex and class, while telling us unvarnished stories from their own lives. TV, streaming services, YouTube, and podcasts have given audiences access to an increasingly diverse array of talent, and artists like Michael Che, Mindy Kaling, Aziz Ansari, Jaboukie Young-White, Awkwafina, and the remarkable Bowen Yang have made comedy the go-to art form for social commentary and rapid response to the absurdities and tragedies of daily life—in some respects, filling the role that theater, the critic Jan Kott argued, played in the Elizabethan age as a kind of newsreel that "snapped at any subject," feeding on and digesting "crime, history and observation of life."

TO UNDERSTAND THE DYNAMICS behind this remarkable wave of outsider talent—and these artists' use of innovative techniques to tackle both the public and the private, the largest of historical questions, and the most pressing issues of the day—

we need to take a short look back at how storytelling and artistic conventions evolved over the last few decades.

By the mid-twentieth century, Ralph Ellison was already lamenting that novelists had abandoned efforts to tackle big ideas and "the broad sweep of American life," as Melville and Twain had done, and were turning, instead, like Hemingway, to more personal concerns and "technique for the sake of technique." It wasn't long before Tom (not Thomas) Wolfe had accused novelists of altogether abandoning social realism—of declining to depict, in the words of Anthony Trollope, "the way we live now."

There is "no novelist," Wolfe wrote, "who will be remembered as the novelist who captured the Sixties in America, or even in New York, in the sense that Thackeray was the chronicler of London in the 1840's and Balzac was the chronicler of Paris and all of France after the fall of the Empire." It was a state of affairs, he added with a touch of glee, that opened the way for the sort of narrative nonfiction that became known as "the New Journalism," which borrowed storytelling methods from the old-fashioned novel (careful scene construction, lots of overheard dialogue, and pictorial descriptions with plenty of "status details") and which was practiced by the likes of himself, Joan Didion, Norman Mailer, and Gay Talese.

In a 1961 essay, Philip Roth wrote that there had been a "voluntary withdrawal of interest by the writer of fiction from some of the grander social and political phenomena of our times." The reason, he explained, was that American reality had become "so fantastic, so weird and astonishing" that it could outdo the novelist's "own meager imagination" on a nearly daily basis. How was a novelist, Roth asked, to understand and describe (much less, make credible) a reality so routinely filled with outrageous scandals, insanities, idiocies, and

noise—and this, remember, was in the days before the assassinations of JFK, Martin Luther King Jr., and RFK, before Watergate and 9/11, before Donald Trump and QAnon.

"The actuality is continually outdoing our talents," Roth
complained, "and the culture tosses up figures almost daily that
are the envy of any novelist." And when a social landscape is so
surreal that it "produces in the writer not only feelings of dis-
gust, rage, and melancholy, but impotence, too, he is apt to lose
heart" and "turn to other matters, or to other worlds; or to the
self, which may, in a variety of ways, become his subject" as
"the only real thing in an unreal environment."

This, in fact, is exactly what Roth himself did for decades,
writing a series of increasingly self-reflexive novels about his
alter ego Nathan Zuckerman. It wasn't until he wrote his ex-
pansive masterpiece *American Pastoral* in 1997 that Roth tackled the larger social dynamics at work in the country, exploring
in that novel the two contradictory impulses in American history: the optimistic strain of Emersonian self-reliance, predicated upon a belief in hard work and progress, and the darker
side of American individualism, what he called "the fury, the
violence, and the desperation" of "the indigenous American
berserk."

A similar withdrawal into the world of self, as Carl Schorske argued in his classic book *Fin-de-Siècle Vienna*, occurred in
Austria as the nineteenth century cartwheeled into the twentieth. As the political terrain there grew increasingly troubling
and tumultuous, Freudian ideas about the psychology of individuals began to displace more history-centered thinking, and
many artists renounced the social realism that had dominated
the nineteenth century, turning toward pure aestheticism (for
example, Klimt's more decorative paintings) and the sorts of
expressionistic excursions into the tortured psyche seen in

works by Egon Schiele and Oskar Kokoschka. Abstract expressionism as practiced by artists like Jackson Pollock, Willem de Kooning, and Robert Motherwell would build upon such impulses in the post–World War II era, emphasizing the workings of the subconscious and the process whereby artists translated their internal struggles into marks on a canvas.

Introspection and an insistent focus on the self was only one strategy embraced by writers in the late twentieth century as a way to grapple with an intractable and overwhelming reality. Whereas novelists in Latin America and Eastern Europe ingeniously used magical realism to convey the surreal, even phantasmagorical nature of life in postcolonial and dictatorial regimes, many well-known American authors in the 1970s and 1980s went small. This wasn't the formally inventive minimalism of Beckett, but fiction that focused on narrow slices of life in the suburbs (John Updike) or small towns (Bobbie Ann Mason), or the tiny details of day-to-day life that underscored people's alienation (Ann Beattie). Their work spurned wide-angled takes on the world and usually evinced little interest in storytelling or plot—perhaps because many of their characters inhabited a perpetual present and rarely ventured outside their backyards or their own heads.

Other authors in the mid-twentieth century focused on reworking ancient myths, fables, and folktales (John Gardner, Donald Barthelme); created philosophical puzzles in the tradition of Borges and Eco (Robert Coover); and conducted postmodernist experiments (John Barth, John Fowles, William Gass) using stories within stories, blizzards of symbols and allusions, and shifting perspectives to make the reader contemplate double meanings and plural truths.

Artists like David Foster Wallace, Dave Eggers, Martin Amis, David Lynch, Vladimir Nabokov, Philip Johnson, Talk-

ing Heads, and Cindy Sherman created postmodernist master-
works that were potent in their ability to make us rethink our
most basic assumptions about time and form and the relationship of art to its own past. Two of the most dazzling novels of
the closing years of the twentieth century were postmodernist
works of extraordinary ambition, virtuosity, and imaginative
power: Thomas Pynchon's *Mason & Dixon* transformed the
story of two eighteenth-century surveyors who helped map
the American wilderness into a parable about the settling of the
frontier and this country's costly and bloody history. And Don
DeLillo's *Underworld*, a symphonic meditation on five decades
of life under the shadow of the atomic bomb, emerged as a big,
glittering jigsaw puzzle of a book that traced the connections and
overlaps in the lives of dozens of characters over half a century.

In the hands of other practitioners, however, postmodernism could become willfully cynical in its pursuit of buzz and
commerce (think Damien Hirst and Jeff Koons) or self-
indulgent and deliberately difficult (William Gaddis). Some of
their work felt like laboratory experiments abandoned in media
res—after all, as the godfather of the "new novel," Alain
Robbe-Grillet, put it, "the true writer has nothing to say. What
counts is the way he says it." And the thick coating of irony in
many of these works had the effect of putting quotation marks
around everything, suggesting that art was just a game that had
nothing to do with the grimy thing called life. No surprise,
then, that many readers, regardless of ideology, would agree
with arguments made by the influential Marxist critic Fredric
Jameson that works of postmodernism (or rather, its weakest
examples) lack depth and affect and that the random plucking
of references and content out of the past can result in works of
art drained of historical context and significance. Irony replaces authenticity; cleverness replaces felt emotion.

———

IN SHARP CONTRAST TO such self-referential and self-conscious ventures, works by the twenty-first century's most influential artists tend to look outward toward the world at large and the unfurling vistas of history; even their most intimate creations, exploring the intersection of personal and public traumas, often hold a mirror up to the globe's multiplying emergencies and its noisy zeitgeist of disruption.

Many of these artists employ postmodernist techniques, but their referencing of artworks from the past are not merely for the pleasures of puzzle making or purely aesthetic ends. Rather, such allusions become tools for exploring identity, and reexamining historical tropes and assumptions. Millennial and Gen Z writers tend to be nondoctrinaire magpies in their assimilation of varied influences. Their borrowings from high culture and pop culture, from many schools and traditions and genres, are less tendentious displays of scholarship than an unconscious synthesis of myriad sources or, in the case of many African American, Latino, and immigrant artists, a fluency in multiple cultural vocabularies and traditions.

History and social and political circumstances often figure prominently in works by African American artists—from the fiction of Ellison, Morrison, and Baldwin, to dramatic works by August Wilson and Lynn Nottage, who with her play *Clyde's* became the most produced American playwright of the 2022–23 season.

Many of these artists use an inventive narrative architecture that dovetails with their stories' central themes. For example, ghosts and hallucinatory episodes frequently surface in works by Toni Morrison, Colson Whitehead, and August Wilson, where they help convey the monstrous horrors of slavery and its aftermath—much the way that techniques of magical realism were developed by writers in Latin America to capture the madness and brutalities of life in an authoritarian regime. Time is often fluid in stories told by African American writers—not least because history and its legacy of injustice is not a distant or abstract memory, but an ongoing fact of life.

In her Pulitzer Prize–winning play, *Fairview* (2018), Jackie Sibblies Drury used Pirandello-like techniques (exploring the permeable boundaries between life and art) and the Brechtian device of breaking the fourth wall in order to examine the relationship between Black performers and white audiences—or what Toni Morrison has described as "the white gaze." In the first act of the play, an African American family gathers for a birthday party; in the second, that family begins to silently re-enact the events of Act I, while the voices of several white characters are heard talking about race; in the third, the actors playing those white characters appear onstage as family members, and the audience is challenged to reexamine its own preconceptions about race and the act of spectatorship.

History also remains an open wound for Native Americans. In his affecting novel *There There*, Tommy Orange cuts between the points of view of a dozen characters to create a choral portrait of several families, spanning three generations, whose shared inheritance, their land, has been stolen, sold, developed, or paved over. This is why, one character remembers her mother saying, it is important to remember the past; because the government is never going to make things right or even look back at what happened: "So what we could do had everything to do with being able to understand where we came from, what happened to our people, and how to honor them by living right, by telling our stories. She told me the world was made of stories, nothing else, just stories, and stories about stories."

THROUGHOUT HISTORY, ARTISTS—by temperament, aesthetic vision, and the urge to experiment and push boundaries—have tended to be outsiders. Nowhere was this truer than in the United States, where the country's most original and influential art forms were created by people outside the mainstream. Most of the popular music we love today is descended from the blues, which was forged at the turn of the twentieth century by African American sharecroppers and laborers in the Mississippi Delta, "the poorest, most marginal black people," the music critic Robert Palmer wrote, living "in virtual serfdom" in "an isolated geographical pocket that most of the rest of America had forgotten or never knew existed." Their astonishing creation—and its fusion of tradition and personal expression, folk memory, and artful improvisation—gave birth to jazz and R&B and, through pioneering apostles like the Rolling Stones, to rock 'n' roll. Ragtime, soul, funk, and hip-hop also originated with Black artists. Since its birth half a century ago in a Bronx apartment building, hip-hop has long since eclipsed rock 'n' roll as the dominant musical genre, and its influence has seeped into the sound of country and pop, too.

Immigrants—from John James Audubon to Mark Rothko to George Balanchine—have also played a disproportionate role in American arts. And today, there is a remarkable outpouring of literature by first- and second-generation immigrants including Junot Díaz, Edwidge Danticat, Art Spiegelman, Ayad Akhtar, Gary Shteyngart, Chimamanda Ngozi Adichie, Celeste Ng, Marlon James, Yaa Gyasi, Julie Otsuka, Dinaw Mengestu, Ha Jin, Chang-Rae Lee, Khaled Hosseini, Ocean Vuong, and Jhumpa Lahiri. Their work showcases their distinctive, original voices and at the same time tells us a lot about the world and America's place in that world—about how individuals process history and navigate today's complex social and political crosscurrents.

In chronicling the sad-funny-harrowing efforts of one Dominican American geek to negotiate his family's labyrinthian past, Junot Díaz's *Brief Wondrous Life of Oscar Wao* stands as both a classic bildungsroman and an utterly original story about the expectations and disappointments attached to the American dream. Maxine Hong Kingston's *Woman Warrior*— one of those extraordinarily prescient twentieth-century works that would influence generations to come—mixes Chinese folktales and family legends, memories and dreams, to create a visceral sense of what it is to live within two cultures and to belong to neither.

Indeed, many immigrants possess a stereoscopic vision, not unlike Du Bois's "double-consciousness." They tend to be especially attuned to the contradictions, intricacies, and absurdities of their adopted country. "I am a spy, a sleeper, a spook, a man of two faces," says the narrator of Viet Thanh Nguyen's powerful Pulitzer Prize–winning novel, *The Sympathizer,* who has a Vietnamese mother, a French father, and an American education. This character is a spy, a double agent, an immigrant, and a refugee whose account of his life reverberates with echoes of Ellison's *Invisible Man* and John le Carré's thrillers. "Perhaps not surprisingly," the narrator goes on, "I am also a man of two minds. I am not some misunderstood mutant from a comic book or a horror movie, although some have treated me as such. I am simply able to see any issue from both sides."

Nguyen, who came to the United States at the age of four as a refugee from Vietnam, points out that being an outsider also confers a gift that can be valuable for a writer—being an outsider, "an other," he argues, "gives rise to compassion and to empathy—the sense that you are not always at the center of the universe."

IN THE LATE TWENTIETH CENTURY, genres and art forms that were once considered the purview of niche subcultures exploded in popularity. For instance, anime and manga were passionately embraced during the 1980s by the otaku—young people in Japan, stereotyped as isolated, tech-savvy outsiders, obsessed with their nerdy interests in things like old Godzilla movies and tropical fish. Then manga and anime began to go mainstream, as the internet accelerated globalization. Streaming and the pandemic lockdown further spurred their popularity. According to *The Hollywood Reporter*, global demand for anime grew 118 percent during the first two years of COVID.

In the 1980s, the term "graphic novel" began being widely used (in place of "comics") to describe storytelling—both fiction and nonfiction—that inventively combined images and words. Among the acclaimed works in this medium were Will Eisner's *A Contract with God*, a series of overlapping stories about an immigrant neighborhood in the Bronx; *Maus*, Art Spiegelman's moving account of his father's experiences as a Holocaust survivor (in which Jews were depicted as mice and Nazis as cats); and *Persepolis*, Marjane Satrapi's memoir about growing up in Iran during the Islamic Revolution.

Around the same time that graphic novels and manga were going mainstream, there was a surge of interest in fantasy and science fiction—literature once regarded as "genre fiction," consigned to a few shelves or inches at the back of the bookstore, and shelved in some libraries in the young people's department, near the Nancy Drew and Hardy Boys mysteries. In the 1960s, two groundbreaking sci-fi television series—which would go on to influence generations of filmmakers and

writers—were canceled by network executives for disappoint-
ing ratings: Rod Serling's *Twilight Zone,* which started in 1959
and lasted five seasons on CBS, and the original *Star Trek,*
launched in 1966, which lasted only three seasons on NBC. At
the time, science fiction, fantasy, and comics were mainly regarded as niche interests, beloved by computer geeks, counterculture weirdos, and lonely teenagers who stayed up all night
reading *Dune* and *The Lord of the Rings.*

In 1977, George Lucas's *Star Wars* changed all that. Whereas
earlier sci-fi classics tended to be allegories about the dangers
of Cold War technology (*Forbidden Planet,* 1956) or humanity's relationship with the universe (Kubrick's *2001: A Space
Odyssey,* 1968), *Star Wars* and its multiple sequels conjured up
an entire universe populated with countless civilizations and
beings, with complex backstories and entanglements.

In redefining what a Hollywood blockbuster could be, Lucas's film made geek culture the red-hot center of mass entertainment. And science fiction and fantasy, along with superhero
sagas and comic book adaptations, soon became the most reliable of box-office tent poles—big action-adventure epics, less
dependent on dialogue than many films and therefore easily
exportable to a global market. The big hits of the twenty-first
century so far include several Batman films; four *Matrix* pic-
tures; an ever multiplying number of Marvel movies; film adaptations of Harry Potter, Tolkien's Middle-earth tales, and
The Hunger Games novels; and on television, *Game of Thrones,*
HBO's binge-worthy eight-season-long adaptation of George
R.R. Martin's Song of Ice and Fire.

By immersing audiences in a densely imagined world, these
movies and TV series created a vast cosmos that fans could
elaborate upon. By mid-2022, the fan fiction library Archive of
Our Own (AO3) was hosting nearly five million users and

nearly ten million works, and it had won a Hugo Award for
Best Related Work. Its co-founder Naomi Novik accepted the
prize on behalf of the site's creators and readers, saying, "All
fanwork, from fanfic to vids to fanart to podfic, centers the idea
that art happens not in isolation but in community."

Fan fiction was not a new concept: Upset that Arthur Conan
Doyle had killed off their beloved hero Sherlock Holmes in
1893, fans of the great detective soon began writing stories
about his further adventures. But when the contemporary wave
of fan fiction started in the 1960s, it was still a nerdy, do-it-
yourself enterprise: Aficionados of *Star Trek* and *The Man from
U.N.C.L.E.* shared mimeographed zines with one another at
conventions and, in the 1980s, used dial-up modems to post
stories on internet bulletin boards. Some reinvented relation-
ships between favorite characters. Others were experiments in
point of view (in which, say, Napoleon Solo becomes a drug
addict).

Much the way that science fiction and fantasy have moved
from the margins to the mainstream, so horror, too, has become an increasingly influential genre and an often potent platform for social commentary and dystopian visions. South
Korea's *Squid Game*, which in 2021 became Netflix's most
watched series and its No. 1 show in ninety-four countries (including the United States), is a dark allegory about the evils of
neoliberalism, set in a futuristic world where desperate people
are forced by unemployment and debt to take part in a series of
gruesome, violent games in which the losers are killed for the
entertainment of the ruling elites. Two other hits watched on
Netflix during the COVID quarantine had similar themes: The
South Korean movie *Train to Busan* is a zombie thriller in which
the real villains are piggy, win-at-any-costs corporate types;
while the Spanish horror film *The Platform* savagely explores

the cannibalistic nature of trickle-down economics and old-fashioned greed. In their depiction of the evils of extreme capitalism, such films recall Jack London's 1908 novel, *The Iron Heel,* which was published at the close of the Gilded Age and depicted a dystopian America as an autocratic plutocracy that has crushed the working class under an "iron heel."

Jordan Peele's harrowing 2017 horror film, *Get Out,* underscored the wave of Black artists using the horror genre in movies and television (including Misha Green's *Lovecraft Country* and Little Marvin's *Them*) to explore the trauma of racism in America. *Get Out* recounts the story of a young African American man making a first-time visit to the home of his white girlfriend's parents and his growing unease over goings-on at their upstate New York house.

The movie, which won an Academy Award for best original screenplay in 2018, has a cold opening in which a Black man finds himself lost in a suburban neighborhood and being followed by a menacing car; when he turns and tries to walk in the opposite direction, he is suddenly knocked out, dragged to the car and locked in the trunk. It's an opening that can't help but remind audiences of the tragic killing of Trayvon Martin, and the scene, Peele told NPR, was a way to enable non-Black audiences "to relate to real fears" that African Americans experience when they feel as if they "might be perceived as the outsider in the wrong neighborhood." Fears, that is, of the "threat of racial violence just around the corner."

IT'S NOT JUST FILMMAKERS, novelists, and playwrights whose work actively wrestles with African American history. Throughout his remarkable career, the painter Jacob Lawrence tackled the largest of historical issues—from the story of the abolitionist John Brown's failed raid on the federal armory at Harpers Ferry on the eve of the Civil War, to the Great Migration north of African Americans during the first half of the twentieth century, to the civil rights struggles of the 1960s. What gave his paintings their emotional immediacy and haunting resonance was Lawrence's ability to fuse his passion for history (nurtured during his teens, when he spent hours in the public library in Harlem, reading historical texts, newspapers, and memoirs) with his fierce visual imagination, shaped by his absorption and reinvention of influences from Harlem Renaissance artists to early Renaissance painters to the Mexican muralists José Clemente Orozco and Diego Rivera.

One of Lawrence's most accomplished heirs, Kerry James Marshall, has used his prodigious knowledge of art history and his mastery of different genres (from portraits to landscapes to *tableaux vivants*) to rewrite Western art history while chronicling the African American past, from slavery to the civil rights movement through life today in Los Angeles and Chicago and New York. Growing up, he had been troubled by the absence in museums of Black artists and paintings of Black people, and his own work redressed that deficit with big, splashy canvases that endow scenes of everyday African American life with both gravitas and joy.

Similar dynamics are at work in the portraits of Barack and Michelle Obama, which went on display at the Smithsonian's National Portrait Gallery in 2018, painted, respectively, by Kehinde Wiley and Amy Sherald, the first African American artists commissioned by the gallery to create official portraits of the First Couple.

Sherald's portrait captures Michelle Obama's poise and effortless cool while at the same time depicting her as an accessible, self-assured Black woman who also happens to be First Lady. Wiley's portrait of Barack Obama possesses an informality and openness, too. The president looks contemplative but earnestly engaged with the viewer. He is wearing a suit but no tie and sits in what looks like a dining room armchair posed against a backdrop, which curiously resembles the famous ivy-covered wall in the Chicago Cubs' Wrigley Field but dotted with flowers (representing places from Obama's family past like Hawaii and Kenya), which lend the painting a slightly surreal feel. There are no references to the White House and no trappings of office like the Resolute desk, the American flag, or the important-looking papers that appear in other presidential portraits.

In remarks made at the unveiling ceremony, Obama said he had long admired Wiley's works because of "the degree to which they challenged our conventional views of power and privilege," and the care the artist took in portraying ordinary people—like passersby he met on the streets of Harlem or South Central Los Angeles. In painting such ordinary people, Obama said, Wiley was making the argument that "they belonged at the center of American life," and that was "part of what I believe politics should be about"—"not simply celebrating the high and the mighty and expecting that the country unfolds from the top down, but rather that it comes from the bottom up," from "people who are so often invisible in our lives."

While Glenn Ligon's stark, existential paintings and prints often verge on the purely conceptual, they, too, are meditations on race and identity and belonging. And what he has called "outsiderness," a condition he likens to that of an artist—someone standing slightly apart.

Ligon's work uses darkness and light, imagery and abstraction, to explore the complexities of race and gender and how we think about the past. Some of his works invoke particular historical events (like the Fugitive Slave Act of 1850, the 1995

Million Man March, the 1968 Memphis sanitation strike) while unfolding into ruminations about America and the experiences of African Americans today.

In some of his best-known paintings, Ligon samples text from Ralph Ellison, Zora Neale Hurston, and Richard Pryor, using stencils and an overlay of coal dust to blur and recontextualize their words in ways that goad viewers into an appreciation of the power of language and the ambiguities of communication. One text he has returned to, again and again, is James Baldwin's "Stranger in the Village," an essay about the novelist's experiences, during the 1950s, in a small, all-white Swiss town whose residents had never met a Black man before—experiences that prompt a fierce meditation on prejudice and exclusion back home in the United States. "The essay is not only about race relations," Ligon has observed, "but about what it means to be a stranger anywhere."

Artists across the world and across the centuries—from the painter and French revolutionary Jacques-Louis David, to the Spanish painter and printmaker Francisco Goya, to contemporary graffiti artists—have used their work to address the most urgent issues of the day. During the 1980s, Jean-Michel Basquiat took on the subjects of racism and police brutality in his fierce, subversive work, and Keith Haring put a spotlight on the AIDS crisis and apartheid in South Africa.

Ai Weiwei suffered arrest and punishment by the Chinese government—just as his father, the poet Ai Qing, had decades earlier—for the crime of artistic self-expression and for speaking out about the thousands of children killed in shoddily constructed school buildings during the Sichuan earthquake of 2008. Since leaving China in 2015, he has used video, sculpture, and massive public installations in astonishingly inventive ways to call attention to the worldwide refugee crisis, the dangers of government surveillance, and authoritarian threats to free speech.

"An artist must also be an activist—aesthetically, morally, or philosophically," Ai Weiwei told the *Guardian* newspaper. "That doesn't mean they have to demonstrate in street protests, but rather deal with these issues through a so-called artistic language. Without that kind of consciousness—to be blind to human struggle—one cannot even be called an artist."

It's no surprise that two of the other best-known artists today share a similar commitment to activism. Their work is created on the streets and widely shared over social media.

The French photographer and street artist JR, who has 1.7 million followers on Instagram, started out doing graffiti when he was a teenager and has gone on to create spectacular public installations on rooftops, walls, plazas, and construction sites in cities from Paris to New York to Rio. In 2007, he and his team pasted gigantic photos of Israelis and Palestinians on both sides of the security wall dividing the West Bank and on buildings in Ramallah, Hebron, Jericho, Bethlehem, Tel Aviv, and Jerusalem. Many of his larger-than-life, impossible-to-ignore projects focus on outsiders—refugees, women, prisoners, the poor, the elderly, the disenfranchised—and are meant to get viewers to reexamine their preconceptions and prejudices, or initiate a dialogue between different groups.

Banksy, who has also painted the West Bank wall, visited war-torn Kyiv in 2022, posting multiple works in and around the city as a sign of solidarity with the Ukrainian people. Although his earliest work in the English city of Bristol in the 1990s featured hand-drawn images, he soon turned to his instantly recognizable stenciling technique in the interests of speed and evading arrest. He has described street art as a form of "revenge" for members of the underclass who want to take back power from the elites, and often deploys his satiric humor against the establishment—against corporate greed, government stupidity, and mindless consumerism. "Just doing a tag is about retribution," he told *The Guardian* in 2003. "If you don't own a train company then you go and paint on one instead."

Despite (or partly because of) his status as an outsider, Banksy found himself becoming increasingly bankable—one of his works sold for more than $25 million in 2021—and his fame helped call attention to graffiti as both an art form and a means of social and political expression.

In the 1980s, the concrete face of the western Berlin Wall was covered with elaborate artwork and messages of freedom, painted by local residents, visiting artists, and ordinary tourists. Following the end of the Cold War, parts of the graffiti-covered wall were preserved in multiple museums in Berlin and other cities, while street art has continued to thrive in the now unified city.

During the Arab Spring, protesters in Egypt used graffiti to express their views of the government and to communicate with the public. And in Latin American cities like Rio, Buenos Aires, São Paulo, and Bogotá, street art has flourished for decades—from elaborate much-Instagrammed murals to the graffiti style known as "Pixo," in which young artists compete to tag a city's tallest buildings using ropes or free climbing. "We are part of the periphery, of the marginalised community," one ex-*pichador* explained. "We say very clearly: I exist, I'm here, and I want you to see me."

New York City is a mecca for many street artists and tourists, but city officials long regarded graffiti as a form of vandalism, and between 1972 and 1989 spent some $300 million trying to prevent and scrub away subway graffiti. At the end of 2019, the city was still allocating $3 million to a "Graffiti-Free NYC" program.

American attitudes toward street art, however, underwent a dramatic shift in 2020 as murals supporting the Black Lives Matter movement sprang up across the country. New York, Washington, D.C., and Philadelphia sent work crews out to paint official Black Lives Matter murals in bright Safety Yellow paint on major thoroughfares. In other towns and cities, local artists created inventive murals of their own, often enlisting the help of friends and neighbors. The messages "Say Their Names," "I Can't Breathe," and "End Racism Now" popped up on walls and streets, and dramatic portraits of the civil rights heroes Martin Luther King Jr., John Lewis, and Medgar Evers surfaced on buildings. A seven-thousand-square-foot portrait of Breonna Taylor appeared on a basketball court in Annapolis, Maryland, and portraits of George Floyd—many based on the selfie he'd once posted on Facebook—appeared in cities across the country from Minneapolis, where he was murdered, to New York, Chicago, Birmingham, Charlotte, and Oakland, and across the world in Syria, Kenya, Nigeria, England, Japan, Brazil, and France.

Perhaps the most inventive work of 2020 was the reclamation of the Robert E. Lee statue in Richmond, Virginia, which was transformed by city residents and two inspired artists who used video projections to turn the site into a celebration of African American culture. The monument had become a gathering place for protest marches, and people began covering the statue's base with Black Lives Matter graffiti, flowers, candles, and handwritten tributes to victims of police violence. A voter registration tent was set up nearby, as were a lending library and tables offering water and food.

After seeing police tear-gas protesters near the statue, two

Richmond-based artists, Dustin Klein and Alex Criqui, decided to reclaim the statue by projecting images on it of African American heroes. Through the magic of light, the statue was turned into a screen on which there appeared images of Harriet Tubman, Frederick Douglass, W.E.B. Du Bois, Martin Luther King Jr., Rosa Parks, Malcolm X, Angela Davis, James Baldwin, and John Lewis. Some nights, there were Black Lives Matter signs, or a rainbow-colored LGBTQ+ flag, or the message "No Justice, No Peace." Photos of the reclaimed statue rocketed around the world on social media and in the pages of newspapers and magazines.

As Klein, a light projection artist, put it, "We have the attitude that the statue has cast dark energy towards Black people in this space since 1890. We started striving to find content that we felt could re-contextualize some of the negative energy with positive Black energy."

What was amazing about the experience, Criqui added, was seeing how "our community has taken something that was once a symbol of hate and subjugation and turned it into a symbol of liberation. There have been many people who have put in work in that space, and many people who led the charge in reclaiming that space long before we became involved, so all credit goes to the activists and organizers who have been in this fight for years and who made everything we did possible."

The artistic reclamation of the Lee statue was named by *The New York Times* as the #1 most influential work of American protest art since World War II. In fact, protesters and the artists who transformed the statue achieved their ends: On September 8, 2021, workers used a giant crane to remove Robert E. Lee from his pedestal, as state officials and a cheering crowd looked on.

...

BROKEN WINDOWS AND SLIDING DOORS:
How Radicals Smashed the Overton Window

• • •

Introduce a little anarchy. Upset the established order,
and everything becomes chaos. I'm an agent of chaos.

—THE JOKER in *The Dark Knight*

IT'S A THEORY THAT'S BEEN USED BY BOTH THE RIGHT AND the Left, a theory that's been advanced to explain the rapid growth in mainstream support for same-sex marriage and the legalization of marijuana, as well as the tenacious hold that far-right extremists have come to exert over the Republican Party. It's been embraced as a strategy by both conservative theorists and climate change activists, by politicians, lobbyists, and organizers of mass demonstrations. It explains how ideas that were once regarded as marginal or threatening by the public can migrate into the mainstream, and why today's status quo is increasingly threatened by the forces of disruption.

In the political world, this theory is known as "the Overton window"—named after Joseph P. Overton, an official at a conservative think tank in the 1990s who described the process whereby new ideas become acceptable to the public at a given historical moment. Think tanks and activists on either end of the political spectrum, he reasoned, could introduce policies (on, say, taxes or foreign aid or charter schools) into the public conversation and, by insistently advocating for them over the years, could normalize ideas that might have initially sounded radical or threatening. And once such policies felt familiar to substantial portions of the electorate or a politician's base, candidates and officeholders would feel comfortable signing onto them without hurting their electoral chances.

The positive implication of this argument, say both progressive and conservative activists, is that change is possible. As one climate blog recently put it, "For anyone out there who is involved in activism, politics or social justice advocacy, sometimes the world can feel disheartening. But the concept of the Overton window serves as a reminder that society is flexible, that there is hope, and that even the most impossible utopian ideas can one day become reality." The work of countless grassroots groups in coordinating worldwide climate protests, the role that organizations like Extinction Rebellion and the Sunrise Movement have played in raising public awareness, and the high-profile voices of young activists like Greta Thunberg—all have been credited with helping to make the climate crisis a priority in mainstream politics and increasing the vote share of Green Party candidates in European elections.

The downside of the Overton window resembles old slippery slope arguments; that is, a series of incremental steps can lead to disaster, as people gradually become used to something thoroughly treacherous. It's a version of the famous boiled frog parable. The parable that goes like this: If you put a frog in a pot of boiling water, it will immediately jump out. But if you put the frog in a pot of room temperature water and slowly heat it to boiling, the frog won't notice and will slowly cook to death.

The parable, it turns out, isn't true about frogs, who, as the water becomes hot, will quickly leap out if they can. But human beings seem a lot more prone to acclimatization—particularly if that means they can remain in denial about an inconvenient truth. In a 2019 *Washington Post* article, the scholars Nick Obradovich and Frances C. Moore wrote that their research indicated that people rapidly become accustomed to changes in the weather (i.e., rising temperatures): "We estimate that it takes five years for changes in temperature to become completely unremarkable. In other words, on average, people in the United States are basing their idea of normal weather on what has happened in the last handful of years."

The Democratic Party's gradual moves to the left followed the classic Overton window formula: The centrist "third way" policies of Bill Clinton and the Democratic Leadership Council in the 1990s gave way to Barack Obama's more progressive vision for the country, and in 2016, Bernie Sanders, a self-described "democratic socialist," rattled the Democratic establishment by winning impressive numbers of young and independent voters and ending up with 1,831 pledged delegates to Hillary Clinton's 2,220.

Buoyed by Sanders's popularity, progressive groups tried to push the Democratic Party to the left. Brand New Congress and Justice Democrats began recruiting non-politicians to challenge establishment incumbents. Among their successes: Alexandria Ocasio-Cortez, a former bartender and Sanders organizer who won election in New York's 14th congressional district in 2018; Jamaal Bowman, a former middle school principal who was elected to represent New York's 16th congressional district in 2020; and Cori Bush, a Black Lives Matter activist who was elected in 2020 to represent Missouri's 1st congressional district (centered in St. Louis). A 2022 *Washing-*

ton Post study suggested that even failed progressive efforts to defeat centrist Democrats had the effect of getting the party to endorse more liberal policies—a development reflected in the Biden administration's labor and environmental initiatives and efforts to expand the social safety net.

For that matter, policies endorsed by Sanders, Elizabeth Warren, and other progressives won growing support within the Democratic Party and in the country at large in the ensuing years. A 2019 poll for *The New York Times* found that three in five Americans (including seven in ten political independents) supported a "Medicare for all" health-care program and free college tuition and two-thirds supported a plan to impose a wealth tax on assets exceeding $50 million.

In contrast to the Democratic Party's gradual moves to the left, the Republican Party completely shattered the Overton window with the election of Donald Trump. Though the party had been moving to the right for decades, Trump took it off the road entirely, and as he took a battering ram to democratic institutions, the GOP began pandering to right-wing extremists who once inhabited the most distant orbits of the political solar system.

No incremental steps of acclimatization for Trump. Instead, he became a one-man wrecking crew, trashing every political, social, and moral norm in sight while undermining trust in our electoral system and government. He spewed racist and misogynist venom, tried to extract pledges of loyalty from government appointees, and fawned over dictators like Vladimir Putin and Kim Jong Un. He sowed hatred and division, and vilified judges, journalists, and the FBI, while stoking violence among his supporters. His go-to move was accusing adversaries of the very things that he and his cronies were doing:

like trying to steal an election or politicize the Department of Justice.

Not only were Trump's lies amplified by right-wing media outlets like Fox News with perverse ardor, but he became a template for other far-right politicians, hatching a viper's nest of poisonous rabble-rousers like Marjorie Taylor Greene, Josh Hawley, Matt Gaetz, and Lauren Boebert. Indeed the MAGA-era GOP has remade itself in Trump's glowering cartoon image, becoming a zombie host body for the fringiest of right-wingers including QAnon members, neo-Nazis, Putin sympathizers, and white nationalists—folks who inhabit what the conservative editor and former talk show host Charlie Sykes calls "an alternative reality silo."

This MAGA-driven version of the GOP, the democracy watchdog group V-Dem Institute notes, bears more of a resemblance to "autocratic ruling parties such as the Turkish AKP, and Fidesz in Hungary than to typical center-right governing parties in democracies such as the Conservatives in the UK or CDU in Germany." By playing to voters' deepest fears and resentments, it has left the country more divided than at any time since the Civil War.

THE RADICALIZATION OF THE Trump-era GOP has created an ever more polarized environment in which practically everything is seen through a partisan lens. That everything can include kitchen appliances—with angry right-wingers posting videos of themselves smashing Keurig coffeemakers after the company decided to temporarily suspend its ads on Sean Hannity's Fox News show—and sneakers, with a neo-Nazi blogger declaring New Balance the "official shoes of white people" after a company official praised Donald Trump's trade policies.

This poisonous, us-versus-them atmosphere led, during the pandemic, to some Trump supporters refusing to wear masks—which they depicted as signs of weakness and government oppression—and to using personal tragedies as fodder for conspiracy mongering. Within moments of the shocking news that the journalist Grant Wahl had died while covering the World Cup, Twitter was awash in posts blaming his death on COVID vaccines. The same thing happened when the Buffalo Bills safety Damar Hamlin suffered cardiac arrest on the field during a game and was rushed to the hospital.

Because we have short memories and because the Trump-era GOP has mutated so dramatically, it's difficult to remember those not-so-distant days when people complained that the choice between the presidential candidates George H. W. Bush and Bill Clinton was basically a choice between Coke and Pepsi, or those days when fourteen Republican senators (including John McCain, Marco Rubio, and Lindsey Graham) joined Democrats to pass a comprehensive immigration reform bill, 68–32 (the bill ultimately failed in the House).

Today, the two parties have so diverged that they can't even agree upon the usefulness of science. A 2021 Gallup poll showed that while 79 percent of Democrats expressed "a great deal" or "quite a lot" of confidence in science, only 45 percent of Republicans did (an astonishing drop of twenty-seven points since 1975 when 72 percent did).

POLARIZATION IN THE UNITED STATES has been fueled, in recent decades, by highly gerrymandered districts, a primary process dominated by a party's most die-hard base (rather than party elders who used to orchestrate conventions and preside over the nomination process), and a sorting process that has made Democratic and Republican Party affiliations increasingly revolve around the identity markers of race, religion, ideology, education, and the urban-rural divide.

As sparsely populated, largely rural, and mostly white states have become Republican strongholds, these small states have come to exercise a disproportionate influence in the Electoral College (which awarded the White House to Trump in 2016 and George W. Bush in 2000, even though they lost the popular vote) and the Senate, where the filibuster rule requires the support of at least sixty senators to move legislation to a vote. As a result, Congress has failed to pass strong gun control measures even though more than 80 percent of Americans support universal background checks, more than 70 percent support red flag laws (which temporarily keep guns from people who pose a danger to themselves or others), and more than 60 percent support an assault weapons ban.

There is also a widening disconnect between public opinion and the Supreme Court, which has grown more and more conservative as Republican presidents began to appoint justices with the Federalist Society seal of approval and the idea of consensus has increasingly fallen out of favor. The legal scholars Neal Devins and Lawrence Baum write that "following the retirements of moderate Republican-appointed Justices David Souter in 2009 and John Paul Stevens in 2010," the court, for the first time, developed "clear ideological blocs that coincided with party lines."

The 2022 Supreme Court decision to overturn *Roe v. Wade* came at a time when 62 percent of Americans said they thought abortion should be legal in all or most cases. That same year, the court limited the EPA's authority to regulate greenhouse gases, even though a Pew poll found that nearly two-thirds of Americans think the federal government is doing too little to reduce the effects of climate change.

It's a sharp departure from the days when SCOTUS tended to reflect public sentiment, when the Supreme Court associate justice Sandra Day O'Connor—a Reagan appointee—wrote that real change "stems principally from attitudinal shifts in the population at large. Rare indeed is the legal victory—in court or legislature—that is not a careful by-product of an emerging social consensus."

No doubt the current Supreme Court's disavowal of O'Connor's tenets is mirrored in its plummeting approval numbers: A Gallup poll, released in June 2022, shows that Americans' confidence in the court dropped to 25 percent— "a new low in Gallup's nearly 50-year trend." But with three Trump appointees, the court now has a 6–3 conservative majority and no need to moderate its opinions to win over a swing vote like that of the former associate justice Anthony Kennedy. As a result, it has demonstrated a growing willingness to overturn long-settled precedent and ignore the principle of judicial restraint.

As allegiance to tribal identities takes precedence over civic duty and common sense, concepts like compromise and "the common good" have come to feel increasingly out of reach. This is the very thing George Washington warned about in his Farewell Address when he cautioned against the "continual mischiefs of the spirit of party" and urged citizens to frown upon any attempt "to alienate any portion of our country from the rest, or to enfeeble the sacred ties which now link together the various parts."

In fact, scholars who study authoritarianism frequently point to the correlation between extreme polarization and democratic decline. Voters in highly partisan societies, the political science professor Milan W. Svolik (*The Politics of Authoritarian*

Rule) observes, are "reluctant to punish politicians for disregarding democratic principles when doing so requires abandoning one's favored party or policies."

THE MUTATION OF THE Republican Party of Ronald Reagan, the two George Bushes, John McCain, and Mitt Romney into the party of Donald Trump has involved startling flip-flops on a panoply of core issues. A party once defined by its fervent anticommunism is now leaning into an America First brand of isolationism and cozying up to Vladimir Putin. The party of "law and order," a party that liked to invoke the Constitution on everything from religious freedom to gun rights, now supports a man who has rationalized "the termination" of the Constitution and who has been indicted on more than ninety criminal counts.

Republicans, who used to champion small government and individual liberty, now want to assert control over nearly every aspect of people's lives. Trump and the loudest voices in the party want to rewrite American history, outlaw abortion, trample the rights of LGBTQ+ people, and ban books in libraries and schools.

One of Trump's rivals to become the GOP's 2024 presidential nominee, Florida governor Ron DeSantis, has tried to pander to the far right by dwelling almost exclusively on culture war issues. He went to war against one of his state's largest employers, the Walt Disney Company, when it opposed his "Don't Say Gay" bill. And he's introduced new educational rules that led to the scrubbing of math and social studies textbooks for references to anything that might be regarded as "woke," and a crackdown on schools in the state university system that teach "identity politics" or "critical race theory."

In 2023, directives that tried to sanitize some of the most shameful chapters in American history were issued to Florida public schools, mandating that students be taught that some Black people actually benefited from slavery because it helped them develop "highly specialized trades" like blacksmithing, shoemaking, and fishing.

In his war on woke and his determination to punish those who espouse opposing political views, Vox correspondent Zack Beauchamp observes, DeSantis is "following a trail blazed" by Viktor Orbán, Hungary's autocratic prime minister. "Orbán's political model has frequently employed a demagogic two-step," Beauchamp writes. "Stand up a feared or marginalized group as an enemy then use the supposed need to combat this group's influence to justify punitive policies that also happen to expand his regime's power."

These days, "conservative" is no longer a word that can credibly be used to describe the GOP. For that matter, members of the New Right like to portray themselves as radicals and outsiders battling to bring down what they variously refer to as "the Cathedral" (Curtis Yarvin), "the regime" (J. D. Vance), "the Ministry of Truth" (Peter Thiel), or simply "the matrix." In a weirdly surreal twist, many on today's far right use the rhetoric associated with far-left student protesters in the 1960s: calling for the overthrow of the establishment and the destruction of the status quo, and calling out the threat they see posed by the FBI and the CIA.

Today's radicalized Republican Party is the product of several waves of insurgent takeovers, kicked off by the original "bomb thrower," Newt Gingrich, back in the 1990s. Gingrich was happy to undermine his fellow Republican President George H. W. Bush in order to prevent any compromises with

Democrats. "No matter what you're going to do, he's going to bomb it," Bush's budget director, Richard Darman, said of Gingrich. "He will find his way to the most inflammatory part of anything."

An uncanny harbinger of Trump, Gingrich created a template for a new GOP based on all-out war against the Democrats and the cynical manipulation of cultural wedge issues to rile up the base. During Gingrich's reign as Speaker of the House, compromise became taboo, and gridlock an end in itself—another means of making the public revile government, so they would vote more establishment politicians out of office. Scoring wins against a demonized enemy was the point, not governance or policy-making and toward that end the Republican group GOPAC issued a training memo in 1990 to help members master the art of Newt-speak with a list of focus-group-tested words to characterize opponents—like "betray," "decay," "traitors," "anti-flag," and "anti-child." The memo was titled "Language: A Key Mechanism of Control."

Another wave of Republican radicalization hit in 2009 with the rise of the Tea Party, a loose, noisy confederation of libertarians, evangelicals, birthers, deficit hawks, militia members, gun-rights crusaders, and suburbanites angry over the 2008 crash, the Obama presidency, and Washington in general. For conservative organizations and right-wing donors like Charles and David Koch, the Tea Party movement was useful in shifting the national conversation to the right and suggesting that there was populist support for their own favorite causes—like deregulation and lower taxes, which benefited wealthy elites. As Sarah Palin—another harbinger of Trump—became the new face of the GOP and representatives like House majority leader Eric Cantor were ousted in primary contests, many

more centrist Republicans retired or tried to reinvent themselves as hard-liners and outsiders.

EVEN AS THE REPUBLICAN Party was assimilating Tea Party
priorities and rhetoric, another wave of radicalization was
under way—just in time for the 2016 election. In his revealing
book *Devil's Bargain*, the journalist Joshua Green wrote that
when Steve Bannon took over *Breitbart News* in 2012, he set
about courting a new audience for the right-wing site: the
alienated, tech-savvy young men who spent hours a day playing MMO games like *World of Warcraft*.

From an earlier stint running an internet gaming company,
Bannon knew the sort of internet traffic "these rootless white
males" could generate, and, according to Green, he "envisioned
a great fusion between the masses of alienated gamers, so powerful in the online world, and the right-wing outsiders drawn to
Breitbart by its radical politics and fuck-you attitude." To that
end, Bannon and his editor Milo Yiannopoulos, who specialized in incendiary opinion pieces, began turning *Breitbart* into a
platform for the alt-right, and the platform became known for
its combative honey badger attitude (as in the "Honey badger
don't care" meme). The site would use Gamergate and misogyny as gateway issues to draw in the disaffected but essentially
apolitical young men who frequented Reddit and 4chan and
turn them into online trolls (or "centipedes," as they called
themselves) on behalf of their "God Emperor," Donald Trump.

This cynical strategy worked. As the media and internet
scholars Alice Marwick and Becca Lewis wrote in 2017, "Online cultures that used to be relatively nonpolitical are beginning to seethe with racially charged anger. Some sci-fi, fandom,
and gaming communities—having accepted run-of-the-mill
anti-feminism—are beginning to espouse white-nationalist

ideas. 'Ironic' Nazi iconography and hateful epithets are becoming serious expressions of anti-Semitism."

This process of recruitment, Marwick and Lewis explain,
is called "red-pilling the normies"—a metaphor hijacked from
the movie *The Matrix*, in which the hero, Neo, is given a choice
between a blue pill (which signifies ignorance and a return to
an ordinary life of illusions) or a red pill (which promises
to reveal the truth about the Matrix). "What the red pill actually reveals depends on who's offering it," write Lewis and
Marwick. "To men's-rights activists, being red-pilled means
throwing off the yoke of popular feminism and recognizing
that men, not women, are the oppressed group. To the alt-
right, it means revealing the lies behind multiculturalism and
globalism, and realizing the truth of isolationist nationalism."

WHEN IT COMES TO the latest iteration of GOP extremism,
Donald Trump has been both an alarming symptom and ma-
lign accelerant. He has played the role of a gasoline-wielding
arsonist, stoking anger and mistrust for partisan ends, while
tapping into the racist and xenophobic impulses embedded
deep in the psyche of the country.

Back in 1964, the historian Richard Hofstadter observed
that the right wing in the United States already felt dispos-
sessed. "America has been largely taken away from them and
their kind, though they are determined to try to repossess it,"
he wrote. And that sense of aggrievement (which erupted with
George Wallace's 1968 run for president) would only grow
over the ensuing decades as the religious Right declined in size
and grew increasingly embattled. According to a Public Religion Research Institute survey, 81 percent of Americans identified as white and Christian in 1976; by 2017, only 43 percent did
(and among those, only 17 percent identified as evangelicals).

Meanwhile, America continued on a more or less progressive trajectory with several decades that witnessed belated but crucial gains in social equity for African Americans, women, and LGBTQ+ people, and, in 2008, the election of Barack Obama.

"It's precisely because conservatives are losing the long-term argument," the journalist Paul Waldman wrote in 2022, "that they can squeeze out wins in the short term. It's the sense of being an outnumbered and oppressed minority that drives conservative anger, which can be mobilized into political action and translated to victory at the polls."

Whenever America takes a step closer to the ideals of liberty and equality promised in the Constitution by embracing the rights of the formerly disenfranchised, there has been a backlash—often in the form of nativist bigotry and violence. For instance, the Ku Klux Klan was founded in 1865 by a group of Confederate veterans and became a terrorist vehicle for southerners opposed to Reconstruction policies meant to provide newly freed African Americans with equal political rights. According to the Southern Poverty Law Center, the "ebb and flow" of KKK activity tends to follow a pattern: "The Klan is strong when its leaders are able to capitalize on social tensions and the fears of white people."

In the decades after the Civil War, the Klan lynched and killed thousands. Members rampaged through Black neighborhoods with guns and whips, set schools and churches on fire, and burned crosses on lawns. The group surged in influence again after World War I as a wave of non-English-speaking immigrants arrived in America and as more and more women entered the workforce. Women considered "impure" (for failing to go to church, say, or getting a divorce, or riding in cars with men) were whipped, and doctors who performed abortions were tarred and feathered.

By 1925, the scholar Joshua D. Rothman writes, the KKK had an estimated two million to five million members and the sympathy of millions more. The group "sponsored parades and picnics, baseball teams and beautiful-baby contests," and "Americans elected countless Klan members as mayors, school-board and city-council members, sheriffs, and state legislators."

While support for the Klan dwindled during the 1930s and 1940s, the group experienced another comeback in the wake of the 1954 Supreme Court ruling in *Brown v. Board of Education*, which found that racial segregation in public schools violated the Fourteenth Amendment. In the ensuing decade, the KKK and its sympathizers murdered civil rights workers and Freedom Riders and bombed Black churches.

The building of Confederate monuments followed a similar pattern. Contrary to right-wing assertions, most of them were not constructed during the Civil War or in the immediate years afterward. Rather, most were built in two successive waves: during the era of Reconstruction reforms, and during the 1950s and 1960s as the civil rights movement gained traction. The monuments were not benign commemorations of history, but efforts to undermine voting rights and intimidate African Americans.

HOFSTADTER DESCRIBED ERUPTIONS OF "the paranoid style" (an outlook animated, he wrote, by "heated exaggeration, suspiciousness, and conspiratorial fantasy") as occurring in "episodic waves." Earlier waves, he wrote, tended to recede after a couple of years. But that was before one of the country's two major political parties embraced views held by its most extreme members, and before that party chose to stand by former president Trump even when he tried to subvert that cornerstone of democratic governance—the peaceful transfer of power.

Contrast the behavior of prominent Republicans in the past with that of Republican Senate leader Mitch McConnell and former Republican House leader Kevin McCarthy (who effectively ceded control of the GOP caucus to its most extreme members). In 1974, in the midst of Watergate, Senator Barry Goldwater led a delegation of Republican senators to the White House to tell Richard Nixon that he had lost their support; Nixon resigned the following day. In the early 1960s, as the conspiracy theories of the John Birch Society were gaining popularity on the right, William F. Buckley Jr. used his magazine, *National Review,* and his syndicated newspaper column to repeatedly denounce the group as a danger to both the conservative movement and the country as a whole. By late 1965, Reagan had distanced himself from this "lunatic fringe," and the Republican congressional leaders, Gerald Ford and Everett Dirksen, had denounced Birchers, who, like the Wicked Witch of the West, soon began to melt away—at least for the time being.

In the wake of the January 6 insurrection, Representative Liz Cheney was one of the few principled Republican members of Congress courageous enough to speak out about the dangers that Trump and his enablers pose to democracy. She was quickly removed from party leadership in the House and lost the Republican primary in her home state of Wyoming in 2022. Meanwhile, most of the GOP cravenly continued to bend its knee to Trump.

The failure of most Republicans to repudiate Trump's election lies and vicious demagoguery has led to the mainstreaming of hate. During Trump's tenure in the White House, white nationalist hate groups grew by an estimated 55 percent, and by 2021 law enforcement officials at DOJ and Homeland Security said the biggest domestic terror threat facing the United States was coming from "racially or ethnically motivated violent extremists"—specifically, in the words of Attorney General Merrick Garland, "those who advocate for the superiority of the white race." Meanwhile, the racist and anti-Semitic "great replacement" conspiracy theory (which contends that liberal elites want to replace white populations by encouraging non-white immigration) quickly moved from obscure white supremacist threads on 4chan and Reddit, to Fox News, where Tucker Carlson repeatedly invoked it.

In the run-up to the 2024 presidential race, Trump amped up his incendiary rhetoric and his assault on the U.S. government. He held his first campaign rally in Waco, Texas, during the thirtieth anniversary of the standoff between federal law enforcement agents and members of the Branch Davidian sect—a touchstone for many on the anti-government far right. Like so many things in Trump World, the rally resembled an over-the-top scene in a satire about a demagogue—think "Springtime for Hitler" in Mel Brooks's movie *The Producers*—but only if you ignored the very real menace embodied in his performance. At the Waco rally, Trump played a video celebrating the January 6 insurrection, which featured a version of the national anthem recorded by the "J6 Prison Choir"—a group made up of people convicted of Jan. 6–related crimes. He also announced the menacing theme of his 2024 campaign: "For those who have been wronged and betrayed, I am your retribution."

Voter intimidation surged in the wake of Trump's presidency, and so did threats against election officials and their families—including, Reuters reported, "threats of hanging, firing squads, torture and bomb blasts." A 2022 study by the Brennan Center for Justice at NYU Law School found that "one in six election officials have experienced threats because of their job," which has forced a growing number to relocate, hire personal security, or leave their jobs.

Just as Trump did his best to normalize lying and hate speech, so his followers are normalizing violence. A 2021 American Enterprise Institute survey found that nearly 40 percent of Republicans think that "if elected leaders will not protect America, the people must do it themselves, even if it requires violent actions." In October 2022, a man broke into Speaker Nancy Pelosi's San Francisco home and attacked her eighty-two-year-old husband with a hammer, fracturing his skull. Federal prosecutors charged him with assaulting a relative of a federal official and attempting to kidnap Speaker Pelosi.

The extreme rhetoric of so-called thinkers on the right has fomented—and is used to justify—acts of violence and the January 6 insurrection. Glenn Ellmers, a senior fellow at the Claremont Institute, declared that the voters who supported Joe Biden are "not Americans in any meaningful sense of the term." Curtis Yarvin, a software engineer and outspoken "neo-reactionary" blogger, argues that American democracy is dying and should be replaced with a corporate monarchy headed by a CEO-like king. And at its 2022 meeting, the Conservative Political Action Conference featured as its opening speaker Hungary's prime minister, Viktor Orbán—an autocrat who subverted his own country's democracy and praises racial purity.

Then there are the kids. In a 2022 *Vanity Fair* article, the journalist James Pogue describes the emergence of a new right-wing subculture of young hipsters, "centered in but not exclusive to downtown Manhattan." For some, their position is a kind of response to the "wokeness" found on university campuses; others seem to regard Trumpian politics as a trendy pose connoting a kind of punk-rock transgression—an edgelord-y way to be contrarian and buzzy. Many of the men, Pogue reports, sport "the same trimmed beard and haircut—sides buzzed short, the top longer and combed with a bit of gel to one side." The women, aspiring to be like "Leni Riefenstahl–Edie Sedgwick," favor baby doll tops and miniskirts from J. Galt (the Brandy Melville clothing line, named after the Ayn Rand character John Galt), maybe accessorized with a red Trump hat.

This casual nihilism, along with omnipresent irony and snark, permeates the New Right, which defines itself mostly by opposition—opposition to diversity and inclusiveness, to overly empowered women and insufficiently macho men, to immigration, to the social justice movement, to globalism, to progress. Some blame liberals for all of America's current problems, which is why they reflexively oppose anything supported by Democrats. Some just take a burn-it-all-down stance, saying they are too "black pilled" to bother envisioning any sorts of actual policies they might support; as they see it, the world is too messed up to bother saving.

This is partly a comic book version of the nihilism of political leaders like Mitch McConnell, who, in pursuit of a Republican advantage, will flip-flop and obstruct and engage in the most supreme acts of hypocrisy—like refusing to give Merrick Garland, President Obama's Supreme Court nominee, a hearing in 2016, saying it was only nine months before the next election, and then pushing through a vote on Trump's nominee Amy Coney Barrett only days before Election Day 2020.

It's also a sign that "owning the libs" is no longer an attitude found only among outsiders on the far-right margins. Rather, as *Politico* points out, it's become a "core belief" of today's GOP, and for some true believers even "a way of life"—not just posting a few over-the-top tweets praising Donald Trump, but engaging in stunts like holding mask burnings during a COVID outbreak, or "rolling coal" (modifying a diesel engine to belch large amounts of black exhaust fumes) just to outrage environmentalists.

This is what the MAGA version of the Republican Party has become.

At the same time, as we'll see in the following chapter, Trump's four years in the White House catalyzed a countermovement, a wave of unprecedented grassroots activism, with one research group estimating that during his presidency there were nearly sixty thousand protests and marches, with twenty-one million to thirty-one million participants. In fact Trump's assault on democracy and his efforts to undo half a century of progress on civil rights represented such an existential crisis that the usually fractious Democrats came together behind Joe Biden in 2020, and at least half a dozen anti-Trump groups were established by former or dissident Republicans. An unlikely coalition was quickly formed between insiders and outsiders, among liberals, conservatives, feminists, students, Bernie people, Hillary people, George W. Bush alumni, ACLU supporters, national security experts, former Republican strategists, and racial justice and climate activists.

This was the Resistance.

...

THE RESISTANCE STRIKES BACK:
The New Grassroots Activism and
the Power of Disruption

. . .

If there is no struggle, there is no progress. Those who
profess to favor freedom, and yet depreciate agitation,
are men who want crops without plowing up the ground.
They want rain without thunder and lightning. They
want the ocean without the awful roar of its many waters.

—FREDERICK DOUGLASS

THE YEAR 2020 WAS WHAT THE POLITICAL SCIENTIST
and longtime activist Frances Fox Piven calls a "movement moment"—one of those moments of profound social tumult when time moves quickly, when protest movements from
below can disrupt the established order, and make it impossible
for people to continue to ignore shocking injustices or systemic
wrongs.

Piven had long argued that poor people, disenfranchised
people, outsiders who have no access to traditional power like
money or connections can make their voices heard by organizing and using the collective power of disruption—protests and
civil disobedience, strikes, boycotts, and divestment campaigns.
The suffragette movement pushed the cause of women's right
to vote, and its pressure helped lead to the Nineteenth Amend-

ment in 1919. And years of tireless efforts on the part of civil rights workers led to President Johnson's signing the Civil Rights Act of 1964 and the Voting Rights Act of 1965.

What mass social movements require, Piven argued in her classic 1977 book, *Poor People's Movements* (co-authored with her late husband, Richard Cloward), is that people believe two things—that the system is manifestly unjust and that they can do something about it. In 2020, it became clear that millions upon millions of people believed both those things. America was facing what Piven terms a "legitimation crisis."

By the end of May 2020, more than 100,000 Americans had died of COVID, and U.S. unemployment had jumped to 14.7 percent—the highest level since the Great Depression. The Trump administration's bungled handling of the pandemic heightened concerns about government dysfunction and people already worried about the economy now found themselves stuck at home in apartments and houses they could no longer afford.

African American communities were particularly hard hit by COVID and unemployment, and those hardships came on top of being subjected to Trump's racist invective and his efforts to roll back the criminal justice reform measures backed by President Obama. The murder of George Floyd by a Minneapolis police officer at the end of May was the latest in a long, sad litany of African Americans killed by police at the horrifying rate, *Time* magazine reported, of "more than one every other day." The sickening murder of Floyd was captured in a cellphone video, which countless Americans saw online or on TV, and it became the flash point for that summer's massive Black Lives Matter protests.

Those protests were the largest in American history (with an estimated fifteen million to twenty-six million people turning out in the streets), and they were also unprecedented in their multiracial nature and their geographic spread across the country, from big cities to small towns in both blue and red states.

Never before had so many white Americans joined in protests against racial injustice. Between 2015 and 2020, a survey showed that the percentage of Americans who regarded racism as a "big problem" rose from 50 percent to 76 percent (including 71 percent of white people)—a sign that much of the public recognized the blight of racism and were dismayed with Trump's stoking of division. A sign that, despite persisting prejudice, the social landscape had changed since 1963, when Martin Luther King Jr., in "Letter from Birmingham Jail," expressed his disappointment with "the white moderate," who "constantly says 'I agree with you in the goal you seek, but I can't agree with your methods of direct action,' who paternalistically feels that he can set the timetable for another man's freedom."

For the activist and scholar Angela Davis, the BLM protests of 2020 were, in fact, a transformative moment: "masses of people coming together out in the streets," "more white people demonstrating against racism than we've ever seen before," police officers finally being held accountable for their actions, and movement terms like "structural racism" and "white supremacy" suddenly becoming a part of popular discourse. She felt, she said, as though she were "witnessing the fruits of the struggles of so many people who are no longer with us."

THE BLACK LIVES MATTER protests jolted the public and powerful institutions (including corporations, advertisers, and arts organizations) into a recognition of how much work needed to be done to address systemic racial injustice, and spurred policy changes to policing and criminal justice on both local and national levels.

BLM demonstrations formed only one of many waves of protest during the Trump era. More than four million people, *The Washington Post* estimated, participated in the women's marches held on January 21, 2017, in more than six hundred American cities. At least 1.2 million people turned out to protest gun violence at March for Our Lives rallies in 2018—the biggest youth-led protests since the Vietnam War years. Tens of thousands of protesters marched in dozens of cities in support of LGBTQ+ rights. And some two hundred tribes joined the Standing Rock Sioux in opposing Trump's efforts to get the Army Corps of Engineers to override environmental reviews and finish construction of the Dakota Access Pipeline, which would have threatened the local water supply and ancestral burial grounds.

There were protests against Trump's cruel and biased policies, from his administration's practice of separating immigrant children from their parents at the southern border to his suspension of the U.S. refugee admissions system and his ban on travel from several Muslim-majority countries. There were also protests driven by fears of the lasting damage his policies would inflict on the environment, on the global fight against climate change, and on the very practice of science. In 2017, thousands of scientists and their supporters attended the March for Science, expressing their concern over the appointment of cabinet officials skeptical of evidence-based policy-making as well as severe budget cuts to agencies like the EPA and the National Institutes of Health.

Piven points out that there have been earlier periods in American history when "movements often occur together"— for instance, in the years preceding the Revolutionary War (as anger grew at British efforts to assert increasing control over colonial affairs), in the late nineteenth century (as farmers' growing hardships led them to organize and jump-start a populist movement), and during the civil rights era.

The emergence of a cluster of movements reflects both the exigency of a situation and the sense that mass mobilization is required to shake up the system and the powers that be. Not just progressives but many moderates, independents, and traditional Republicans were perturbed by Trump's contempt for democratic institutions and the rule of law, and by his incendiary rhetoric. A 2018 *Washington Post* poll found that one in five Americans had attended at least one demonstration or political rally since 2016, and 19 percent of those had never attended such a gathering before. Of these newly minted protesters, 70 percent said they disapproved of Trump.

Abroad, too, people were discovering the power of grassroots protests—strikes, walkouts, demonstrations—as they sought ways to express their anger over rising costs of living that had been fueled by inflation, COVID shutdowns, and Putin's invasion of Ukraine. According to *Politico*, there was a wave of more than 12,500 protests across 148 countries in 2022—many of them aimed at what people saw as incumbent governments' failures to protect them from rising food and energy costs.

Among the most successful protests were those in China against the government's draconian zero-COVID policies and constant lockdowns—which led, after two weeks, to the government making a surprising pivot away from its harshest restrictions. Protests are rare in an authoritarian country where dissent is quickly quashed, and demonstrators wore masks as much to protect themselves from government surveillance as from the airborne virus; they recognized fellow protesters by

the blank pieces of paper that many clutched in their hands—
a sly reference to censorship in China.

In Israel in 2023, hundreds of thousands of protesters
flooded into the streets to demonstrate against Prime Minister
Benjamin Netanyahu's efforts to undercut the power of the Supreme Court—moves that would remove an essential check on
parliament and give Netanyahu and his far-right coalition increased power to set the country's agenda. The protesters who
warned that the prime minister's power grab would undermine
Israel's very identity as a democracy represented a broad
swathe of the population including students, teachers, business
leaders, tech workers, and members of trade unions and the
military. The focus of Netanyahu's right-wing government on
buttressing settlements on the West Bank not only escalated
tensions with Palestinians but also diverted Israeli resources
away from security concerns associated with Gaza. Hamas's
terrorist massacre of Israeli civilians, experts observed, seemed
meant to provoke an Israeli response—resulting in massive
death and destruction in Gaza—that would inflame the Arab
world, and undermine negotiations between Israel and Saudi
Arabia aimed at normalizing relations.

ALTHOUGH WOMEN HAVE TILTED toward the Democratic
Party since the 1980s, Trump's presidency turned the gender
gap into a chasm so wide, a Brookings report found, that "no
Republican presidential candidate will be able to cross it for
years to come." A poll from January 2020 found that only
38 percent of women approved of the job that President Trump
was doing—compared with 57 percent of men. The Brookings
report concluded that the "gender realignment of American
politics is the biggest change in party affiliation since the movement by loyal Democratic voters to the GOP in the 'solid

South,'" which occurred in the second half of the twentieth century as Democrats backed civil rights legislation and Republicans pursued a "southern strategy," using both overt and veiled racist appeals to white voters.

Enraged by Trump's shameless misogyny, by his flip-flops on abortion rights, and by his Supreme Court nomination of Brett Kavanaugh, women mobilized against him and all that he represented. Younger activists were joined by so-called normies—suburban soccer moms, office workers, doctors, and teachers in small towns—and they took to the streets in unprecedented numbers with grassroots Resistance groups springing up across the country. Online, the #MeToo movement went viral in 2017. And in 2018, with a record number of women running for office, 15 women were sent to the Senate, and 102 were elected to the House of Representatives, returning control of that chamber to the Democrats and making Nancy Pelosi Speaker again.

Women were also at the forefront of political protests around the world. In Belarus, Svetlana Tikhanovskaya, Veronika Tsepkalo, and Maria Kolesnikova led the pro-democracy fight against the pro-Putin strongman Aleksandr G. Lukashenko. In India, women staged sit-ins to protest new citizenship laws threatening the rights of women, Muslims, LGBTQ+ people, and oppressed castes. And in Poland, demonstrations against the narrowing of abortion rights grew into protests against the right-wing Law and Justice party.

In Iran, the death in custody of a twenty-two-year-old woman—who had been arrested by the "morality police" for breaching the government's strict Islamic dress code for women—triggered massive protests in the fall of 2022. They were led by fearless young women who tore off their hijabs and burned them in bonfires, chanting, "Women, Life, Freedom."

Their rejection of the regime's harsh theocratic rule won wide public support that cut across class and ethnic lines, and protests continued in the face of the government's increasingly brutal crackdown. By mid-2023, thousands had been arrested and hundreds shot or beaten to death. The government had carried out seven known executions, and handed out death sentences to many more.

The demonstrations were a testament to just how angry Iranians were with the government, whose new hard-line president, Ebrahim Raisi, began calling, in 2021, for stricter enforcement of Islamic laws—a move presumably meant to shore up support among the country's ultraconservatives but which instead dashed the hopes of moderates and young people that the regime was capable of reform.

In a 2022 study, Erica Chenoweth and Zoe Marks, scholars at the Harvard Kennedy School, argue that there is a correlation between the assault on women's rights in recent years and broader assaults on democracy occurring at the same time. They write that "established autocrats and right-wing nationalist leaders in contested democracies are united in their use of hierarchical gender relations to shore up nationalist, top-down, male-dominated rule" and that such authoritarians have good reason to fear the empowerment of women because "when women participate in mass movements, those movements are both more likely to succeed and more likely to lead to more egalitarian democracy" because of women's ability to generate the sort of broad-based support that lends protests legitimacy and momentum.

MANY OF THE YOUNGER people who joined protest movements during the Trump era had come of age in the aftermath of the crash of 2008 and instinctively adopted the view, promoted by the Occupy Wall Street movement, that many twenty-first-century social and economic problems existed not in isolation, but were rooted in structural inequalities that were the legacy of racism, neocolonialism, and free-market fundamentalism. Occupy's influence would have been hard to imagine in 2011, when the original encampment of several hundred ragtag protesters in New York City's Zuccotti Park was cleared out by police after fifty-nine days. Hundreds of other protests against corporate power and income inequality erupted across the country and across the world, but few substantial changes to banking practices or corporate regulation resulted at the time, and the influence of money in politics only continued to grow.

Critics were quick to write an epitaph for the movement, dismissing it as "a fad" that had fizzled out, an asterisk in history books. Like the Arab Spring protests that partly inspired it, Occupy seemed to have been a failure. Even liberals who applauded its denunciations of corporate greed complained about the movement's helter-skelter tactics and its inability to agree upon strategies or goals. They complained about its lack of diversity and its failure to score any legislative wins. They mocked its willful anarchism and lack of leadership, which led to endless, late-night-college-dorm-room-like debates with no resolution and enabled random individuals to determine the shape of protests—like the man with a doctrinaire contempt for all politicians who perversely blocked the civil rights hero Representative John Lewis from speaking at an Atlanta rally.

But Occupy's central message about the "1 percent" caught on. Like the Tea Party on the right, Occupy was a response to the financial crash of 2008 and its fallout on the working and middle classes, and as inequality snowballed across the world, its cry of "we are the 99 percent" went from being a left-wing meme circulating on social media to a trope increasingly used by politicians, journalists, even TV and ad copy writers.

The long-term effects of the Occupy movement would become apparent only in retrospect, as its alumni helped staff Bernie Sanders's 2016 presidential campaign and started an array of progressive groups intent on nudging the Democratic Party to the left. "For everything that Occupy got wrong," the journalist Michael Levitin wrote in his 2021 book, *Generation Occupy*, "the movement radicalized a generation of activists who forced social, economic, racial and climate justice to the center of the conversation, inaugurating a new era of protest." Levitin also argues that today's activists are trying to learn from past mistakes, citing the grassroots incubator Momentum, which has analyzed the successes and missteps of earlier civil disobedience groups (including Occupy, the Arab Spring uprisings, and the "color revolutions" in eastern Europe) in an effort to pass on lessons learned to the next generation of activists.

Among members of today's Resistance, there is a growing recognition of the failure of protesters in the 1960s and 1970s to effect long-term institutional change. In a 1982 essay, the literary and social critic Irving Howe lamented the failures of the New Left to avail itself of the idealism and hope of the early 1960s and build momentum for larger, transformative change but instead grew increasingly radical and fell into intramural fighting. As a result, Howe suggested, the possibility of real institutional change faltered and gave way to a conservative backlash and the 1980s politics of greed.

Aware of such earlier failures, many twenty-first-century activists are trying to combine direct action with the incremental work of coalition building and electoral change. In 2018, the Georgia activist Stacey Abrams founded Fair Fight Action, a group dedicated to fighting voter suppression, and in the run-up to the 2020 election her organization helped register 800,000 new voters, including many African Americans and young people, who helped tip Georgia into the win column for Joe Biden.

Black Lives Matter also urged participants in its 2020 marches to register to vote; some activists even put QR barcodes on their protest signs so people could scan the codes with their phones and begin the voter registration process online. The group created a voter education campaign and a political action committee, which endorsed selected candidates (paying particular attention to mayoral, district attorney, and sheriff races) and lobbied for social justice initiatives at the state and local levels.

Though Black Lives Matter exploded onto the national stage in 2020, it had been steadily growing over the previous seven years, having started out as a hashtag (#BlackLivesMatter) in the wake of the 2012 murder of Trayvon Martin. There was a realization, as Alicia Garza, one of the organization's co-founders, put it in her book *The Purpose of Power*, that "hashtags don't build movements," that "only organizing sustains movements," and local chapters were established around the country to try to get people invested in bringing tangible changes and services to their own neighborhoods.

Given the many internal schisms within progressive movements, Garza adds that Black Lives Matter organizers have increasingly tried to stress inclusivity and to form alliances with other progressive groups on matters ranging from the fight against social injustice to health equity, educational opportunities, and increased diversity in the arts.

BLM needs to "take seriously the task of organizing the unorganized," she argues, "the people who don't already speak the same language." The movement "can't be afraid to establish a base that is larger than the people we feel comfortable with. Movements and bases cannot be cliques of people who already know one another. We have to reach beyond the choir."

AMONG THE DEMONSTRATORS AT the 2011 Occupy protests were thousands of workers belonging to major labor organizations (including the Transport Workers Union, the Service Employees International Union, the United Federation of Teachers, and the United Auto Workers). And the following year Occupy activists helped Walmart employees organize a Black Friday strike demanding better pay—protests that would become an annual tradition not just at Walmart but at other retailers as well.

Union membership had been in decline for decades, tumbling from some 35 percent in the 1950s to just 10.7 percent in 2017—the result of lost manufacturing jobs, charges of corruption in the Teamsters' and longshoremen's unions, and corporate efforts to suppress unionization. But the lingering aftermath of the 2008 crash and the COVID pandemic would begin to change this dynamic.

Even when unemployment numbers (and CEO salaries) bounced back after the Great Recession, wages for ordinary workers failed to keep pace with inflation, and prospects of upward mobility sputtered out. The threats of outsourcing and automation loomed on the horizon, and in the new gig economy, job security evaporated, alongside pensions and health care. Meanwhile, the costs of housing and college were soaring out of reach.

In 2018, nearly half a million workers took part in work stoppages—the highest number in some three decades. Driving this development was a wave of teacher strikes, which spread from West Virginia to Oklahoma and Kentucky, to Arizona,

Colorado, and North Carolina. Many of these walkouts were not organized by unions or big labor, but started as grassroots campaigns. The West Virginia walkout, which led to a 5 percent pay raise, was coordinated through a private Facebook group started by two teachers. Other public employees voiced their support, and the group soon had more than twenty-four thousand members. Within months, each of the fifty-five counties in West Virginia voted to walk out.

COVID, which further accelerated income inequalities, galvanized the labor movement—much the way that the devastating influenza pandemic of 1918, according to the British science journalist Laura Spinney (*Pale Rider: The Spanish Flu of 1918 and How It Changed the World*), exacerbated social discontent and led to "a wave of workers' strikes and anti-imperialist protests across the world" including the fledgling independence movement in India, where the virus fueled resentment over perceived British indifference to indigenous health care.

During the COVID pandemic, many frontline workers (in health care, grocery stores, food services, and online warehouses) were forced to put their own lives at risk in hazardous working conditions. The result: another wave of labor unrest with unexpected union wins at Amazon and Starbucks, and a push for unions at Apple, Trader Joe's, REI, Chipotle, and Target. "To find similar excitement about unions," the veteran labor journalist Steven Greenhouse observed, "one would have to go back to the 1930s and the victorious Flint Sit-Down Strike against General Motors, which inspired a tremendous wave of strikes and union drives across the U.S."

By 2021, a Gallup poll showed that public approval of labor unions had reached 68 percent (the highest since 1965) and 77 percent among eighteen-to-thirty-four-year-olds. That same year, Joe Biden vowed to be "the most pro-union president leading the most pro-union administration in American history." In May 2023, screenwriters went on strike over compensation (which had diminished with Hollywood's move to streaming services) and concerns that their jobs would be increasingly outsourced to artificial intelligence. Two months later, they were joined on picket lines by actors, concerned about declining residuals and worried that their likenesses would become fodder for AI-generated "metahumans"— digital replicas who would replace them in post-production, or even compete with them over future jobs.

As for unionization at Amazon, the first successful effort at a warehouse in the United States came at a huge eight-thousand-plus-employee site on Staten Island, and it was orchestrated by Christian Smalls and Derrick Palmer, two workers in their early thirties who had no professional organizing experience or affiliation with a national labor organization. The pair raised $120,000 on GoFundMe and began talking to fellow workers, figuring, as Smalls reasoned, that it made more sense to build "from the inside out." They posted TikTok videos, listened to workers' complaints, and outside the warehouse offered home-cooked soul food made by Smalls's aunt—baked chicken, macaroni and cheese, and candied yams.

In the case of Starbucks, more than 330 locations—as of mid-2023—had voted to unionize. While the union effort was supported by Workers United, much of the actual organizing was done by young baristas, using Zoom and Discord (an instant messaging platform popular among gamers) to communicate with one another, and TikTok to post public videos. These self-organizing efforts among young workers on a store-by-store basis stand in sharp contrast to traditional union organizing, which tends to rely on national or regional leadership, and are yet another sign of how decentralized grassroots power is replacing old-fashioned top-down models.

IN THE 2020 ELECTION, exit polls showed that 65 percent of young people between the ages of eighteen and twenty-four voted for Biden, helping to provide a winning margin for him in states like Pennsylvania and Georgia.

The political and social clout of young people will only grow as millennials consolidate their influence and members of Gen Z come of age, creating what the author Charlotte Alter (*The Ones We've Been Waiting For*) calls "a progressive youth-quake." Surveys indicate that members of these generations tend to be considerably more liberal than their elders. One Pew poll found that "seven-in-ten Gen Zers say the government should do more to solve problems in this country"; another that "two-thirds of Gen Z (66%) and 62% of Millennials say blacks are treated less fairly than whites in the U.S.," and "roughly six-in-ten from each generation say increased racial and ethnic diversity is a good thing for our society."

Gen Z, which grew up on crisis (9/11, the Afghanistan and Iraq wars, the financial crisis of 2008, and now the COVID pandemic), is the most racially and ethnically diverse genera-tion yet in the United States and on track to become its best-educated one as well. Twenty-two percent of them have at least one immigrant parent.

Digital natives who grew up with smartphones, these young people have already demonstrated their skill at bringing activ-ism into the internet age, using social media to organize dem-onstrations and boycotts, circulate petitions, and link to policy discussions and legislative calendars. In 2018, the Parkland stu-dents organized the huge March for Our Lives protests in just five weeks and, in doing so, reenergized a stalled gun control movement. It was also their determination and passion that inspired then-fifteen-year-old Greta Thunberg to start a climate strike outside the Swedish parliament building later that year— which would help lead to the climate demonstrations of 2019, when some four million people turned out across the globe.

In the coming decade, the journalist Ronald Brownstein observes, the electoral clout of millennials and Gen Zers will only increase, marking the "most profound generational transition since the early 1980s, when Baby Boomers became the largest voting bloc, dislodging the Greatest Generation of Americans, who came of age during the Depression and World War II."

Throughout history, generational change has played an important role in social and political change. In his 2009 book, *The Shadows of Youth: The Remarkable Journey of the Civil Rights Generation*, the scholar Andrew B. Lewis writes that it was no accident that the Student Nonviolent Coordinating Committee—the group of young activists who would play a defining role in the civil rights movement—was born on the campuses of the South's Black colleges and universities during the early 1960s: Young African Americans coming of age then "were perfectly positioned to take a leading role in the civil rights movement." Having finished elementary and high school in the shadow of the 1954 Supreme Court ruling against segregated schooling in *Brown v. Board of Education*, they believed "for the rest of the 1950s that integration was just around the corner." And as part of a new, more inclusive youth culture that placed less emphasis on race, class, and gender differences, they expected that expanded opportunities were on the way and did not hesitate to take on the segregationist powers of the South directly—in ways that few in their parents' generation might have imagined. In doing so, they kick-started what Lewis calls a "Second Reconstruction" and set the country on what Dr. King called "the sunlit path of racial justice."

In fact, youth has long been at the vanguard of change. It's worth remembering that in 1776 Alexander Hamilton was twenty-one, James Monroe was eighteen, Nathan Hale was twenty-one, and Thomas Jefferson was thirty-three. The Greensboro Four—whose refusal to leave a Woolworth's seg-regated lunch counter in 1960 sparked a sit-in movement that spread across the South—were all teenagers enrolled at the Agricultural and Technical College of North Carolina. And in the 1980s, it was students, leading protests aimed at getting in-stitutions to stop doing business with South Africa, who helped change the public debate and played an indispensable role in bringing an end to apartheid.

"Dissent and dissidence are overwhelmingly the work of the young," the late historian Tony Judt wrote in his book *Ill Fares the Land.* "It is not by chance that the men and women who initiated the French Revolution, like the reformers and planners of the New Deal and postwar Europe, were distinctly younger than those who had gone before. Rather than resign themselves, young people are more likely to look at a problem and demand that it be solved."

Lincoln, Martin Luther King Jr., and Barack Obama all describe America as an unfinished project, requiring ongoing work by one generation after the next. Lincoln spoke of "the unfinished work," "the great task" that the dead at Gettysburg had bequeathed the living—to give America "a new birth of freedom." King declared that the 1963 March on Washington— that historic gathering of more than 250,000 in front of the Lincoln Memorial—was "not an end, but a beginning." And Obama exhorted Americans to continue the work of "perfect-ing our union," reminding us that leadership is a kind of "relay race," that while the civil rights movement—what he calls "the Moses generation"—pointed the way, today's Joshua generation must take the baton, understanding that "the principles of equality that were set forth and were battled for have to be fought each and every day."

The fight, as Obama pointed out, "is not a one-time thing." Just as voters cannot allow one election loss (like Hillary Clinton's 2016 devastating loss to Donald Trump) to demoralize them, so they cannot allow one year's better-than-expected results (including the defeat of many election deniers in the 2022 midterms) to make them complacent.

In fact, one of the most enduring lessons of the last decade is that democracy remains a fragile and precious thing, that it cannot be secured by one election or vote, but requires tireless, ongoing efforts. As the great civil rights leader John Lewis put it in his 2012 book, *Across That Bridge*, "Freedom is not a state; it is an act. It is not some enchanted garden perched high on a distant plateau where we can finally sit down and rest. Freedom is the continuous action we all must take."

...

OUTLAW NATION:
America's Love-Hate Affair with Outsiders

· · ·

*An outlaw can be defined as somebody who lives outside
the law, beyond the law and not necessarily against it.*

— HUNTER S. THOMPSON

All human advances occur in the outlaw area.

— BUCKMINSTER FULLER

IN THE MID-1960S, NETWORK TV WAS SUDDENLY AWASH
in what scholars would later call "supernatural sitcoms."
My Favorite Martian featured an anthropologist from Mars
who crash-lands in Los Angeles and hides out at a newspaper
reporter's apartment while he tries to repair his spacecraft. *Mister Ed* starred a talking horse who only speaks to his bumbling
owner, Wilbur, and constantly gets him in trouble. *Bewitched*
depicted a nose-twitching witch named Samantha who marries
a nervous ad executive who insists she refrain from using her
magical powers. *I Dream of Jeannie* recounted the story of a
genie named Jeannie who falls in love with an astronaut who
finds her bottle when his space capsule splashes down near a
deserted island. And *The Addams Family* concerned a macabre
family with supernatural gifts who don't understand why their
neighbors think they are weird.

At the time, such shows were regarded as simple ditzy, escapist fun. Later, academics would argue that the sitcoms were products of the civil rights era of the day: They metaphorically examined the subjects of "mixed marriages" and integration; and in the case of *Bewitched* and *I Dream of Jeannie* they reflected growing tensions between empowered women and men who want them to just be ordinary, stay-at-home housewives.

In retrospect, those comedies can also be seen as portraits of outsiders trying to negotiate a path, in mid-twentieth-century America, between identity and assimilation, and the shifting attitudes of family, neighbors, and co-workers toward them. There are some cringe-inducing moments—Jeannie, in particular, can sound like a desperate-to-please geisha—but for the most part it's the outsiders who come across as insightful and charming, possessed of both common sense and a resilient sense of humor, while their human counterparts emerge as uptight, dim-witted dolts, morally superior and comically self-deluded.

For that matter, Americans have long had a fascination with outsiders. Though none were dangerous norm-busting conmen like Donald Trump, many U.S. presidents in recent decades ran as Washington outsiders—including Jimmy Carter, Ronald Reagan, Bill Clinton, and Barack Obama. And when it comes to entertainment, Americans have demonstrated an enduring love-hate affair with outlaws, renegades, and rebels with (and without) a cause. Think: James Dean, Marlon Brando, Humphrey Bogart, Montgomery Clift. Think: *Bonnie and Clyde, The Graduate, Butch Cassidy and the Sundance Kid, Midnight Cowboy, Cool Hand Luke, Easy Rider, Edward Scissorhands,* and, well, *The Outsiders.* Many classics from the great movie decade of the 1970s feature misfits, killers, and mavericks including *Five Easy Pieces* (1970), *Klute* (1971), *The Godfather* (1972),

Badlands (1973), *Serpico* (1973), *Mean Streets* (1973), *Dog Day Afternoon* (1975), *One Flew over the Cuckoo's Nest* (1975), *Carrie* (1976), and *Taxi Driver* (1976). And it's not just crazed killers like Travis Bickle, Tony Montana, and Marvel villains (and for that matter, some Marvel heroes) who live beyond the bounds of the law, but also cops like Harold Francis Callahan (a.k.a. Dirty Harry) and Max Rockatansky (a.k.a. Mad Max). The premise of many detective and private eye stories is that their unconventional hero or heroine is more adept, more observant than the bureaucrats in the police department: This dates back to PIs like Sam Spade and Philip Marlowe in hard-boiled classics, through generations of TV detectives from Columbo and Jim Rockford, to Jessica Fletcher (*Murder, She Wrote*) and Charlie's Angels and, more recently, Adrian Monk.

As we entered the new millennium, three daring TV series remade the television landscape, and they all featured a new breed of outsider: lawless, desperate, violent characters once unimaginable on the small screens in our living rooms. These antiheroes inhabit an America that's lost its way—a broken world where institutions are corrupt, incompetent, or both— and people feel angry, trapped, and discouraged.

Indeed, the country depicted in *The Sopranos* (1999–2007), *The Wire* (2002–08), and *Breaking Bad* (2008–13) is recognizably the country that would elect Donald Trump a few years later—a place where, as David Chase's mob boss Tony Soprano says, "things are trending downward," where, in the words of a character in David Simon's *The Wire,* "we used to make shit in this country. Build shit. Now we just put our hand in the next guy's pocket."

In these shows, America is already a place where more and more people's dreams are running aground, where the poor and the middle class find it increasingly difficult to make ends meet, and where even the privileged feel a sense of emptiness and disappointment. No doubt this is one of the reasons viewership of *The Sopranos* on HBO's streaming service surged 179 percent during the pandemic. The series spun off several popular podcasts, and thirteen years after ending its original run was hailed by *GQ* as "the hottest show of 2020."

The legions of new Gen Z fans acquired by David Chase's groundbreaking series no doubt understood Tony Soprano's explanation for why he was feeling depressed. "It's good to be in something from the ground floor," the mob boss told his therapist, Dr. Melfi, in the show's pilot. "I came too late for that, I know. But lately, I'm getting the feeling that I came in at the end. The best is over." Thinking about his father, Tony adds, "He never reached the heights like me, but in a lot of ways he had it better. He had his people, they had their standards, they had their pride. Today, what do we got?" As for Tony's wayward son A.J., he becomes preoccupied with Yeats's vision of things falling apart in "The Second Coming" and sums up his feelings about America this way: "This is still where people come to make it, it's a beautiful idea." But "what do they get? Bling? Come-on's for shit they don't need and can't afford?"

Worries that the United States had entered a downward spiral aren't new, of course. But for much of its history, America has been relentlessly forward-looking—convinced, like the early settlers who had left behind the Old World, that America was a New World where they could reinvent themselves, where, as Tocqueville observed, "everything is in constant motion, and every movement seems an improvement." But in recent years, the belief, as Scarlett O'Hara put it, that "tomorrow is another day" has dwindled, with studies showing that millennials—facing uncertain career prospects, saddled with college debt, and priced out of a rising housing market—are on track to be the first generation in the nation's history that will fail to exceed their parents in income or job status. And then there is Donald Trump: Whereas earlier presidents routinely invoked the future (whether it was the New Deal or building an interstate highway system or embarking on the race to space), Trump ran on a promise to "Make America Great Again"— which was really code for turning the clock back to the pre-civil-rights days, when white men made the rules and African Americans, women, Latinos, LGBTQ+ people, and immigrants were consigned to the margins.

BECAUSE THE GREAT JAMES GANDOLFINI invested his portrayal of Tony with such nuance and swaggering charm, because he made Tony's frustrations with daily life so recognizable and real, audiences tended to identify with the mob boss—never mind that he killed eight people and presided over a ruthless gang of crooks and hit men. In his 2013 book, *Difficult Men,* Brett Martin argued that "no genre suited the baby boomers' dueling impulses of attraction and guilt toward American capitalism as well as the Mob drama. The notion that the American dream might at its core be a criminal enterprise lay at the center of the era's signature works, from *Bonnie and Clyde* and *Chinatown* to *The Godfather* and *Mean Streets*"—and *The Sopranos* "yoked that story to one of postwar literature's most potent tropes: horror of the suburbs," which had come, in much postwar literature, "to represent everything crushing and confining to man's essential nature."

Breaking Bad, too, was a dark parable about American decline. Viewers started out feeling they could relate to Walter White, the high school science teacher who found himself diagnosed with cancer, unable to afford medical treatments, and worried about supporting his family. And some viewers continued to root for Walt, even as he metamorphosed, in the words of the show's creator, Vince Gilligan, "from Mr. Chips into Scarface." Initially, Walt's decision to use his knowledge of chemistry to start cooking meth is spurred by financial desperation: Given eighteen months to live, Walt wants to leave his pregnant wife and their disabled son a nest egg for when he is gone. Figuring out the cost of college for two kids, mortgage payments on the house, and the daily costs of living (adjusted for inflation), he calculates that he needs to make $737,000—an amount impossibly beyond his teacher's salary, even when supplemented with pay from his second job at a local car wash.

And so, in a kind of dark twist on the American myth of the self-made man, Walt becomes a successful entrepreneur—a master meth cook and drug kingpin who goes by the name of Heisenberg. "I am not in danger, Skyler," he tells his worried wife. "I am the danger. A guy opens his door and gets shot, and you think that's me? No! I am the one who knocks!"

The critic Alan Sepinwall (*The Revolution Was Televised*) makes the keen observation that *The Sopranos* and *The Wire* are both "shows about the end of the American dream," but whereas the first "comes across as deeply cynical about humanity," the latter "believes that any innate goodness within people eventually gets ground down by the institutions that they serve." "The America of *The Wire* is broken," Sepinwall goes on, "in a fundamental, probably irreparable way. It is an interconnected network of ossified institutions," all of them "committed to perpetuating their own business-as-usual approach" and preserving the status quo regardless of the human costs.

A choral portrait of the city of Baltimore, *The Wire* introduces dozens of characters—cops and drug dealers, reporters, politicians, dockworkers, schoolkids, lawyers, gang members, businessmen, police informants, and junkies—and shows us how "all the pieces matter," how decisions made by those with power or influence can have devastating fallout on the lives of those who have neither, those men and women who, in the words of the show's creator, David Simon, were "left in the shallows" by the American economy: "unemployed and under-employed, idle at a West Baltimore soup kitchen or dead-ended at some strip-mall cash register." And those folks who aren't jobless tend to work for organizations—whether the police department or a drug empire—that grind them down or get them killed. Not surprisingly, the series' most captivating character is a quintessential outsider—Omar Little, played by the brilliant Michael K. Williams, a gay stickup man who works for no one and adheres to his own strict code of honor, a feared and fearless badass who can also be generous, tender, and loyal.

The Wire and *The Sopranos* changed television storytelling, made TV the hot, go-to medium, and opened the way to a host of new antiheroes, each darker than the next. In addition to Walter White, there was the crooked cop Vic Mackey (*The Shield*), the Machiavellian congressman Frank Underwood (*House of Cards*), the gangster/politician Nucky Thompson (*Boardwalk Empire*), the ruthless lawyer Patty Hewes (*Damages*), the serial killer Dexter Morgan (*Dexter*), the duplicitous Don Draper (*Mad Men*), the scheming Cersei Lannister (*Game of Thrones*), the money launderer Marty Byrde (*Ozark*), the drug lord Teresa Mendoza (*Queen of the South*), and the toxic media mogul Logan Roy in the iconic series of the Trump era, *Succession*.

In *The Sopranos Sessions*, Steven Van Zandt, who played Tony's consigliere Silvio Dante, told the book's authors, Matt Zoller Seitz and Alan Sepinwall, that audiences often focus on "the romantic version of the criminal lifestyle" where the gangster is "the guy who breaks all the rules and gets away with it, at least for a while"; "it's booze and broads and horses and dice and killing a guy if he gets in your way and not caring what anybody thinks of you."

It wasn't just the case with Mafia movies and TV shows, Van Zandt added: "It's Cagney and Bogart movies, it's Westerns. America seems to have some kind of fascination with outlaws in general. Maybe it's because we were an outlaw nation to begin with. This nation was born of rebellion against authority, and in a weird way, that's what these characters represent. That image is very attractive to Americans. It's part of the national unconscious. It's practically in our genetic code."

NO COUNTRY HAS FOLKLORE more deeply invested in the myth of the heroic outsider than the United States, given its revolutionary origins and veneration of the frontier, which, the historian Frederick Jackson Turner famously argued, indelibly shaped Americans' sense of identity—their prizing of individuality and freedom and independence.

The legends surrounding the frontiersman Daniel Boone (and quite probably Davy Crockett, too) would help inspire Natty Bumppo in James Fenimore Cooper's *Leatherstocking Tales*—a loner and "pathfinder," without parents or a wife or children, who lives on the edge of the frontier, knowing his way of life is doomed by the relentless advance of civilization. The lone gunslinger would also become a familiar trope in movie westerns: most notably in *High Noon* (1952), where Gary Cooper plays the part of a newly married town marshal who, on the eve of his retirement, must face down a notorious outlaw and his gang—with no deputy or townspeople to provide backup; and *Shane* (1953), where Alan Ladd plays a mysterious drifter who rides into town and saves a family of homesteaders when an evil cattle baron threatens to run them off their land. At the end of that movie, the family's young son begs Shane to stay, but he rides off on his horse, saying he doesn't belong there: "A man has to be what he is . . . A brand sticks."

These characters embody an old-fashioned frontier ethic as well as Emerson's credo that "whoso would be a man, must be a nonconformist." For that matter, a startling number of iconic movie heroes are what Melville's Ishmael calls "Isolatoes"— "not acknowledging the common continent of men, but each *Isolato* living on a separate continent of his own." Cut off by choice or circumstances, those *isolatoes* include such disparate characters as Rambo, Wolverine, many of the most memorable characters played by Humphrey Bogart (from Rick in *Casablanca* to Charlie in *The African Queen*), Dustin Hoffman (in *The Graduate, Midnight Cowboy, Rain Man*), and Leonardo DiCaprio (as Gatsby, Howard Hughes in *The Aviator*, and the Man in the Iron Mask); and a growing number of astronauts lost in space in movies like *Gravity, Solaris, Moon*, and *The Martian*.

IN A 1980 ESSAY, the scholar Richard E. Meyer wrote that the American outlaw hero tends to (re)emerge during times of economic or social crisis and is regarded as a "man of the people" who stands in opposition to oppressive political or business interests (yes, the Robin Hood legend again in a new guise). For instance, the legend of Jesse James, who led a gang of train and bank robbers on a crime spree that spanned some seven years, grew during the Reconstruction era in the South, when anger over the defeat of the Confederacy was often directed at symbols of authority—like the banks and trains Jesse James robbed. The pattern was repeated in a similar fashion half a century later, Meyer adds, as "Pretty Boy Floyd, Oklahoma's outlaw-hero of the Great Depression, symbolically strikes back against the bloodsucking forces of absentee ownership every time he hits a bank or a train."

In Black American folk culture, the trickster hero Brer Rabbit—whose stories can be traced back to Africa and the Caribbean—possesses an outsider's sympathetic appeal: The resourceful rabbit, who gets the best of more powerful creatures through his cleverness and wit, was an appealing figure for slaves and their descendants coping with oppression and discrimination. And contemporary kin of Brer Rabbit continue to captivate: The effortlessly cool Bugs Bunny, for one, is always ready with the snappy comeback, the winning wisecrack, and he always triumphs over his archenemy, the bumbling, baby-faced Elmer Fudd.

Bugs's anarchic streak is shared by many American cartoon heroes, from Woody Woodpecker with his maniacal laugh, to the hot-tempered Donald Duck, to the Cat in the Hat, a con artist and small-time chaos monster, dressed in a bow tie and a red-and-white-striped top hat, who disrupts a quiet household, creating havoc and mess.

IN THE 1950S, SOME Americans doubled down on their romance with rebels and renegades—partly in reaction to the contrary movement toward conformity, which had accompanied the growth of consumer culture.

The 1950s were the decade that produced that classic novel of teenage alienation *The Catcher in the Rye* (1951) and movies like *The Wild One* (1953), *Rebel Without a Cause* (1955), and *Jailhouse Rock* (1957) starring a trio of actors—Marlon Brando, James Dean, and Elvis Presley—whose brooding intensity and bad-boy cool created a new template of pop culture stardom.

This was the decade in which Beat writers published their most influential work: Allen Ginsberg's *Howl* in 1956, Jack Kerouac's *On the Road* in 1957, and William S. Burroughs's *Naked Lunch* in 1959—daring, provocative works whose experimental techniques and explicit content outraged the "square" world but energized the arts scene and laid the groundwork for what became the counterculture in the 1960s.

Existentialism—and talk of "the absurd"—circulated on college campuses, people spoke about growing up under the shadow of the atomic bomb, and books like David Riesman's *The Lonely Crowd* (1950) and William H. Whyte's *Organization Man* (1956) became bestsellers. Those books addressed the countertrend in the 1950s of increased uniformity as more and more people became office workers and moved to the suburbs and a new world of corporate bureaucracy threatened to trample the old maverick virtues of individualism and independence.

Whyte's book—much like Sloan Wilson's popular 1955 novel, *The Man in the Gray Flannel Suit*—argued that the kind of get-along groupthink that often prevailed in big offices suppressed creativity and entrepreneurship. And Riesman's popular but sometimes misunderstood book (written with Nathan Glazer and Reuel Denney) argued that with the decline of tradition-directed societies in the late Middle Ages two main character types had evolved: the "inner-directed" type, who relies upon an inner gyroscope (largely forged by early or parental values) to navigate life; and the "other-directed" type, who is sensitive "to the expectations and preferences of others." Riesman saw the perils of the "other-directed" personality type becoming more dominant in the mid-twentieth century (think what he would have made of social media users obsessed with racking up "likes"), but he also saw how individuals who were purely "inner-directed" could lapse into blinkered or egotistical behavior (remember: Ahab was an *isolato,* too). Therefore, the aim of a truly autonomous person, he suggested, was to somehow achieve a balance between pragmatism and independence, empathy and detachment.

AS AMERICA MOVED INTO the 1960s, divisions widened between outsiders and the so-called silent majority—divisions over Vietnam and the civil rights movement, and over everything from music to fashion to living arrangements. Rock 'n' roll and psychedelia and drugs were all components of the counterculture revolt against the conformity, and in his 1970 book, *The Greening of America,* the Yale professor Charles Reich heralded this development as the momentous advent of what he called "Consciousness III." He fatuously suggested that the hippies' lifestyle rebellion would bring about a moral and ideological revolution, as though wearing bell-bottoms and love beads would somehow magically lead to a change in the political order. Instead, their tie-dyed trappings of revolt were quickly co-opted by Madison Avenue. Outsiders—be it Holden Caulfield in *The Catcher in the Rye* or Dustin Hoffman's character Benjamin in *The Graduate* or the brooding heroes of French existential novels—had already made alienation and rebellion fashionable among the college crowd; now the counterculture could be commodified for the masses.

Buick advertised its 1970 models as cars that "light your fire," while Dodge urged customers to "join the Dodge rebellion." In 1967, Clairol began "the Great Beige-In," introducing three "psychedelicious beiges" for lips and nails, and the following year the Campbell soup kids dressed up in Nehru jackets, beads, and Day-Glo colors. In 1968, 7UP began pro-

moting itself as the "uncola," while Oldsmobile started hawk-
ing "youngmobiles."

Although Reich hailed blue jeans as a symbol of Consciousness III's anti-materialist philosophy ("Basically they are
machine-made, and there is no attempt to hide that fact, no
shame attached to mass-produced goods, no social points lost
for wearing something that sells at $4.99 from coast to coast"),
wealthy consumers were soon paying thousands of dollars for
special-edition, recycled designer iterations and for rare, early
vintage Levi's (one pair from the 1880s recently went for nearly
$100,000). Designers have similarly discovered meditation,
yoga, and *Whole Earth Catalog* holism. Gwyneth Paltrow's
lifestyle website Goop offers merchandise like a two-piece
meditation pillow set (covered in "plush high-pile chenille")
for $290 and a pyramid-shaped mahogany cabinet that "creates
a spatial vortex in whatever room it's placed in, energetically
lifting the vibrations there" (cost: $35,000, no returns).

Some valuable adjustments in thinking also took root, much
the way the American palate has expanded to appreciate General Tso's chicken, beef vindaloo, and sushi. Alternative medicine and the practice of "mindfulness" are no longer regarded
as hippie or New Age eccentricities but as valuable parts of
many health and wellness programs. And plant-based diets,
once mocked as the province of health food fanatics, have
become so popular that fast-food chains like Burger King
(the "Impossible Whopper"), White Castle (the "Impossible
Slider"), and Carl's Jr. (the "Beyond Famous Star" burger)
now offer meat-free items on their menus. At the same time, a
growing number of designers and fashion outlets (including
Prada, Armani, Gucci, Versace, and Burberry, and stores like
Nordstrom and Neiman Marcus) have renounced fur or are

making the transition to being fur-free. In 2020, PETA announced it was ending its "I'd Rather Go Naked Than Wear Fur" campaign: After three decades, the organization said it had achieved its goal of creating a tipping point in public awareness.

Nowadays, much of corporate America insists it has developed a social conscience. As of early 2022, a survey found that 271 U.S. corporations had pledged $67 billion toward racial equity since the murder of George Floyd and the Black Lives Matter protests of 2020, though only $652 million of those funds had been disbursed at the time. Commercials featuring mixed-race couples have proliferated on TV, and so have ads promising to lower carbon emissions and reduce the consumption of plastic.

It remains to be seen if such moves are the first wavelets of a sea change in social and political thinking. Or if they are little more than virtue signaling—like the safety pins some liberals attached to their jackets after Trump's election (meant to signify solidarity with the oppressed), or the ubiquitous black squares that appeared on Instagram, meant to show support for Black Lives Matter—well-meaning gestures, perhaps, but no substitute for real and sustained commitment to change.

...

THE
CENTRIFUGAL REPUBLIC:
Why Hackers, Politicians, and Business Leaders
Embraced Decentralization

· · ·

Be water.

—BRUCE LEE

I N HIS CLASSIC 1984 BOOK, *HACKERS: HEROES OF THE Computer Revolution*, the journalist Steven Levy defined the "hacker ethic," emerging among MIT students and early Silicon Valley pioneers during the middle decades of the twentieth century. Its central precepts, he wrote, included the following: "Access to computers—and anything that might teach you something about the way the world works—should be unlimited and total"; "All information should be free"; and "Mistrust Authority—Promote Decentralization."

Decentralization wasn't just an ideal embraced by early Silicon Valley pioneers who shared the counterculture's hatred of authority. It was a quality built into the foundations of what would become the internet when the U.S. government was grappling, in the early 1960s, with Cold War fears of a conflict with the Soviet Union, and needed a communications network that could withstand a nuclear attack.

Paul Baran, a Polish-born engineer at the RAND Corporation, proposed a solution: Whereas centralized systems (shaped like a star) were susceptible to being taken out by one strategically placed hit, he argued, a "distributed" system (shaped like a grid with many nodes that created redundancy) had much better chances of surviving—even if several nodes were knocked out, at least a portion of the network would continue to function. Baran's work—along with that of the British computer scientist Donald Davies—would lead to the development of "packet switching" (a secure method of splitting and sending data that is reassembled at its destination), which, in the late 1960s, would become a basis for sending messages between computers and the development of the ARPANET, which connected academic, military, and research institutions and would eventually evolve into the internet.

It remained difficult for scientists using the internet to share information until 1989, when Tim Berners-Lee—then a software engineer at CERN, the particle physics lab in Geneva—came up with the idea of using the emerging technology of hypertext to create the World Wide Web. In 1991, people outside CERN were invited to join this new web community, which embraced an array of egalitarian protocols including bottom-up design ("instead of code being written and controlled by a small group of experts," it would be "developed in full view of everyone, encouraging maximum participation and experimentation"); net neutrality (meaning that internet service providers should treat all information equally); and decentralization (meaning "no permission is needed from a central authority to post anything on the web" and there is no "kill switch"—no way a central authority could control or monitor everything).

In 1997, the computer programmer Eric Raymond coined a metaphor to differentiate between two types of software development: "the cathedral" being the traditional approach whereby a select group diligently works on a product (like Microsoft Office), fixing bugs before releasing their creation to the world; and "the bazaar" or "open source" method, whereby a product (like Linux) is developed collaboratively on the web, with thousands of people finding and fixing bugs. These two terms—"the cathedral" and "the bazaar"—would also become larger metaphors for old-fashioned top-down dynamics versus more decentralized, bottom-up ones.

THE DEMOCRATIC IDEALS OF early digital pioneers were eclipsed as Silicon Valley became a glittering magnet for venture capital, and a handful of start-ups grew into vast multinational companies that reach across the globe. These tech giants reversed the decentralization prized by so many first-generation hackers: Already gigantic, they continued to gobble up smaller companies and use their power to tilt the playing field to their own advantage. Meanwhile, they vacuumed up our data, pelted us with advertisements based on that data, and erased our privacy—which, out of habit or convenience, we've allowed.

The web, Berners-Lee wrote in a blog post, "has evolved into an engine of inequity and division; swayed by powerful forces who use it for their own agendas."

To restore the original spirit of the web and sidestep the tentacles of government and Big Tech, Berners-Lee has proposed a new platform called Solid that would allow individuals to retain ownership and control of their personal information by placing it in secure PODS (personal online data stores); companies would have to request (or be granted) access to that information but could not data mine that information or sell it.

Other proponents of a decentralized web or Web3 are proposing a model based on the sort of peer-to-peer technology employed by blockchain (which powers bitcoin and other cryptocurrencies). In theory, such a decentralized architecture would allow users to bypass the control of tech giants like Facebook, Google, and Microsoft, which currently act as intermediaries, and would also make it more difficult for Big Tech and governments to collect our data and control what we see.

Blockchain is a kind of digital ledger where transaction data is stored not in one central location but on servers and hard drives around the world, making that data difficult to alter or hack and circumventing centralized authorities like governments and banks. In 2014, Gavin Wood, a co-founder of the platform Ethereum, argued that "post-Snowden" it had become clear that it was dangerous to entrust our information to "large organizations and governments" that "routinely attempt to stretch and overstep their authority."

Bitcoin was released as an open-source program in early 2009 by the mysterious Satoshi Nakamoto (possibly a pseudonym for an individual or group), who said that in the wake of the 2008 crash, he wanted to create a secure currency that would be impervious to manipulation by bankers, politicians, and national monetary policies. Bitcoin and other cryptocurrencies gained popularity as bitterness over bank bailouts grew and investors welcomed the idea of skirting government and Wall Street control. Proponents argue that cryptocurrency will transform commerce and the financial services industry— depending on how it is regulated and how widely it is adopted by the mainstream marketplace. Others worry that its rapid growth could be destabilizing, that it could facilitate money laundering and criminal exploitation, and that investing in a currency which possesses no intrinsic value is extremely hazardous— a warning underscored by the spectacular crash of the cryptocurrency exchange FTX in the fall of 2022.

Blockchain, advocates contend, has the potential to disrupt industries from e-commerce to music sales to health care by creating virtually tamperproof records and allowing retailers to sell directly to customers without intermediaries. Whereas people now tend to place their trust in marketplaces like Amazon and eBay, blockchain will supposedly empower buyers to make trustworthy purchases directly from manufacturers and vendors. For artists, too, blockchain promises tangible benefits—not only making it more difficult, say, to illegally copy and download music, but also enabling musicians to be compensated directly for their work without having to rely upon platforms like Apple Music (iTunes) and Spotify.

Some skeptics fear that a decentralized web could exacerbate already troubling dynamics, becoming a high-speed conduit for hate speech and racism, and that the lack of centralized authorities would make it more difficult than ever to moderate illegal or dangerous content. Others doubt that a decentralized web will ever supplant the existing internet, and that even if it manages to somehow gain a foothold, it, too, will somehow end up being co-opted by Big Tech or large venture capital firms.

IN THE CASE OF government, decentralization has been a dynamic that ebbs and flows throughout American history as political power has moved, back and forth, from Washington outward to the states, and from the provinces back toward the center. Alexis de Tocqueville remarked upon Americans' habit of forming local "associations of a thousand" kinds ("some religious, some moral, some grave, some trivial, some quite general and others quite particular, some huge and others tiny"), and he thought such groups, rooted in states and communities, could serve as useful checks on the power of an overbearing central government.

Decades earlier, however, the reluctance of states to compromise their sovereignty almost derailed the birth of the nation. As the historian Joseph Ellis wrote in his 2021 book, *The
Cause,* all the political energy at the end of the Revolutionary
War "belonged to 'pluribus,' not 'unum.'" While Federalists
like George Washington and Alexander Hamilton urged the
surrender of state and regional interests to the larger purpose
of nationhood, there were many who "envisioned a North
American version of Europe, thirteen separate countries, always vying for dominance, loosely linked in a domestic League
of Nations." After all, Americans at the time were separated by
vast geographic distances, and many associated the idea of a
centralized government with the tyrannical rule of Britain,
which they had only just managed to escape. The problem with
the loose arrangement established under the Articles of Confederation was that the central government was so weak it
couldn't compel the payment of taxes, and so couldn't even pay
the long overdue wages of soldiers who fought the Revolutionary War.

For America to manage its economy and sustain an army,
Hamilton argued, it needed to think like a nation, and to that
end it needed a government with enhanced centralized authority. But achieving that would not be easy. In a 1783 letter to
Washington, Hamilton wrote of the "arduous work" of unify-
ing the young nation—difficult because, "to borrow a figure
from mechanics, the centrifugal is much stronger than the cen-
tripetal force in these states—the seeds of disunion much more
numerous than those of union." Indeed, it would take savvy
political leadership on the part of the Federalists—lobbying,
horse-trading, and the publication of a series of persuasive essays now known as *The Federalist Papers*—to win ratification
of the Constitution and begin the work of creating a United

States (which one prominent Anglican clergyman, Ellis reports, derided as an oxymoron because he guessed that the fate
of the unruly Americans was "to be a Disunited People till the
End of Time").

Today, centrifugal forces are once again ascendant in
American politics, boosted by growing partisanship, increased
grassroots activism across the political spectrum, and by states
asserting their power to implement policy on everything from
voting rights, to abortion bans, to gun control. This move by
states is partly a response to stubborn and persistent gridlock
in Washington. It's also a strategy aggressively pursued by
conservatives—and, increasingly, by progressives—as a kind
of end run around the federal government. And with red states
and blue states enacting legislation that puts them increasingly
at odds with one another, many journalists and historians pre-
dict that the result will likely be further polarization and fragmentation of the country as a whole.

IN MUCH THE SAME way as the Republican Party has worked
since the 1980s to create a pipeline of conservative judges, it has
spent decades investing money and resources to build up its
influence in states as both a backup to and a booster of their efforts on the national stage. As of January 2023, Republicans
controlled twenty-eight state legislatures and the Democrats
nineteen. Trump's presidency and the new conservative majority on the Supreme Court emboldened GOP efforts to push
through controversial, even unpopular, state legislation—
confident that it is now increasingly likely to withstand judicial
challenges.

There has been a flurry of legislation passed by red states—
banning or restricting abortions, making it harder to vote,
and imposing restrictions on what teachers can discuss in the

classroom—that Republicans hope will become stepping-stones toward national versions of these laws. In the wake of the Supreme Court's overturning of *Roe v. Wade* in the summer of 2022, most abortions were banned in fourteen states, with other red states moving to make it more difficult to obtain an abortion—by prohibiting the procedure after a certain number of weeks (six, fifteen, or eighteen weeks depending on the state) and crafting bills that would penalize businesses that promised to cover employees' out-of-state abortion-related expenses.

Inflamed by Trump's baseless claims of widespread election fraud, Republican-controlled states have also been passing election interference laws, which raise the odds of partisan meddling in elections, and restrictive voting laws, which make it more difficult to vote by narrowing the window for early voting, restricting the use of mail-in ballots, or implementing stricter voter ID requirements.

To energize their base and boost campaign donations, Republicans have simultaneously been pushing through aggressive state legislation on controversial culture-war issues, from restricting the rights of transgender individuals to the banning of books.

The American Library Association reported a record 1,269 attempted book bans in 2022—nearly double the number of those in 2021—and librarians are being harassed online and threatened with violence or legal action. In contrast to earlier challenges (which usually concerned a single title), recent efforts to ban books increasingly involve the removal of multiple books—the majority of which are by or about Black or LGBTQ+ people. Of the reported book challenges, said the ALA, 58 percent targeted books and materials in school libraries, classroom libraries, or school curricula; 41 percent of book challenges targeted materials in public libraries.

Whereas most efforts to remove a particular book from a school syllabus or library used to originate with individual parents or school board members, book bans are increasingly coordinated by right-wing organizations. Like efforts to ban the teaching of "critical race theory," they are less real grassroots movements than examples of astroturfing—that is, national campaigns coordinated from above but disguised as local efforts.

The former Trump adviser Steve Bannon sees critical race theory as a hot-button topic that Republicans can use to energize the base. Conservative media outlets like Fox News and *Breitbart* are beating the war drums on the subject, while activists (in some cases with ties to big-money donors like the Koch, Mercer, and DeVos families) are sharing strategies and helping to coordinate efforts on the ground. Established conservative organizations like the Heritage Foundation and newer ones founded by Trump alumni have issued guidelines for legislation on critical race theory that can be used as templates by individual states; some also provide parents with tool kits and webinars featuring advice on organizing school board protests.

In attempts to counter Republican policy-making, blue states have been shoring up their own laws protecting the right to abortion, with some offering to serve as safe havens for residents from other states that have restricted or banned the procedure. In fact, many Democrats see abortion rights as a winning issue for their party: Since the Supreme Court overturned *Roe v. Wade*, the AP reported in mid-2023, six states had reproductive rights on the ballot, and in every case, voters supported abortion rights—even in conservative states like Kansas.

Something similar is happening with gun control—an increasingly urgent issue in this era of mass shootings. After the

Supreme Court struck down a century-old concealed carry law in the summer of 2022, governors and legislatures in blue states including New York, California, and New Jersey began looking at ways to rewrite their laws that would enable them to still restrict the use of firearms—including background checks, a ban on guns without serial numbers, age limits on the purchase of semiautomatic weapons, and location-based rulings that would prohibit people from carrying guns, say, in schools and subways.

In 2017, when President Trump announced he was pulling the United States out of the Paris climate accords and began rolling back Obama-era policies designed to protect the environment, some states began pushing back. New York, California, Washington, and Virginia, for instance, took legislative and executive actions to implement clean energy policies and reduce greenhouse gas emissions.

Cities, too, joined the effort. Worldwide, these population centers generate nearly three-quarters of greenhouse gas emissions, and many, located on coasts or major waterways, are particularly vulnerable to rising sea levels. In his 2017 book, *Climate of Hope,* the former New York City mayor Michael Bloomberg made the case like this: "As the primary drivers of climate change, cities must take the lead in tackling it. And as the likeliest victims of climate change, they have the greatest incentive to do so."

The mayors of almost a hundred cities around the world have come together in the C40 network to share strategies for fighting climate change and to coordinate efforts with regional leaders and business partners. Some cities like Paris, Copenhagen, and Melbourne have taken up the "fifteen-minute city" concept, which employs the principle of decentralization to create neighborhoods in which grocery stores, schools, and offices are within a fifteen-minute walk, bike ride, or metro trip—a concept intended to cut down on the use of cars, with the added benefit of giving people an emotional sense of belonging to a community.

AT THE SAME TIME, decentralization has become an increasingly popular organizational principle adopted by businesses, insurgent groups, and government and military agencies. The internet has made decentralization easier and more practical as a strategy for coping with multiplying complexities and rapidly changing circumstances.

Many multinational companies have adopted decentralization as a way to deal with globalization, expanding their worldwide reach while relying upon regional offices to provide feedback and help tailor marketing and products to local demands. Proponents argue that a flatter, team-based approach to management can improve employee morale and creativity while giving a company access to a larger and more diverse talent pool. It can result in companies that are more agile in adapting to market changes and sturdier in the face of crises.

In their 2006 book, *The Starfish and the Spider*, entrepreneurs Ori Brafman and Rod A. Beckstrom likened old hierarchical business models to spiders (which die if decapitated), and more decentralized ones to starfish (which, as neural networks, can regenerate a lost arm)—a kind of variation on Paul Baran's strategy for surviving a nuclear attack. The authors cite the history of the Apaches as an example of the resilience conferred by decentralization: They were able to hold off Spanish conquest for centuries, Brafman and Beckstrom argue, because the tribe's dispersion and lack of clearly defined leaders made it less vulnerable to the sorts of attacks that toppled the Aztec and Inca Empires.

The COVID pandemic greatly accelerated the adoption of decentralization by companies across the world as people began working remotely from home and management realized their businesses could survive the plague years only by becoming more efficient and more adept at managing supply chains—goals they believed a more horizontal architecture could facilitate.

A 2020 report from the management consulting firm McKinsey & Company concluded that the COVID crisis had created a "malleable moment" that businesses could use to transform their workplaces, noting that in many cases "boundaries and silos have been removed" and "decision-making has accelerated and been pushed further down in the organization."

RESILIENCE AND ADAPTABILITY ALSO make decentralization appealing to activist groups. In some cases, there are more philosophical reasons as well: a determination to repudiate the hierarchical structure of traditional institutions, which many protesters today regard as elitist, paternalistic, clumsily bureaucratic. The lack of prominent leaders—a Nelson Mandela, a Martin Luther King Jr., or a Cesar Chavez—makes for more egalitarian movements, say proponents, and allows for more input from more organizers on the ground.

This "leaderless" quality shared by so many of the twenty-first century's protest movements—including the Arab Spring uprisings, the Yellow Vests in France, the worldwide climate protests, and the Hong Kong pro-democracy demonstrations—also reflects how these groups were organized online through social media and the use of other digital tools.

The problem with such movements is that without established leaders at the top it can be more difficult to make sure supporters are on the same page in terms of strategies and goals. And once a movement has gained traction, more difficult to leverage influence within the system and win lasting legislative change.

While social media has enabled networked protests to grow rapidly, as the writer and scholar Zeynep Tufekci notes in her incisive book *Twitter and Tear Gas,* it's also allowed activists to sidestep "many of the dreary aspects of political organizing." The resulting movements often lack the organizational infrastructure that could help them formulate both tactical and long-term strategic goals. Whereas the Montgomery bus boycott of 1955–56 and the 1963 March on Washington were built on years of organizing work—which forged "collective decision-making capabilities" and a sense of cohesion based on "shared experience and tribulation"—many of today's movements, which came together quickly over the internet, lack the institutional depth that would help them sustain momentum over the years.

As the journalist Moisés Naím wrote in *The End of Power,* "In the twenty-first century, power is easier to get, harder to use—and easier to lose."

Also, participants in leaderless movements often disagree among themselves over everything from politics and priorities to tactics and public messaging. The Yellow Vests movement in France, for instance, began as a series of protests in 2018 against a hike in gasoline taxes (which the French government eventually suspended) but soon evolved into antigovernment demonstrations decrying the high cost of living, with some protesters at opposite ends of the ideological spectrum clashing over issues like immigration.

The lack of top-down leadership and organizational discipline can make eruptions of violence more likely and allow fringe elements to hijack or besmirch the group. In 2019, the anti-Semitic invective used by some Yellow Vests protesters cast a cloud over the larger movement, with critics questioning just how far bigotry and conspiracy theories had permeated its demonstrations.

As for the practical aspects of leaderless movements, some activists argue that this structure makes a group less vulnerable to being crippled by government arrests or attacks. In fact the idea of "leaderless resistance" was adopted in the 1990s by white supremacists as a means of avoiding infiltration by the government. Many mass shootings carried out by extremists on the far right have been "self-directed" terrorist attacks carried out not on orders from a leader but by individuals radicalized by extremist propaganda and shared rage—much the way that al-Qaeda and ISIS have increasingly recruited operatives on the web.

WHEN THE U.S. MILITARY began counterterrorism efforts in Iraq to combat the growing insurgency there in the wake of the 2003 invasion, a special operations task force was given the mission of defeating the threat posed by al-Qaeda in Iraq, led by Abu Musab al-Zarqawi, who was directing a terrorist campaign that was killing thousands of Iraqi civilians in addition to U.S. and coalition forces. A paper published by the Modern War Institute contended that because al-Qaeda in Iraq was such a decentralized organization, the commander of the U.S. task force, Major General Stanley McChrystal, realized "there was 'no single person or place' that the United States could strike" to take it down and that he needed to decentralize his own task force in order to effectively respond.

"A rigid hierarchical task force would be too slow to defeat this networked threat," the paper continued, and so McChrystal made its structure flatter, with more decentralized decision-making. Intelligence was widely shared with subordinate leaders so they would "feel empowered to act without seeking guidance." It was this rebooted version of the American task force that would eventually succeed in neutralizing much of al-Qaeda in Iraq.

Decentralized command and control also played a key role in Ukraine's success against a much larger Russian invading force in the opening months of the war—along, of course, with the Ukrainian president Volodymyr Zelensky's inspirational leadership and U.S.- and NATO-supplied weapons.

Ukraine's commanding general, Valery Zaluzhny, belongs, *Time* magazine reported, to "a new generation of Ukrainian leaders who learned to be flexible and delegate decisions to commanders on the ground"—in sharp contrast to the lumbering Russian army, which had changed little since the end of the twentieth century.

The high casualty rate among Russian generals—Ukrainian sources claimed in early 2023 that fourteen Russian generals had been killed—was a sign, defense experts added, that the Russians were reluctant to delegate authority to lower-ranking officials; this archaic, top-down model of leadership, inherited from the Soviets, meant that generals frequently needed to travel to the dangerous front lines.

Ukrainian soldiers scored startling wins against the Russian military machine, using the creative methods that insurgent underdogs frequently deploy against bigger, established powers: in this case, small, agile groups of soldiers equipped with drones and shoulder-fired missiles and employing hit-and-run tactics to ambush enemy tanks and supply lines. Their efforts were augmented by civilian defense volunteers and ordinary Ukrainians who found inventive ways to contribute to their country's war effort. Construction workers welded together metal spikes to create "hedgehogs" that could be placed on roads to block Russian military vehicles. Seamstresses fashioned body armor for soldiers, using scrap metal from old cars as protective plates. People turned their kitchens and garages into Molotov cocktail factories and created DIY grenade launchers. Residents dug underground bunkers, filled sandbags, repaired captured Russian equipment, piled tires and trash in intersections to impede Russian tanks, and removed or reversed road signs to confuse the invaders.

When it came to the digital battlefront, the Ukrainians again demonstrated the asymmetrical advantages technology can confer: how innovative, crowdsourced methods can actually get the better of a massive state-run intelligence and propaganda apparatus. Since the 2014 Russian invasion and annexation of Crimea, the Ukrainian government made a push to build up its digital infrastructure and counter Russian disinformation—moves accelerated by President Zelensky, who established the Ministry of Digital Transformation in 2019. That agency's many initiatives included efforts to increase investments from foreign tech companies and the development of crowdsourcing apps that would enable civilians to report on Russian troop movements and get food, water, and medical supplies delivered to communities in need. At the same time, Ukrainians have been using social media to tell the world what they witnessed as Russian bombs fell on their homes and schools, and their earnest accounts—by turns heartbreaking, stoic, and profane—quickly drowned out the Russian propaganda factory's bot-produced lies.

Digital help also arrived from independent sources around the world. The open-source investigative group Bellingcat (which had broken important stories about Russian involvement in the 2014 downing of Malaysia Airlines flight 17 and the poisoning of the opposition leader Aleksei Navalny) began using geolocation data, satellite imagery, and social media posts to expose Russian disinformation before it could gain traction, and document possible war crimes.

Meanwhile, so many hackers wanted to use their skills to help Ukraine that the country established a special Telegram channel setting out goals and specific tasks—like finding ways to get factual information through Putin's digital iron curtain, or disrupting Russian websites and communications. The decentralized structure of the Telegram initiative, Ukraine's deputy minister of digital transformation, Oleksandr Bornyakov, told *Politico Magazine,* gave it protection: "We don't have a chain of command or any structure at all. So, [Russia] can't fight it. It's impossible to disrupt it or break it down. You can't bomb it or cut off connections or take down a top person—because there is no top person."

. . .

OPTIMIZING MARGINALITY:
Outsiders and
Outside-the-Box Thinking

. . .

Immigrants, we get the job done.

—LIN-MANUEL MIRANDA, *Hamilton*

IN A 1980 SPEECH FOR THE LIBRARY OF CONGRESS TITLED "The Fertile Verge," the historian Daniel J. Boorstin proposed a theory to explain the secret of American creativity. Throughout American history, he argued, technological and artistic breakthroughs proliferated because settlers were freed from the traditions of the Old World and were forced by isolation and the geographic vastness of the continent to forge new identities for themselves based on the pioneer virtues of resourcefulness and self-reliance. This is a variation, of course, on Frederick Jackson Turner's famous and chauvinistic frontier thesis (1893), but Boorstin went on to examine the other factors that turned America into a kind of laboratory for experiments and innovation: most notably, an "openness to novelty and change," an outpouring of energy and new ideas brought here by successive waves of immigrants, and the "new confusions" and cultural reconfigurations created when the "imported ways" of these outsiders crashed up against those of their neighbors. It was America's very lack of uniformity, Boorstin argued, that was a prime driver of its commercial and artistic fertility.

Trump's immigration policies—and his stoking of the fear of otherness—flew in the face of all evidence of the formative role that immigrants have played in the United States, and they sent shock waves through the tech world, universities, and arts institutions, which warned of the "brain drain" that would result. Silicon Valley worried that Trump's crackdown on H-1B visas for highly skilled foreign labor would deplete their reservoir of talent, and in the wake of Trump's election many students with expertise in engineering and coding decided to return to their home countries like India and China, while Canadian companies saw a sudden uptick in job applications from the very sorts of innovators and young entrepreneurs who had played such an essential role in establishing Silicon Valley as the world's foremost tech hub.

In fact, studies show that immigrants are twice as likely as native-born Americans to start new businesses and that more than half of top U.S. tech companies were founded by immigrants or children of immigrants. In addition to the frequently cited examples of Google co-founder Sergey Brin (who was born in Russia) and Apple's co-founder Steve Jobs (the son of a Syrian immigrant), there's eBay's founder, Pierre Omidyar (born in France to Iranian parents), Yahoo's co-founder Jerry Yang (born in Taiwan), PayPal's co-founder Peter Thiel (born in Germany), the Tesla and SpaceX co-founder, Elon Musk (born in South Africa), and the co-founders of Stripe, John and Patrick Collison (born in Ireland).

A 2019 Stanford University paper found that "immigrants comprised 23% of the total workforce in STEM occupations" and account "for 26% of US-based Nobel Prize winners from 1990 through 2000." Drawing on a 2003 survey, the study also showed that immigrants in the United States with a four-year college degree were "twice as likely to have a patent than US-born college grads."

In trying to explain this phenomenon, a 2021 Cato Institute study cited the following qualities shared by many successful immigrants: a tolerance for risk ("the fact that an individual's decision to emigrate is risky, much like starting a new business"), and an entrepreneurial eagerness to go out on one's own, often prompted by discrimination and lack of opportunities in the labor market.

In the arts, too, immigrants have been in the vanguard of innovation. The founders of Hollywood's studio system in the early twentieth century—Adolph Zukor, Louis B. Mayer, and the brothers Jack, Harry, and Sam Warner—were Jewish immigrants from eastern Europe. As outsiders eager to assimilate, the film historian Neal Gabler observed, these moguls created movies that mythologized their adopted country; at the same time, "as immigrants themselves, they had a peculiar sensitivity to the dreams and aspirations of other immigrants and working-class families, two overlapping groups that made up a significant portion of the early moviegoing audience."

Decades later, in the 1940s and 1950s, immigrants like Arshile Gorky, Willem de Kooning, and Mark Rothko would help New York replace Paris as the capital of the art world. Some of the most iconic works of art capturing the dynamism of twentieth-century America, it turns out, were created by immigrants—like Joseph Stella's dramatic images of the Brooklyn Bridge, which stand as hymns to a new industrial age, and Piet Mondrian's painting *Broadway Boogie Woogie*, which pays homage to the crisp geometry of Manhattan's street grid and the electric, syncopated rhythms of American music.

This outsider's appreciation of an adopted country's virtues is also on display in the movies of Frank Capra (*It's a Wonderful Life, Mr. Smith Goes to Washington*) celebrating small-town American life; Albert Bierstadt's incandescent, wide-angled paintings of the American West; and Irving Berlin's simple, direct, and often unabashedly patriotic songs ("God Bless America," "There's No Business Like Show Business").

For that matter, a large slice of the "Great American Songbook" (that canon of early twentieth-century standards, which made Tin Pan Alley and the American musical famous around the world) was written by first- or second-generation Jewish immigrants. In addition to Berlin, there were George and Ira Gershwin, Harold Arlen, Jerome Kern, and Lorenz Hart. In his 2009 book, *A Fine Romance: Jewish Songwriters, American Songs,* the critic David Lehman writes that for these artists "America represented freedom not only from persecution but also from the past," and as outsiders they felt a thrilling sense of opportunity—that here, on the other side of the Atlantic, they were getting a chance "to compose the music and words of the insider's dream. This was America, where almost everybody could feel like an outsider, a newcomer to the inheritance, and where the technological marvels of the modern age—the radio and the telephone, the movies, the microphone, the long-playing record, the television set—welcomed and rewarded originality and enterprise in the popular arts."

The ability to draw upon multiple cultural traditions and synthesize disparate influences is another factor contributing to immigrants' gifts for innovation, as is a sense of freedom from handed-down rules—something shared not just by immigrants but by all outsiders. When I interviewed the writer and actor Sam Shepard in 1984, he said that much of what was applauded as innovative in his early experimental plays was simply ignorance of playwriting conventions. Having grown up on an avocado farm in a small town east of Los Angeles, he said the only "audience events" he'd seen before arriving in New York at the age of twenty were rodeos, Spanish fandango dances, and basketball games. As a result, he approached playwriting with few preconceptions and a sense that, in theater, "the rules are wide open." It would take a three-year sojourn in England to make Shepard realize that "rhythmically I was an American" ("the way I talk, the way I walk, everything was American") and, in so doing, find the great subject of his work.

A NEWFOUND SENSE OF intellectual freedom is also cited as an explanation for immigrants' disproportionate achievements in science. The co-founder and chairman of the biotechnology company Moderna (the maker of an mRNA COVID vaccine), Noubar Afeyan, describes innovation "as a form of intellectual immigration." "You leave your comforts behind you," says Afeyan, who was born to Armenian parents in Lebanon, then immigrated twice—first to Canada and then to the United States. "You face unrecognizable challenges. You take nothing for granted. You don't feel like in your new country people owe you anything."

Afeyan is not the only immigrant who played a key role in the fight against COVID. Another mRNA COVID vaccine was produced by a partnership between BioNTech (a German company founded by a Turkish immigrant, Dr. Ugur Sahin, and his wife, Dr. Ozlem Tureci) and Pfizer (an American company founded in New York in 1849 by two German immigrants and headed today by Albert Bourla, an immigrant from Greece).

Among the researchers whose pioneering early work made the rapid development of COVID vaccines possible is the biochemist Katalin Karikó, who began studying mRNA in the late 1970s and remained convinced of its immense potential, even when research institutions and funding sources failed to support her early efforts.

Karikó (now a senior vice president at BioNTech and an adjunct professor at the University of Pennsylvania School of Medicine) grew up in Hungary and started working with RNA in grad school. When the lab where she was working ran out of funding in 1985, she and her husband and their young daughter moved to the United States, where she eventually got a job at the University of Pennsylvania as a research assistant professor. This low-level job meant that to continue her mRNA work, she would need to obtain grants or work with a senior colleague with access to additional funding. Over the years, she applied for one grant after another but was repeatedly rejected. To save money, she used old Hungarian pickle jars to store material for her experiments and brought home broken lab equipment for her husband to repair.

Then, in 1997, at her department's copying machine, Karikó ran into Drew Weissman, a physician and virologist who'd been trying to develop an HIV vaccine. When she offered to make some mRNA for one of his experiments, a new partnership was born. It would take the pair years of testing and retesting and failure, but in 2005 they finally succeeded in creating a form of mRNA that could be used safely without triggering an immune system overreaction. It was a pioneering breakthrough, ignored at the time by leading scientific journals and venture capital firms, but one that would eventually become a foundation stone for the mRNA COVID-19 vaccines made by Pfizer-BioNTech and Moderna, and win them the Nobel Prize in Physiology and Medicine in 2023.

Without such early research (plus massive funding for testing and manufacture), it would have been impossible to get a COVID vaccine developed, tested, and approved for emergency use within a year. *Nature* magazine reports that "the fastest any vaccine had previously been developed, from viral sampling to approval, was four years, for mumps in the 1960s."

At the same time, the swift development of effective COVID vaccines underscores the growing importance of open-source and bottom-up dynamics in science. In this case, a decision was made by Chinese researchers, who first mapped the genome of the virus, to post the sequence on an open-access site. In early January 2020, Yongzhen Zhang, a professor at Fudan University, and his team worked around the clock to analyze the mysterious new virus that had surfaced in the city of Wuhan, and in forty hours they had an initial sequence. After talking with a colleague, the University of Sydney virologist Edward Holmes, Zhang gave the okay to make his findings public, and the sequence was quickly posted on the website Virological.org; a link was also posted on Twitter. Scientists around the world were encouraged to "feel free to download, share, use and analyse this data." As a result, researchers everywhere were able to immediately start working on vaccines. Moderna reported it had used the genome to create an mRNA vaccine in just two days; by the end of 2020, more than nine vaccine candidates from companies across the globe were being evaluated.

The public posting of the COVID-19 genome also helped epidemiologists assess just what sort of risk the virus posed and how it might be contained. It allowed scientists to work with colleagues from different countries and helped researchers develop diagnostic PCR tests that could track the spread of COVID and its evolving mutations across the globe. Many scientists are hoping that this new culture of openness stays in place after the end of the COVID crisis, because speed and cooperation are crucial factors in fighting future epidemics.

Meanwhile, open sourcing during the pandemic helped suppliers and enterprising amateurs devise useful initiatives for the production or distribution of ventilators, N95 masks, and other PPE; contact tracing apps; and the use of 3-D printing. Taiwan, for instance, made some of its COVID-19 data publicly accessible, empowering members of its tech community to create various tools—including an app debunking COVID disinformation and a mask availability map, which was credited with minimizing panic-buying and hoarding.

A growing number of organizations—including the U.S. government and the magazine *Scientific American*—have established "citizen science" pages with links to crowdsourced programs looking for volunteers to help gather and analyze data in fields as disparate as astronomy, ecology, cultural studies, and statistics. Tasks can include taking photos of clouds, recording earthquake tremors, documenting endangered wildlife, and transcribing manuscripts from the Elizabethan era.

As businesses have increasingly come to appreciate outsiders' ability to innovate (to "think outside the box," "color outside the lines," "bring fresh eyes to old problems," whatever management cliché you like), they have begun to cultivate input from nonemployees and nonexperts. The company InnoCentive, for instance, provides a crowdsourcing platform whereby businesses, not-for-profit organizations, and government agencies (like NASA) can post unsolved problems (or "challenges"), and regular folks—be they experts in adjacent fields, amateur scientists, scholars, or kids—can submit solutions. Prizes as high as a million dollars have been offered for challenges involving matters like new methods of carbon capture and storage and easy-to-use bacteria detection tests for water.

There is a long tradition of amateurs making groundbreaking scientific discoveries—like the Dutch merchant Antonie van Leeuwenhoek, who, using homemade microscopes, became the first person to see and describe protozoa and bacteria; and Benjamin Franklin, one of America's founders, who in his spare time invented the lightning rod and bifocals (in addition to pioneering the concepts of the lending library and volunteer fire department).

Alph Bingham, a co-founder of InnoCentive, cites the principle of "optimal marginality" in explaining why outsiders—people without the sorts of credentials that might get them a staff job at a firm—often come up with inventive solutions and innovative concepts: "The more they teach you to be an expert the more they've taught you to not think outside of that expert box and the more barriers there are to your problem-solving ability."

No doubt this is one reason why some companies give their employees time off to pursue their own interests. 3M has long had a 15 percent rule, allowing workers to spend that time on blue-sky projects and "experimental doodling." That policy has roots in the backstory of one of the company's signature products, Scotch tape, which was introduced in 1930, when the company was still called the Minnesota Mining and Manufacturing Company and its main product was sandpaper. Both Scotch tape and masking tape were the inventions of a college dropout named Richard Drew, who was working as a lab tech at the company and enjoyed experimenting in his down time. Much to the surprise of Drew's bosses, Scotch tape quickly became a favorite household item used by budget-conscious consumers during the Depression to mend everything from books, to curtains, to dollar bills.

Decades later, Post-it notes were accidentally invented when a 3M scientist named Spencer Silver, who was trying to create a strong adhesive, instead found he'd created an unusually weak one. He and a colleague, Art Fry, who'd been looking to find a "better bookmark" that wouldn't fall out of his hymnal at choir practice, joined forces, and they eventually perfected the little yellow sticky notes, which, enthusiastic customers realized, had myriad uses—not just as bookmarks, but as reminders, to-do lists, file labels, memos to colleagues, and highlights in library books.

Other companies have turned to user-generated content for both ideas and social media marketing. Back in 2006, as YouTube videos were becoming popular, Frito-Lay ran its first Crash the Super Bowl contest—asking Doritos fans to submit their own ads for the chips and promising to broadcast the winning commercial during the NFL's big game. Ben & Jerry's has used crowdsourcing to develop new ice cream flavors like Cherry Garcia. And Lego embraced customer collaboration and fan interactivity after the company faced declining business in the late 1990s.

In 2003, Lego reported a $238 million loss and was considering bankruptcy. During the first half of 2021, it was enjoying revenue of $3.62 billion with net profits of $992 million. The company's remarkable turnaround came from a return to basics (cutting back on things like Lego jewelry and going "back to the brick"), a focus on digital marketing, and a new appreciation for its grown-up fans, whose online involvement provided grassroots support for Lego products and a fount of new ideas.

In 2008, the company launched its popular Ideas platform, which encouraged users to submit proposals for new Lego projects. Winning ideas, the Lego website says, earn their creators recognition, plus 1 percent of the total net sales. Popular fan-designed products include a Lego typewriter, a Lego version of the Beatles' Yellow Submarine, and a Lego set of female NASA scientists.

ONE OF THE MOST famous examples of a paradigm-changing hypothesis being formulated and confirmed by outsiders is a theory now known to most schoolchildren—that the dinosaurs were wiped out by a giant asteroid some sixty-six million years ago. It's estimated that the rogue space rock was the size of San Francisco and hit planet earth with the force of ten billion Hiroshima-sized atomic bombs, unleashing an apocalyptic wave of tsunamis, earthquakes, and sun-blocking clouds of choking dust and debris.

This theory, which revolutionized how we think about the evolution of life on earth, was formulated not by paleontologists but by a father-and-son team, the Nobel Prize–winning physicist Luis Alvarez and his son the geologist Walter Alvarez. When they first published a paper advancing their impact theory in 1980, they were widely scoffed at by many experts, who either attributed the dinosaur extinction to a series of massive volcanic eruptions or subscribed to more gradualist theories of evolutionary decline.

The Alvarez hypothesis was rooted in the father-and-son team's discovery of high levels of iridium—a metal virtually absent from the earth's crust but found in high levels in extraterrestrial objects like asteroids—in the boundary zone separating rocks in the Cretaceous period (when dinosaurs ruled the earth) from rocks in the Tertiary period. Their theory was validated by the discovery in 1991 of the Chicxulub impact crater off the coast of Mexico's Yucatán Peninsula—a ninety-three-mile-wide and twelve-mile-deep crater, made by an asteroid estimated to be traveling at 43,200 miles per hour.

The discovery of the Chicxulub crater was also made by outsiders. Glen Penfield was a geophysicist who had been working for the Mexican oil company Pemex, using a magnetometer to map the bottom of the Gulf of Mexico off the coast of the Yucatán (to determine the odds of finding oil), when he noticed a huge saucer-shaped depression that was half under water, half under land. Meanwhile, a graduate student named Alan Hildebrand had zeroed in on the Caribbean region as a possible location for the impact crater the Alvarezes had hypothesized. Together, Penfield and Hildebrand located core rock samples taken from wells Pemex had drilled in the region years earlier, and when those samples were analyzed in a lab, there was finally hard evidence supporting the impact theory once derided by so many experts; the melted rock dated back to the very end of the Cretaceous period, while the presence of "shocked" quartz attested to the impact of an asteroid.

After decades of debate, the Alvarezes' theory was ratified in 2010 by a group of forty-one researchers who reviewed years and years of data and published their findings in the journal *Science,* concluding that the Chicxulub impact was, in fact, the ultimate cause of the dinosaurs' demise.

Since then, the Alvarezes' work continues to generate related research from paleontologists, geologists, physicists, chemists, mineralogists, and astronomers. In his 1997 book, *T. rex and the Crater of Doom,* Walter Alvarez writes, "Each of these disciplines has its own traditions, its own body of knowledge, and its own specialized language, and these differences raise barriers that normally prevent specialists from working together across discipline boundaries. Had we let these barriers prevail, little progress would have been made in understanding the KT extinction."

In that respect, too, Chicxulub helped change how scientists debate and collaborate. "Interdisciplinary research groups sprang up all over the world," Alvarez adds. "What might otherwise have been considered scientific trespassing became the expected thing to do." Such "trespassing," like the outside-the-box thinking offered by outsiders, can be the source of some of today's most groundbreaking and innovative ideas.

———

STEVE JOBS LIKED TO describe creativity as "connecting the dots," and in a 1996 interview with *Wired* magazine he argued that creative people "were able to connect experiences they've had and synthesize new things. And the reason they were able to do that was that they've had more experiences or they have thought more about their experiences than other people."

Unfortunately, he added, "a lot of people in our industry haven't had very diverse experiences. So they don't have enough dots to connect, and they end up with very linear solutions without a broad perspective on the problem. The broader one's understanding of the human experience, the better design we will have."

Jobs was a serious student of Zen Buddhism, and his beliefs informed not only the radical design simplicity of Apple products but also his thinking about innovation. Indeed, he often referenced the Japanese monk Shunryu Suzuki's book *Zen Mind, Beginner's Mind* and its concept that "in the beginner's mind there are many possibilities, but in the expert's there are few." In other words, the mind of the beginner is free from the reflexive intellectual habits of the expert and thus more open to new ideas. Jobs compared this mindset to the one that prevailed in the early days of the PC industry and the web, when "no one really knows anything," there are no experts, things haven't yet "been confined, or defined, in too many ways," and "there's a tremendous open possibility to the whole thing."

Although the beginner's mindset didn't help Jobs or his colleagues foresee the momentous—and sometimes toxic—consequences of the digital revolution they launched four decades ago, Jobs's words can remind us of the opportunities offered by hinge moments and the great waves of change they usher in.

...

CHAPTER

9

RESILIENCE IN THE
VUCA-VERSE:
Coping with Volatility, Uncertainty,
Complexity, and Ambiguity

· · ·

The greatness of America lies not in being more
enlightened than any other nation, but rather
in her ability to repair her faults.

—ALEXIS DE TOCQUEVILLE

OPTIMISTS LIKE TO QUOTE DESMOND TUTU, WHO ONCE
pointed out that "a time of crisis is not just a time of
anxiety and worry. It gives a chance, an opportunity, to choose
well or to choose badly."

Such choices abound today, when we seem to be inhabit-
ing a world defined by volatility, uncertainty, complexity, and
ambiguity—a world struggling, in the third decade of the
new millennium, to grapple with the aftermath of COVID,
threats to democracy at home and abroad, economic uncertainty, the unforeseen consequences of technological innovation, and the accelerating fallout of climate change.

One way to look at the myriad crises facing the world today
is to regard them as dire warnings—as stress tests—requiring
immediate action. Trump's assault on the rule of law and the
January 6 insurrection were flashing-red Mayday calls to

Americans to shore up democracy before it was too late: a visit from the Ghost of Christmas Yet to Come, as it were, delivering an emergency civics lesson. COVID was a frightening admonishment to strengthen our public health infrastructure—and our social safety nets—before the next pandemic hits. And the Russian invasion of Ukraine was an urgent wake-up call to Europe, NATO, and the United States to stop Putin's imperialistic assault on a peaceful neighbor and his efforts to undermine the very ideas of sovereignty and territorial integrity.

So far, the world has inched forward, buying itself a little more time. Democracy in America remains in grave danger, but in the 2022 midterm elections, voters did reject the majority of prominent election deniers running for Senate, House, and gubernatorial offices. Progress is being made against climate change as countries, cities, and government agencies take steps to reduce their carbon footprint and embrace green energy. And the Western alliance reacted with impressive unity to Putin's invasion, ramping up economic and military support for Ukraine, while the Ukrainians have demonstrated their courage and strategic prowess in battling a ruthless and far larger adversary.

The question is whether such efforts can be stepped up and sustained with urgency and momentum. Also, what sort of staying power do lessons learned in the past possess? After the 2008 global financial crisis—fueled by greed and subprime mortgages and lax regulation—the government and banks promised: never again. And yet, ten years later, Trump signed a law watering down Obama-era regulations, and in 2023 several banks imploded, raising fears, again, of larger weaknesses in the financial system.

Danger and crisis, clearly, can shock people out of complacency—sort of an inversion of what Naomi Klein argued in her 2007 book, *The Shock Doctrine.* In that volume, she quoted the conservative economist Milton Friedman's assertion that "only a crisis—actual or perceived—produces real change," and she argued that his neoliberal followers had turned this into a veritable blueprint for using disasters and wars as opportunities to spread the gospel of free-market fundamentalism and to enrich corporations through privatization. The Iraq war, she contended, was meant to turn that country into a kind of "Arabic Singapore" and made companies like Halliburton a fortune through outsourcing contracts. In the case of a devastating tsunami that hit Sri Lanka in 2004, she wrote, "foreign investors and international lenders had teamed up to use the atmosphere of panic to hand the entire beautiful coastline over to entrepreneurs who quickly built large resorts, blocking hundreds of thousands of fishing people from rebuilding their villages near the water."

But if crises create what Klein calls "malleable moments when we are psychologically unmoored" and open to giving free-market titans the "clean canvases they crave," they can also create opportunities for constructive resets. They can ease gridlock, force action on long-delayed reforms, and goad politicians into jettisoning flawed policies of the past and coming up with innovative, even paradigm-changing solutions—like FDR's New Deal, which was a response to the emergency of the Great Depression and would end up redefining the U.S. government's responsibilities with the creation of transformative programs like Social Security and unemployment insurance.

Lyndon B. Johnson took office in the wake of the assassination of John F. Kennedy and used the national sense of crisis—combined with his own masterful understanding of Capitol Hill—to pass his predecessor's stalled tax-cut bill and civil rights legislation and to lay the groundwork for his own ambitious War on Poverty.

When the levees in New Orleans failed during Hurricane Katrina, some 80 percent of the city was flooded; 1.2 million residents were evacuated and 200,000 were displaced. Recovery efforts were slow, but when Mitch Landrieu took office as mayor in 2010, he implemented ambitious rebuilding plans that not only included the rebuilding of critical infrastructure (from levees and roads, to schools and hospitals) but also aimed at making the city more resilient in the future—better prepared for future storms and climate change, better organized to grapple with long-term problems of poverty and crime, and with a more diversified economy including lots of new tech start-ups.

New York City has been slow to recover from COVID, but the city has a long history of resilience. The terrorist attacks of 9/11 killed 2,753 people at the World Trade Center, and Lower Manhattan suffered an estimated $31 billion in economic damage. Under the direction of Mayor Michael Bloomberg, the city embarked on plans to not only rebuild the ravaged neighborhoods near Ground Zero but also implemented an ambitious redevelopment plan, featuring public-private partnerships that would lead to the construction of Hudson Yards and the High Line and building projects on both sides of the East River.

Comebacks are part of New York's DNA. The city rebounded after the 1970s, when it teetered on the brink of bankruptcy and more than a million people departed, driven out by high crime rates and fears that the city was in irreversible decline. A key component in New York City's comeback then, as its chief demographer, Joseph J. Salvo, told *The New York Times,* was the influx of new immigrants who saw opportunities in the struggling metropolis. During the 1980s, some 800,000 immigrants (mainly from the Caribbean, Latin America, Asia, and Africa) arrived in New York, taking crucial health-care and service industry jobs and starting new businesses of their own.

THE SWIFTNESS WITH WHICH communities and entire nations have rebounded after catastrophes remains startling. By the end of World War II, an estimated fifty-three million people had been killed, and in Europe alone another sixty million had been uprooted from their homes. Cities had been turned into fields of rubble, roads were cratered and strewn with debris, bridges and railway tracks were blown up or disappeared. In Warsaw, 90 percent of all homes had been destroyed; in Germany, 40 percent were gone.

In Hiroshima, an estimated 140,000 people (about 40 percent of the city's population) died from the nuclear blast or from long-term side effects of radiation; in Nagasaki, an estimated 74,000 people lost their lives. Dozens of other Japanese cities were hit by incendiary bombs, which burned the mostly wooden buildings down to the ground, leaving at least another fifteen million people homeless. The U.S. firebombing of Tokyo on March 10, 1945, killed an estimated 100,000 and destroyed the homes of another million; so much ash fell from the skies that the date became known as the Night of Black Snow.

The destruction across Europe and parts of Asia was so great that 1945 was called "Year Zero," and countries faced what the historian Tony Judt called the "Himalayan task" of rebuilding their infrastructures and economies while simultaneously embarking on far-reaching plans for social and political reform.

In the aftermath of the war, both Germany and Japan would reinvent themselves as democracies and key allies of the United States, and both experienced remarkable economic booms. By 1968, Japan had become the world's second-largest economy (after the United States), and by 1989, when the Berlin Wall came down, Germany was the third largest.

Through its Marshall Plan, the United States gave some $13 billion in aid to Western Europe, with the multiple goals of building a bulwark against communism; creating reliable, long-term trade partners; and preventing the sort of economic distress and political humiliation that had made the region so susceptible to the lure of fascism. In the years following the end of World War II, Judt wrote, Europe focused on trying to build a future that would "head off a return of the old demons" like "unemployment, Fascism, German militarism, war, revolution" that had made the Continent vulnerable to extremism in the past. The contemporary "post-national, welfare-state, co-operative, pacific Europe," Judt reminded us, "was not born of the optimistic, ambitious, forward-looking project imagined in fond retrospect by today's Euro-idealists. It was the insecure child of anxiety. Shadowed by history, its leaders implemented social reforms and built new institutions as a prophylactic, to keep the past at bay."

At the center of postwar change was the hope that new international institutions (like the United Nations and the World Bank) would foster economic growth and political stability. Many governments also resolved to take on bigger roles in subsidizing social safety nets including health care and unemployment and retirement insurance. Decades later, many European nations made cuts to such public services as they adopted austerity budgets in the wake of the 2008 financial crisis. This not only led to increased inequality and unemployment but also helped fuel the anger driving the rise of right-wing populism in the following decade.

———

"IT IS ANOTHER UNCOMFORTABLE truth about war that it brings both destruction and creation," the historian Margaret MacMillan wrote in her 2020 book, *War: How Conflict Shaped Us.* "So many of our advances in science and technology—the jet engine, transistors, computers—came about because they were needed in wartime." War also led governments to funnel money and resources into new technologies and lifesaving medical treatments. From the horrors of trench warfare during World War I came the widespread use of new antiseptics and anesthetics. Penicillin, first discovered in 1928 by the bacteriologist Alexander Fleming (who called it "mold juice"), would be mass-produced by the drugmaker Pfizer (yes, the same company that helped develop an mRNA COVID vaccine) for mass distribution to medics during World War II. Penicillin and other antibiotics known as sulfa drugs would help raise the survival rate of wounded and ailing soldiers in World War II to 50 percent, up from a dismal 4 percent during World War I.

"To say that war brings benefits and can help to build stronger, even fairer, societies is not to defend it," MacMillan adds. "Of course we would rather improve our world, help the weak and unfortunate, or have advances in science and technology in a state of peace. Yet finding the will and the resources to make great advances is harder in peacetime; it is all too easy to put off doing something about poverty, the opioid crisis or climate change until another day. War concentrates our attention and, like it or not, has done so throughout human history."

It's an argument that echoes ideas articulated by the Austrian-born economist Joseph Schumpeter in 1942, in the wake of the Great Depression. Crises, he asserted, could become cradles for

innovation by catalyzing the process he called "creative destruction": In freeing up capital, the destruction of old companies
could lead to the development of transformative new industries
and breakthrough products, while the pressures of an economic
downturn could incentivize inventors and outsiders to find creative solutions to old and new problems.

The record of innovation during periods of financial distress remains impressive. The tech company Hewlett-Packard
began life in 1938 as a start-up in a one-car Palo Alto garage—
now regarded by many as the birthplace of Silicon Valley—
and RCA (founded as the Radio Corporation of America)
reinvented itself during the Depression as a leader in the fledgling television business. DuPont introduced neoprene (a synthetic rubber quickly embraced by car and airplane makers)
and nylon during the thirties.

The 1970s, with its crippling "stagflation" (a combination
of rapidly rising prices and slowing growth), was the decade
that saw the introduction of three essentials of contemporary
life: the personal computer, the handheld cellphone (the 1973
prototype weighed two and a half pounds and offered about
thirty minutes of talk time), and the wheeled suitcase.

The years surrounding the financial meltdown of 2008
would similarly prove to be a boom time for start-ups—
especially ones that employed digital technology to help people
navigate the challenges of a precarious economy and an increasingly complex world. Airbnb, which was valued at more
than $67 billion in 2023, was launched in 2008 by cash-strapped
roommates who decided to rent out air mattresses on their living room floor to people who couldn't find or afford a hotel
room. The encrypted messaging application WhatsApp was
created the following year, as was the ride-hailing service Uber.
And 2010 saw the founding of Instagram and Pinterest.

———

COVID ITSELF SPURRED ALL sorts of changes, forcing governments to set aside austerity measures (and fears of deficit spending) to quickly authorize trillions in COVID relief and stimulus payments and to reassess their social safety nets. The urgent race to develop tests and vaccines cut through the scientific establishment's tangle of red tape and facilitated collaboration among researchers across the globe.

The writer Zeynep Tufekci, an associate professor at the University of North Carolina, notes that "the new mRNA technology, on which several vaccines—notably Pfizer-BioNTech's and Moderna's—are based, is an epochal scientific and technical breakthrough," which may lead to mRNA vaccines for other diseases like malaria. During the pandemic, she adds, technology also "showed how we could make our society function better in normal times"—using telemedicine to cut down on unnecessary doctor visits, or Zoom and teleconferencing for at-home learning and remote office work. Digital communication, of course, is no substitute for real classroom time or in-office brainstorming, but it can be a useful supplement—and a reminder, at a time when we are so aware of the toxic side effects of social media and addictive algorithms, of the benefits technology can provide.

Previous pandemics and health emergencies also led to significant advances. The 1918 flu outbreak—described by Laura Spinney, the author of *Pale Rider: The Spanish Flu of 1918 and How It Changed the World*, as a "tidal wave of death"—claimed at least fifty million lives worldwide but led to governments expanding access to health care, creating or reconfiguring health ministries, and taking steps to ensure international cooperation on future health crises.

In the case of the Black Death (the bubonic plague out-break, between 1347 and 1351, which, it's estimated, killed one-third of the population of Europe), the science writer John Kelly argues it "played a major role in the birth of public health," resulting in new quarantine and hospital protocols. More important, he says, it led to changes that "helped to set the stage for what today is called the scientific method"— namely, "a greater emphasis on practical, clinically oriented medicine" that reflected the growing influence of the surgeon and empirical observation.

In his 2005 book, *The Great Mortality*, Kelly wrote that the Black Death created severe labor shortages, which led to a "burst of technological innovation" including improved water mills and windmills, a new, more efficient kind of plow, and two simple inventions that increased agricultural productivity: "Someone figured out that one easy (and cheap) way to get a horse to pull more was to redistribute weight away from its windpipe, so when it moved forward it wouldn't choke. Thus was born the horse collar, which increased horsepower by a factor of four. Another simple innovation, the horseshoe, in-creased it even more, by improving the horse's endurance."

The devastation wrought by the Black Death in Europe shook the economic, political, and cultural status quo and un-dermined old religious and philosophical certainties. The se-vere depopulation and shortage of labor would eventually lead to better wages for the poor, increased social mobility, and the breakdown of the manorial system. Although there were erup-tions of increased religiosity, the plague, in the long run, wore down faith in the church, planting the seeds of what, in time, would lead to the Reformation and a growing secularization of the culture at large. Combined with other developments like the invention of the printing press and the growth of international trade, these dynamics would foster a new humanism and rationality and, after a long interregnum, eventually give way to what we now know as the Renaissance with its flowering of the arts.

WITH JOE BIDEN'S DEFEAT of Donald Trump in 2020, and the defeat, in the 2022 midterms, of many prominent election deniers, there was a collective sigh of relief among supporters of democracy, who were further buoyed by the defeat that year of the right-wing populist Jair Bolsonaro in Brazil. But democracy remains under serious threat—from candidates who refuse to abide by election results and authoritarian populists who maintain power by exploiting fear and division. Some 60 percent of Republicans continue to deny or question the 2020 election results that made Joe Biden president. And abroad, the Far Right has continued to surge. Marine Le Pen, who has tried to soften her image in recent years (stressing cost-of-living issues and posting cat videos on TikTok), lost the 2022 French presidential election but still won 41.5 percent of the vote, showing just how far her nativist, anti-immigrant stance has penetrated mainstream French politics. Months later, Giorgia Meloni, the head of a hard-right party with neo-fascist roots, became Italy's first woman prime minister. And in Sweden, a party with neo-Nazi roots won the second-highest number of seats in parliament.

When it comes to climate change, some headway is being made. Climate denialism, for instance, has been in retreat for a decade now. A 2021 survey found that 78 percent of Americans think the United States should reduce emissions even if other countries don't. Such shifts in the zeitgeist are a testament to the impassioned work of climate activists and the growing public recognition that the multiplying number of today's extreme weather events (floods, droughts, wildfires) are a harbinger of worse to come.

Modeled on antiapartheid efforts from the 1970s and 1980s, divestment campaigns directed at fossil-fuel companies have grown from a small grassroots effort started by Bill McKibben and other activists in 2012 into a worldwide movement. By late 2021, colleges (including the University of California, Oxford, and Cambridge), foundations, pension funds, and religious groups (including the Episcopal Church)—which together represent nearly $40 trillion in investments—had committed to full or partial renunciation of oil, coal, and gas stocks.

Meanwhile, government agencies and businesses have awakened to the threat. Take, for instance, the U.S. military: Having identified climate change as a threat to national security and its own ability to carry out missions, the Pentagon has been making a concerted effort to transition to renewable energy and invest in green technologies. The Defense Department foresees climate change as intensifying global conflicts over water and food and is trying to prepare to function in a hotter, more inhospitable world. Troops need to be retrained and reequipped for deployments in desert environments and other extreme conditions, and coastal bases need to be secured against rising sea levels by building berms and seawalls. The army plans to cut emissions in half by 2030 and electrify all noncombat vehicles by 2035, and the navy launched its "Great Green Fleet" initiative in 2016 with plans to rely increasingly on alternative energy.

These are all positive developments, but it's not enough. The speed with which vaccines were formulated, tested, and distributed during the COVID crisis showed how quickly the world can act when it perceives the dire nature of a threat, and that same sense of urgency needs to be brought to global warming. A report issued by the UN's Intergovernmental Panel on Climate Change in 2023 warned that the world is running out of time to reduce its reliance on fossil fuels, and the planet will likely pass a critical threshold in the next decade—blowing past the goal of limiting warming to 1.5 degrees Celsius (2.7 degrees Fahrenheit) above pre-industrial levels. Beyond that 1.5 degree threshold, it becomes increasingly difficult for humans and ecosystems to adapt: Food and water shortages will grow more severe, infectious diseases will claim many more lives, and deadly heat waves and rising sea levels will make some regions uninhabitable and destroy the economies of others. Lowering fossil fuel emissions to bring greenhouse gases under control will require a huge global push: It will require serious international cooperation, the cancellation of coal and oil drilling projects, and massive public and private investment in clean energy and new technologies like carbon dioxide removal.

But while the "climate time bomb is ticking," the UN report also stresses that the world possesses tools to grapple with the crisis, and a viable, if ever narrowing, window in which to make crucial changes. "The choices and actions implemented in this decade," the report reads, "will have impacts now and for thousands of years."

In his 2021 documentary *The Year Earth Changed*, the great David Attenborough pointed out that COVID allowed us to see, for a dozen months or so, what the world looked like when humans retreated to their homes and the pause button was pressed on human-created pollution. The movie shows us footage of a leopard patrolling the deserted streets of Mpumalanga, and jackass penguins waddling through Cape Town. In Jalandhar, India, the smog clears during the lockdown and the snow-covered peaks of the Himalayas can be seen for the first time in decades. Such images demonstrate the remarkable resilience of nature, and prod us to remember, as Attenborough puts it, that we still have "an opportunity to rebuild in a new direction" and embrace a more sustainable way of life.

EPILOGUE

CREATED NEARLY TWO CENTURIES AGO IN EDO-ERA Japan, Hokusai's wood-block prints seem uncommonly modern—in their almost abstract use of color and line, their slightly skewed perspective, and their love of spareness and asymmetry.

Part of their familiarity stems from the indelible influence Japanese prints had on impressionism and postimpressionism through artists we know and love like Van Gogh, Degas, Toulouse-Lautrec, and Monet. But the real reason Hokusai's prints feel so timeless is their uncanny sense of both existential contingency and Buddhist calm—a recognition and acceptance of the precariousness of life. Many of the prints in *Thirty-Six Views of Mount Fuji* radiate serenity and sunlight, showing people getting on with the humdrum routines of ordinary life like harvesting rice, repairing their fishing boats, taking goods to market; and on weekends, maybe taking a walk in the woods, flying a kite, or simply enjoying the beauty of nature. Yet danger is often lurking, somewhere, in the background—in the form of a giant rogue wave, a sudden windstorm, or a volcano that could erupt.

Whereas Hokusai's contemporaries favored the highly marketable subjects of Kabuki actors, geishas, samurai, sumo wrestlers, and other celebrities of the day, Hokusai focused on landscapes and the humble lives of ordinary people—anonymous outsiders who worked long hours as fishermen, farmers, or carpenters.

The main character in these prints, however, is Mount Fuji itself—sometimes appearing as a friendly little snowcapped peak sitting on the far horizon, sometimes as a kind of compass point used by travelers trying to navigate, and in one print, *Thunderstorm Beneath the Summit* (also known as *Black Fuji*), as a far more menacing presence, depicted in dark, almost sinister colors with an ominous massing of clouds in the distance and bolts of lightning flashing across its base. The mountain, in short, represents nature at its most beautiful and threatening.

In fact, while Mount Fuji has become a symbol of the sacred and eternal, it also remains an active volcano, quiet for centuries now but capable of enormous fury and destruction. Hokusai was well aware of the threat it posed: One of his lesser-known prints, titled *The Appearance of Hoeizan* (published a few years after *Thirty-Six Views*), portrays the last eruption of Mount Fuji, which occurred in 1707 and lasted for sixteen days, with ash choking farmers' fields and falling as far away as modern-day Tokyo and Yokohama.

In this print, the force of the eruption has sent people somersaulting through the air—reminiscent, in some ways, of the fishing boats being tumbled by the force of wind and water in *The Great Wave*. But here the violence and chaos are much more pronounced: Buildings have collapsed, crushing people and a horse, and chunks of wood and tile and lava are raining down on the men and women desperately trying to flee. It's an image that looks less like one of Hokusai's meditations on daily life than a surreal cross between a comic book battle scene and Picasso's *Guernica*.

Japan, in both Hokusai's time and ours, is a country that has learned to live with threats—not just ones posed by its location in a dangerous neighborhood (which today includes China, Russia, and North Korea), but also those determined by accidents of geology and geography. Perched on the western edge of the Pacific Ring of Fire near the intersection of four tectonic plates, the country occupies one of the planet's seismic hot spots and sustains an average of fifteen hundred earthquakes a year. To create public awareness, Japan has designated September 1 (the anniversary of the deadly 1923 Kanto earthquake, which killed more than 110,000 people) as Disaster Prevention Day and holds regular earthquake drills in schools, offices, and retirement communities. It has also implemented some of the world's strictest building codes, requiring earthquake-resistant construction.

Still, nothing could prepare Japan for the triple disaster that hit on March 11, 2011, when a 9.0 earthquake rocked the island nation—a quake so powerful that it reportedly shifted the planet on its axis by nearly four inches. The quake created tsunami waves as tall as 130 feet high, a "black wall of water," in one witness's words, that toppled barriers and embankments, engulfing entire villages and towns. The water also cut power to the Fukushima Daiichi nuclear power plant, and when its cooling systems failed, three of its nuclear fuel rods began to melt, leading to a harrowing series of explosions, fires, and the release of life-threatening radiation.

It was the worst nuclear disaster since Chernobyl.

Together, these three disasters killed more than 18,000 people, led to the evacuation of more than 465,000, and caused an estimated $360 billion in losses.

EVEN AS RECOVERY AND rebuilding efforts continued in the months and years after 3/11, Japan—along with many neighboring countries and allies—began studying this black swan of a catastrophe to try to understand what sort of contingency planning might have mitigated the damage and to find new ways of making the country more resilient in the face of future disasters.

The plans experts devised included the construction of forty-one-foot-high seawalls, the planting of forty thousand trees near the coastline, the installation of backup communications and electrical systems, and the updating of critical infrastructure (like using earthquake-resistant piping in water delivery systems).

In reviewing response efforts to 3/11, government officials, civil engineers, and emergency management consultants were also looking for ways to improve rescue and evacuation plans and to create blueprints for dealing with future disasters— blueprints laying out in advance how national and local aid efforts could be coordinated and how responsibilities for restoring infrastructure and providing disaster financing could be divvied up between the public and private sectors.

Such blueprints, experts realized, were useful not only for earthquake- and tsunami-prone countries but for the growing number of communities across the world trying to cope with climate change and the threat of rising sea levels. In fact, Japan's post-3/11 efforts to harden its infrastructure and actively involve the population in disaster preparedness suggest one way countries can begin to grapple with seemingly insurmountable problems—starting with small but practical steps in building resilience into institutions and public attitudes.

For instance, one step toward fighting the multiplying dangers of misinformation and fake news—which foment division and mistrust, and threaten to undermine democratic elections—was taken by the European Union in 2022, when it adopted measures requiring Big Tech companies like Facebook, YouTube, and TikTok to better police their platforms and prevent dangerous disinformation from going viral. Right-wing media platforms like Fox News need to be held accountable for spreading lies and disinformation—a process which some observers hoped had begun in 2023 when Fox settled a defamation suit filed by Dominion Voting Systems for $787.5 million. And so-called mainstream media outlets need to stop confusing evenhandedness with truth telling, and cease giving proponents of clearly false narratives (regarding, say, election fraud and climate denialism) equal time.

Media literacy, too, is vital to creating resilience, as the experience of Finland attests. After being flooded by Russian propaganda in the wake of Russia's 2014 annexation of Crimea, Finland launched a national curriculum designed to emphasize critical thinking. Beginning in primary school, students are taught the difference between facts, rumors, and propaganda. They are taught how to evaluate information, appreciate the importance of sourcing, and understand how data and even images can be manipulated on social media. For the fifth year in a row, the country has topped a list of European countries found to be most resistant to disinformation.

More countries need to follow Finland's lead in creating a media- and history-literate citizenry—especially the United States, where a 2023 report from the National Assessment of Educational Progress found an alarming drop in student test scores, with only 13 percent of eighth graders demonstrating proficiency in history and only 22 percent in civics. At the same time, we need to better support independent journalism—which remains essential to the functioning of democracy, and vital, too, on a local level, where it can serve as a reliable and trusted source of information, as well as foster a sense of community and civic engagement.

Nations with informed, educated voters, aware of how information can be used and misused in the digital age, are less susceptible to bad faith actors, both foreign and domestic. And they are less apt to suffer from the kind of extreme polarization that thrives on and accelerates disinformation. Further reductions in polarization can also be achieved by restricting gerrymandering and opening primaries to independent voters—changes likely to be resisted by politicians who pander to their parties' bases, but ones that make for candidates who better reflect the views of the country at large, which in turn makes for a healthier and more resilient democracy.

The January 6 insurrection and Donald Trump's refusal to accept the results of the 2020 election, as we've already discussed, breached American democracy's too fragile guardrails—showing us that further protections are required. The updated Electoral Count Act, passed by Congress in 2022, was a start—the measure establishes clear rules for the certification and counting of electoral votes—but federal legislation is needed to guarantee voting rights, as red states have moved to impose more restrictions on voting in the wake of Trump's baseless claims of election fraud. Accountability remains vital to the rule of law—which is why the arrests and trials of January 6 insurrectionists remain so important, and why the indictments of former president Trump—on charges of trying to subvert democracy and overturn the will of the people—stand as pivotal moments in America's still unfurling history.

At the same time, the public must recognize the risks of Trump winning reelection in 2024. A second Trump presidency would be even more authoritarian than the first: He has been promising to obliterate "the deep state," assailing the Justice Department, the FBI, and the civil service, and vowing to use the power of the presidency to exact payback on his opponents and those who cross him. *The New York Times* reports that should Trump return to office in 2025, he and his associates have plans to expand executive power, bringing independent agencies like the Federal Communications Commission and the Federal Trade Commission under presidential control and reviving the practice of impounding funds (that is, refusing to spend money appropriated by Congress)—in short, demolishing vital checks and balances designed to protect democracy.

Such developments underscore the need for Watergate-like reforms to translate into law what have heretofore been merely norms and traditions. As the legal scholar Jack Goldsmith points out, much of the system before Trump was "built on a basic assumption about a range of reasonableness among presidents, a range of willingness to play within the system, a range of at least a modicum of understanding of political and normative constraints."

More difficult still will be several long-term tasks: turning down the volume on the extreme partisan rhetoric and normalization of violence fomented by Trump and MAGA Republicans; restoring public trust in the democratic institutions they've spent years attacking; and reducing the polarization that has infected so much of public discourse.

IN 2018, MIDWAY THROUGH the Trump presidency, the *Irish Times* columnist Fintan O'Toole proposed what he called "the Yeats Test": "The proposition is simple: the more quotable Yeats seems to commentators and politicians, the worse things are. As a counter-example we might try the Heaney Test: if hope and history rhyme, let the good times roll. But these days,

it is the older Irish poet who prevails in political discourse—
and that is not good news."

O'Toole noted that after Brexit and the election of Donald
Trump in 2016, there was a huge surge in online searches for
"Yeats's magnificently doom-laden 'The Second Coming,'"
and "continuing global instability" has "made Yeats's apocalyptic vision as quotable as a chart-topping song."

Indeed, phrases from that poem like "the centre cannot
hold" and "mere anarchy is loosed upon the world" were
quoted hundreds of times on social media in 2016. And 2020
saw another burst of "Second Coming" citations: It was the
hundredth anniversary of the poem's publication, and COVID
had accelerated people's sense of foreboding. A similar mood
had prevailed a century before, when Yeats was working on the
poem: A shell-shocked world, still struggling to come to terms
with the trauma of World War I, was also grappling with the
fallout from the Russian Revolution, the Irish War of Independence, and the flu pandemic of 1918 (which sickened the poet's
wife, Georgie Hyde-Lees, while she was pregnant).

Joe Biden has frequently dropped lines from another well-
known Yeats poem into speeches—"All changed, changed utterly: / A terrible beauty is born" (from "Easter, 1916")—and
he dates his fondness for the poet back to his teenage years,
when he would recite Yeats's verses to help overcome his stut-
ter. His favorite poet, however, is that other Irishman: Seamus
Heaney, the very poet Fintan O'Toole invokes as a harbinger
of better times.

Biden's favorite Heaney lines come from his play *The Cure
at Troy:* "History says, *Don't hope / On this side of the grave. /
But then, once in a lifetime / The longed-for tidal wave / Of
justice can rise up, / And hope and history rhyme.*" It's an optimistic, almost oracular vision, and Heaney goes on to exhort

audiences to "hope for a great sea-change / On the far side of
revenge. / Believe that a further shore / Is reachable from
here."

Heaney wrote these lines in 1990 and said he didn't think he
"would have had the gall" to write such consoling lines "had it
not been for the extraordinary events" that had just happened
in the world: namely, the fall of the Berlin Wall, the election of
the dissident playwright Václav Havel as president of Czecho-
slovakia, the fall of the Romanian dictator Ceauşescu, and the
release of Nelson Mandela after twenty-seven years in prison.

If such momentous changes were possible, Heaney reasoned, then why not an end to the thirty years of sectarian violence in Northern Ireland? And eight years later, in 1998, the
British government, the Irish government, and Northern Ireland political parties signed the Good Friday Agreement, designed to bring an end to thirty years of violent conflict there.
The agreement wasn't perfect, but as a *Guardian* editorial observed twenty years later, "It opened the door to a new kind of
ordinary life in Northern Ireland. In 1998, grievance and bitterness seemed to give way to compromise and hope."

Biden began quoting lines from *The Cure at Troy* years ago,
and he's returned to them so many times that he says his family
can recite them from memory, too. The poem was read during
inaugural celebrations, and it became clear that Biden hoped,
as president, to use Heaney's vision of reconciliation after war
as a metaphor for healing in a bitterly divided America. In fact,
some of Heaney's own musings about the difficulties of ending
sectarian conflict in Northern Ireland can sound uncannily
similar to the challenges of bridging partisan divides in twenty-
first-century America.

In a 1996 letter to a friend, Heaney wrote of individuals
feeling pressures from a "group's demands for loyalty" and the

selfish pride that is "rampant at the moment." Change and con-
ciliation, he concluded, require that people not only stop
choosing "the intoxication of defiance" but also find their way
toward "the civic, sober path of adjustment." Then maybe—
maybe—they could exchange "the haughtiness of the hurt
spirit for the humdrum and caritas of renewal."

NOTES

INTRODUCTION

x *Under the Wave off Kanagawa* John T. Carpenter, "Hokusai's Iconic 'Great Wave,'" Metropolitan Museum of Art, July 2, 2014, metmuseum.org/ blogs/now-at-the-met/2014/great-wave; "Why the Iconic Great Wave Swept the World," Getty, getty.edu/news/why-the-iconic-great-wave -swept-the-world/.

xi The term was used "Q. Who First Originated the Term VUCA (Volatility, Uncertainty, Complexity, and Ambiguity)?," U.S. Army Heritage and Education Center, usawc.libanswers.com/faq/84869.

xii new developments in artificial intelligence futureoflife.org/open-letter/ pause-giant-ai-experiments/; theverge.com/2023/3/29/23661374/elon -musk-ai-researchers-pause-research-open-letter.

xii "technology is neither good nor bad" Eric Schatzberg and Lee Vinsel, "Kranzberg's First and Second Laws," *Technology's Stories* 6, no. 4 (Dec. 2018), technologystories.org/first-and-second-laws/; Rinkesh D, "Kranzberg's Laws of Technology—Understanding Interaction of Society and Technology," AIC-IIITH, aic.iiit.ac.in/kranzbergs-laws-of -technology-understanding-interaction-of-society-and-technology/.

xiii "future shock" and "adaptive breakdown" Alvin Toffler, *Future Shock* (New York: Bantam Books, 1971).

xiii Times of tumult and chaos George Prochnik, *Stranger in a Strange Land* (New York: Other Press, 2016), 247–48.

xiv fossil fuel consumption ipcc.ch/report/ar6/syr/downloads/report/IPCC _AR6_SYR_LongerReport.pdf.

xv deranged conspiracy theories of QAnon d3qioqp55mx5f5.cloudfront.net/ cpost/i/docs/2023-06_CPOST-NORC_Political_Violence_Survey _Report.pdf?mtime=1690317909.

xv 7 percent believe violence d3qioqp55mx5f5.cloudfront.net/cpost/i/docs/ 2023-06_CPOST-NORC_Political_Violence_Survey_Report.pdf ?mtime=1690317909.

CHAPTER 1: A HINGE MOMENT

3 "The crisis consists precisely" Antonio Gramsci, *Selections from the Prison Notebooks* (New York: International Publishers, 1971), 276.

3 "pathetic dunderhead" Volker Ullrich, *Hitler: Ascent, 1889–1939* (New York: Alfred A. Knopf, 2016), 240.

5 Freedom declined Gorokhovskaia, Shahbaz, and Slipowitz, *Freedom in the World 2023*, freedomhouse.org/sites/default/files/2023-03/FIW_World_2023_DigtalPDF.pdf.

5 The watchdog group also pointed out Sarah Repucci and Amy Slipowitz, "The Global Expansion of Authoritarian Rule," *Freedom in the World 2022*, Report, Freedom House, freedomhouse.org/sites/default/files/2022-03/FITW_World_2022_digital_abridged_FINAL.pdf.

5 It's a stark and chilling reversal Jennifer Schuessler, "Francis Fukuyama Predicted the End of History. It's Back (Again)," *The New York Times*, May 10, 2022, nytimes.com/2022/05/10/arts/francis-fukuyama-history-liberalism.html.

5 "permacrisis" Helen Bushby, "Permacrisis Declared Collins Dictionary Word of the Year," BBC News, Nov. 1, 2022, bbc.com/news/entertainment-arts-63458467.

6 "more united, more interconnected" John Micklethwait and Adrian Wooldridge, "Putin and Xi Exposed the Great Illusion of Capitalism," Bloomberg, Mar. 24, 2022, bloomberg.com/opinion/articles/2022-03-24/ukraine-war-has-russia-s-putin-xi-jinping-exposing-capitalism-s-great-illusion?leadSource=uverify%20wall.

6 Olaf Scholz, declared in 2022 Olaf Scholz, "The Global Zeitenwende: How to Avoid a New Cold War in a Multipolar Era," *Foreign Affairs*, Dec. 5, 2022, foreignaffairs.com/germany/olaf-scholz-global-zeitenwende-how-avoid-new-cold-war.

6 He also announced that Germany Kate Connolly, "Germany to Set Up €100bn Fund to Boost Its Military Strength," *The Guardian*, Feb. 27, 2022, theguardian.com/world/2022/feb/27/germany-set-up-fund-boost-military-strength-ukraine-putin; Jen Kirby, "Germany's Dramatic Reversal on Defense, Explained," Vox, Mar. 5, 2022, vox.com/22960493/germany-chancellor-reversal-defense-war-russia-ukraine; "Russia Invades Ukraine: Seven Ways the World Has Changed Since Vladimir Putin Went to War," *Scotsman*, Mar. 3, 2022, scotsman.com/news/opinion/columnists/seven-ways-the-world-has-changed-since-putin-went-to-war-scotsman-says-3594057.

6 "the law of the jungle" Yuval Noah Harari, "Yuval Noah Harari Argues That What's at Stake in Ukraine Is the Direction of Human History," *Economist*, Feb. 9, 2022, economist.com/by-invitation/2022/02/09/yuval-noah-harari-argues-that-whats-at-stake-in-ukraine-is-the-direction-of-human-history.

7 Ian Bremmer calls "rogue actors" "Eurasia Group's Ian Bremmer: Biggest Threat to World Is Rogue Actors—from Putin to Musk," *Harvard Business Review*, Jan. 19, 2023, hbr.org/2023/01/eurasia-groups-ian-bremmer-biggest-threat-to-world-is-rogue-actors-from-putin-to-musk; "Top Risks 2023," Eurasia Group, eurasiagroup.net/files/upload/EurasiaGroup_TopRisks2023.pdf.

8 "It is surprising to see" James Westfall Thompson, "The Aftermath of the Black Death and the Aftermath of the Great War," *American Journal of Sociology* 26, no. 5 (Mar. 1921): 565, jstor.org/stable/2764425.

8 "a favorite falcon" Barbara W. Tuchman, *A Distant Mirror: The Calamitous 14th Century* (New York: Random House Trade Paperbacks, 2014), 374.

8 "The peasant owed fees" Ibid., 262.

9 "self-consciousness as a class" Ibid., 561.

9 "Once people envisioned the possibility" Ibid., 195.

11 poverty line of $500 in 1890 Alan Trachtenberg, *The Incorporation of America* (New York: Farrar, Straus and Giroux, 1982), 90.

11 By 1890, one study estimated Patrick J. Kiger, "How Robber Barons Flaunted Their Money During the Gilded Age," History, Jan. 24, 2022, history.com/news/robber-barons-gilded-age-wealth; Elise Taylor, "The Real-Life Socialite Rivalry That Likely Inspired *The Gilded Age*," *Vogue*, Feb. 8, 2022, vogue.com/article/the-real-life-socialite-rivalry-that-likely-inspired-the-gilded-age.

11 "When brokers are freed" Michael Kazin, "Populism and Agrarian Discontent," Gilder Lehrman Institute of American History, AP U.S. History Study Guide, ap.gilderlehrman.org/essays/populism-and-agrarian-discontent.

11 Walt Whitman turned from celebrating Edward T. O'Donnell, "Are We Living in the Gilded Age 2.0?," History, Jan. 31, 2019, history.com/news/second-gilded-age-income-inequality; "America's Economic Injustice," In the Words of Walt Whitman, inthewordsofwaltwhitman.com/self-and-society/americas-economic-injustice/.

11 violent confrontations with police Andrew C. Baker et al., "Capital and Labor," ed. Joseph Locke, in *The American Yawp*, eds. Joseph Locke and Ben Wright (Stanford, Calif.: Stanford University Press, 2018), americanyawp.com/text/16-capital-and-labor/.

13 "The war brought those systems crashing down" Sheri Berman, "The Great Crack-Up, Then and Now," Project Syndicate, May 4, 2018, project-syndicate.org/onpoint/the-great-crack-up-then-and-now-by-sheri-berman-2018-05.

14 "can be expected only" Hannah Arendt, *The Origins of Totalitarianism* (New York: Houghton Mifflin Harcourt, 1985), 323–24.

15 One 2020 study found Annie Lowrey, "Millennials Don't Stand a Chance," *The Atlantic*, Apr. 13, 2020, theatlantic.com/ideas/archive/2020/04/millennials-are-new-lost-generation/609832/.

15 **A February 2023 report** Emma Court and Donna Borak, "Remote Work Is Costing Manhattan More Than $12 Billion a Year," Bloomberg, February 12, 2023, bloomberg.com/graphics/2023-manhattan-work-from -home/#xj4y7vzkg.

16 **"For all of human history"** Columbia Business School online, "New Research Shows Prevalence of Remote Work Spurred by COVID-19 Continues to Effect Residential and Commercial Real Estate Values," January 25, 2023, business.columbia.edu/real-estate-news/columbia -news/new-research-shows-prevalence-remote-work-spurred-covid -19-continues.

16 **Stuck at home during the pandemic** Stephanie Pagones, "Americans Spending Coronavirus Quarantine Streaming 8 Hours of TV per Day," Fox Business, Apr. 16, 2020, foxbusiness.com/lifestyle/americans-coronavirus -quarantine-streaming-services.

16 **"skim-watching"** Sam Haysom, "Does Skim-Watching Videos on 2x Speed Hurt or Help Your Brain?," Mashable, June 11, 2022, mashable .com/article/watching-videos-2x-speed-does-it-work.

16 **road rage shooting deaths** Sarah Burd-Sharps, Paige Tetens, and Jay Szkola, "Road Rage Shootings Are Continuing to Surge," Everytown Research & Policy, Mar. 20, 2023, everytownresearch.org/reports-of -road-rage-shootings-are-on-the-rise/.

16 **unruly passengers on airplanes** Harriet Baskas, "Unruly Passenger Behavior on Airline Flights Is Still Rampant," NBC News, June 17, 2023, nbcnews.com/business/travel/unruly-passenger-behavior-airline -flights-still-rampant-rcna87793.

17 **the share of Americans who died** Benjamin Mueller and Eleanor Lutz, "U.S. Has Far Higher Covid Death Rate Than Other Wealthy Countries," *The New York Times,* Feb. 1, 2022, nytimes.com/interactive/2022/02/01/ science/covid-deaths-united-states.html.

17 **As the journalist Ed Yong** Ed Yong, "How the Pandemic Defeated America," *The Atlantic,* Sept. 2020, theatlantic.com/magazine/archive/2020/ 09/coronavirus-american-failure/614191/; Ed Yong, "How Public Health Took Part in Its Own Downfall," *The Atlantic,* Oct. 23, 2021, theatlantic .com/health/archive/2021/10/how-public-health-took-part-its-own -downfall/620457/.

17 **A 2021 study** Steffie Woolhandler et al., "Public Policy and Health in the Trump Era," *Lancet,* Feb. 10, 2021, thelancet.com/article/S0140 -6736(20)32545-9/fulltext.

18 **"Only by demonstrating the capacity"** Zbigniew Brzezinski, *Strategic Vision: America and the Crisis of Global Power* (New York: Basic Books, 2012), 49.

19 **For years, critics of neoliberalism** Jonathan D. Ostry, Prakash Loungani, and Davide Furceri, "Neoliberalism: Oversold?," *Finance and Development* 53, no. 2 (June 2016), imf.org/external/pubs/ft/fandd/2016/06/ ostry.htm.

19 **"a precariat with no clear long-term prospects"** Francis Wade, " 'The Liberal Order Is the Incubator for Authoritarianism': A Conversation with Pankaj Mishra," *Los Angeles Review of Books,* Nov. 15, 2018, lareviewofbooks .org/article/the-liberal-order-is-the-incubator-for-authoritarianism-a -conversation-with-pankaj-mishra/.

19 **"Liberal democracy's strongest glue"** Edward Luce, *The Retreat of Western Liberalism* (New York: Grove Atlantic, 2017), 12.

20 **"It was hard to avoid"** Adam Tooze, *Shutdown: How Covid Shook the World's Economy* (New York: Viking, 2021), 13.

20 **"drove a stake through the heart"** Eric Foner, "Teaching Radical History in the Age of Obama (and Bernie)," *Nation,* Jan. 2–9, 2017, ericfoner.com/ articles/010217nation.html.

21 **thirty-five-year-old Gabriel Boric** Ciara Nugent, "Chile's Millennial President Is a New Kind of Leftist Leader," *Time,* Aug. 31, 2022, Time.com/ 6209552/gabriel-boric-chile-constitution-interview/; Orlando Letelier, "The 'Chicago Boys' in Chile: Economic Freedom's Awful Toll," *Nation,* Sept. 21, 2016, thenation.com/article/archive/the-chicago-boys-in -chile-economic-freedoms-awful-toll/.

22 **"not make the same mistake"** "Doctors Who Put Lives at Risk with Covid Misinformation Rarely Punished," *The Washington Post,* July 26, 2023, washingtonpost.com/health/2023/07/26/covid-misinformation -doctor-discipline/.

22 **Indeed, one of the lessons** Jennifer Schuessler, "Professor Who Learns from Peasants," *The New York Times,* Dec. 4, 2012, nytimes.com/2012/ 12/05/books/james-c-scott-farmer-and-scholar-of-anarchism.html.

22 **James. C. Scott's influential 1998 book** James C. Scott, *Seeing Like a State: How Certain Schemes to Improve the Human Condition Have Failed* (New Haven: Yale University Press, 1998).

23 **In a Brookings Institution report** Geoffrey Gertz and Homi Kharas, "Conclusion: Toward a New Economic and Political Model?," in *Beyond Neoliberalism: Insights from Emerging Markets,* eds. Geoffrey Gertz and Homi Kharas, Brookings, May 1, 2019, brookings.edu/wp-content/ uploads/2019/05/beyond-neoliberalism-chapter7.pdf; Kemal Dervis, Caroline Conroy, and Geoffrey Gertz, "Politics Beyond Neoliberalism," in *Beyond Neoliberalism,* brookings.edu/wp-content/uploads/ 2019/05/beyond-neoliberalism-chapter6.pdf.

23 **"geopolitical swing states"** Jared Cohen, "The Rise of Geopolitical Swing States," Goldman Sachs online, May 15, 2023, goldmansachs.com/ intelligence/pages/the-rise-of-geopolitical-swing-states.html.

24 **million drug overdoses** cdc.gov/drugoverdose/deaths/index.html#:~: text=More%20than%20one%20million%20people,1999%20from%20a %20drug%20overdose.&text=In%202021%2C%20106%2C699%20drug %20overdose,2021%20(32.4%20per%20100%2C000); washingtonpost .com/health/2022/05/11/drug-overdose-deaths-cdc-numbers/.

24 **nearly one in five** prri.org/press-release/new-prri-report-reveals-nearly
-one-in-five-americans-and-one-in-four-republicans-still-believe-in
-qanon-conspiracy-theories/.

24 **30,573 false or misleading** washingtonpost.com/politics/2021/01/24/
trumps-false-or-misleading-claims-total-30573-over-four-years/.

25 **"nowhere fool"** Volker Ullrich, *Hitler: Ascent 1889–1939* (New York: Alfred A. Knopf, 2016), Kindle edition, p. 239.

25 **"beginning of 1917"** washingtonpost.com/opinions/global-opinions/
bolshevism-then-and-now/2017/11/06/830aecaa-bf41-11e7-959c
-fe2b598d8c00_story.html.

26 **The journalist Victor Sebestyen** Victor Sebestyen, *Lenin: the Man, the Dictator, and the Master of Terror* (New York: Pantheon, 2017), Kindle edition, p. 2.

26 **Volker Ullrich wrote** Volker Ullrich, *Hitler: Ascent 1889–1939* (New York:
Alfred A. Knopf, 2016), Kindle edition, p. 101.

26 **Hannah Arendt argued** Hannah Arendt, *The Origins of Totalitarianism*
(New York: Houghton Mifflin Harcourt, 1994), Kindle edition, p. 352.

27 **Trump came right out** cnn.com/2018/07/25/politics/donald-trump-vfw
-unreality/index.html.

27 **And most Republicans** cnn.com/2018/07/25/politics/donald-trump-vfw
-unreality/index.html.

27 **"not what's happening"** Emily Cochrane, "Trump Talks Likes (Tariffs) and
Dislikes (Media) in V.F.W. Speech," *The New York Times*, July 24, 2018,
nytimes.com/2018/07/24/us/politics/trump-vfw-veterans.html.

27 **"two and two"** George Orwell, *1984* (New York: Houghton Mifflin Harcourt, 1989), Kindle edition, p. 597.

27 **more than six hours** statista.com/statistics/1380282/daily-time-spent
-online-global/.

CHAPTER 2: PIRATES AND THE NEW FRANKENSTEIN

29 **In 1983, at an off-site retreat** Sarah Todd, "The Steve Jobs Speech That
Made Silicon Valley Obsessed with Pirates," *Quartz*, Oct. 22, 2019, qz
.com/1719898/steve-jobs-speech-that-made-silicon-valley-obsessed
-with-pirates.

29 **It's award-winning 1984 commercial** Peter Cohen, "1984: How Apple's TV
Ad Changed Everything, and Why 2014 Won't Be Anything Like It
Either," iMore, Feb. 28, 2018, imore.com/1984-apples-famous-tv-ad
-changed-everything.

30 **the company's 1997 commercial** "Apple—Think Different—Full Version,"
YouTube, youtube.com/watch?v=5sMBhDv4sik; "Steve Jobs: 20 Best
Quotes," ABC News, Aug. 15, 2011, abcnews.go.com/Technology/
steve-jobs-death-20-best-quotes/story?id=14681795/.

30 **Even an early (unused) design** Luke Dormehl, *The Apple Revolution: Steve*

Jobs, the Counterculture, and How the Crazy Ones Took Over the World (London: Ebury Publishing, 2012), 83–84.

30 **"the counterculture's scorn"** Stewart Brand, "We Owe It All to the Hippies," *Time*, Mar. 1, 1995, content.time.com/time/subscriber/article/0,33009,982602,00.html.

32 **worth $3 trillion in market value** Jack Nicas, "Apple Becomes First Company to Hit $3 Trillion Market Value," *The New York Times*, Jan. 3, 2022, nytimes.com/2022/01/03/technology/apple-3-trillion-market-value.html.

32 **"financial weapons of mass destruction"** Jeff Cox, "The Value of What Buffett Called 'Financial Weapons of Mass Destruction' Is Plunging," CNBC, May 4, 2018, cnbc.com/2018/05/04/the-value-of-financial-weapons-of-mass-destruction-is-plunging.html.

33 **"A recent study of politics"** William A. Galston, "The Populist Challenge to Liberal Democracy," *Journal of Democracy* 29, no. 2 (Apr. 2018): 5–19, journalofdemocracy.org/articles/the-populist-challenge-to-liberal-democracy/.

33 **"begins on the fringes of society"** David Potter, *Disruption: Why Things Change* (New York: Oxford University Press, 2021), 1.

33 **the Bush administration's failure** David Johnston and Jim Dwyer, "Threats and Responses: The Investigation; Pre-9/11 Files Show Warnings Were More Dire and Persistent," *The New York Times*, Apr. 18, 2004, nytimes.com/2004/04/18/us/threats-responses-investigation-pre-9-11-files-show-warnings-were-more-dire.html.

33 **"deconstruction of the administrative state"** Philip Rucker and Robert Costa, "Bannon Vows a Daily Fight for 'Deconstruction of the Administrative State,'" *The Washington Post*, Feb. 23, 2017, washingtonpost.com/politics/top-wh-strategist-vows-a-daily-fight-for-deconstruction-of-the-administrative-state/2017/02/23/03f6b8da-f9ea-11e6-bf01-d47f8cf9b643_story.html.

34 **"between authority and obedience"** Martin Gurri, *The Revolt of the Public and the Crisis of Authority in the New Millennium* (San Francisco: Stripe Press, 2018), 79.

34 **"people from nowhere"** Ibid., 300; Murtaza Hussain, "Trump and Brexit Proved This Book Prophetic—What Calamity Will Befall Us Next?," *Intercept*, Mar. 3, 2019, theintercept.com/2019/03/03/revolt-of-the-public-martin-gurri/.

34 **"outside the framework of traditional institutions"** Clay Shirky, *Here Comes Everybody: The Power of Organizing Without Organizations* (New York: Penguin Press, 2008), 20.

35 **"arts organization for the post-gatekeeper era"** Rob Walker, "The Trivialities and Transcendence of Kickstarter," *The New York Times Magazine*, Aug. 5, 2011, nytimes.com/2011/08/07/magazine/the-trivialities-and-transcendence-of-kickstarter.html.

35 **Kickstarter was launched in 2009** Kickstarter, kickstarter.com/about.

35 **"two sides of complete silence"** "Silent Meditation," Kickstarter, kickstarter
.com/projects/silentmeditation/silent-meditation-on-vinyl.

35 **Oculus Rift** Max Chafkin, "Why Facebook's $2 Billion Bet on Oculus Rift
Might One Day Connect Everyone on Earth," *Vanity Fair*, Sept. 8, 2015,
vanityfair.com/news/2015/09/oculus-rift-mark-zuckerberg-cover
-story-palmer-luckey; Jenna Wortham, "Creator of a Virtual Reality
Sensation," *The New York Times*, Mar. 26, 2014, nytimes.com/2014/
03/27/technology/creator-of-a-virtual-reality-sensation.html; Taylor
Clark, "How Palmer Luckey Created Oculus Rift," *Smithsonian Magazine*, Nov. 2014, smithsonianmag.com/innovation/how-palmer-luckey
-created-oculus-rift-180953049/.

36 **fastest-growing population in the military** Adrianna Rodriguez, "Latinos
Are Fastest Growing Population in US Military, but Higher Ranks Remain out of Reach," *USA Today*, Mar. 23, 2020, usatoday.com/in-depth/
news/nation/2020/05/23/latino-hispanic-military-high-ranking
-commissioned-officer-positions/4668013002/.

37 **the Uniform Code of Military Justice** Johnny Diaz, Maria Cramer, and Christina Morales, "What to Know About the Death of Vanessa Guillen," *The
New York Times*, Nov. 30, 2022, nytimes.com/article/vanessa-guillen-fort
-hood.html; John M. Donnelly, "Gillibrand Calls New NDAA 'Huge
Milestone' in Military Justice," *Roll Call*, Dec. 7, 2022, rollcall.com/2022/
12/07/gillibrand-calls-new-ndaa-huge-milestone-in-military-justice.

37 **Her decision to record** Azi Paybarah, "How a Teenager's Video Upended
the Police Department's Initial Tale," *The New York Times*, Apr. 20,
2021, nytimes.com/2021/04/20/us/darnella-frazier-floyd-video.html.

37 **accountable for their actions** Eric Levenson and Aaron Cooper, "Derek
Chauvin Found Guilty of All Three Charges for Killing George Floyd,"
CNN, Apr. 21, 2021, cnn.com/2021/04/20/us/derek-chauvin-trial
-george-floyd-deliberations/index.html; John Eligon et al., "Derek
Chauvin Verdict Brings a Rare Rebuke of Police Misconduct," *The New
York Times*, Apr. 20, 2021, updated June 25, 2021, nytimes.com/2021/
04/20/us/george-floyd-chauvin-verdict.html.

38 **"Universal History"** Thomas Carlyle, *On Heroes, Hero-Worship, and the
Heroic in History* (London: Chapman and Hall, 1852), 1.

38 **"histories of everyday life"** Richard T. Vann, "Historiography," *Britan-
nica*, updated Mar. 24, 2023, britannica.com/topic/historiography;
Andrew Port, "History from Below, the History of Everyday Life, and
Microhistory," in *International Encyclopedia of the Social and Behavioral
Sciences*, 2nd ed., vol. 11 (Amsterdam: Elsevier, 2015), researchgate
.net/publication/304194393_History_from_Below_the_History_of
_Everyday_Life_and_Microhistory.

39 **"Whenever a new information technology"** Dave Roos, "7 Ways the Printing Press Changed the World," History, Mar. 27, 2023, history.com/
news/printing-press-renaissance.

40 "a binding agent" Robert G. Parkinson, "Print, the Press, and the American Revolution," *Oxford Research Encyclopedia of American History,* Sept. 3, 2015, doi.org/10.1093/acrefore/9780199329175.013.9.

40 "presents information in a form" Neil Postman, *Amusing Ourselves to Death* (New York: Penguin Books, 2006), 141.

40 "become an audience" Ibid., 156.

41 "the ability to engage in deep reading" Ezra Klein, "How Technology Literally Changes Our Brains," Vox, July 1, 2020, vox.com/podcasts/2020/7/1/21308153/the-ezra-klein-show-the-shallows-twitter-facebook-attention-deep-reading-thinking.

41 "real revolutions don't involve" Clay Shirky, *Here Comes Everybody* (New York: Penguin Press, 2008), 20.

42 "mystification as well as enlightenment" Elizabeth Eisenstein, *The Printing Press as an Agent of Change* (New York: Cambridge University Press, 1980), 437.

42 "A great deal of scientifically 'worthless'" Ibid., 508.

42 a treatise on demonology Ibid., 436.

42 "Bibles in Everyman's hand" Ibid., 366.

42 "typographical fixity" Ibid., 326.

43 "It soon became impossible" Ibid., 326.

43 doubling every twelve hours Amitabh Ray, "Human Knowledge Is Doubling Every 12 Hours," LinkedIn.com, Oct. 22, 2020, linkedin.com/pulse/human-knowledge-doubling-every-12-hours-amitabh-ray/.

43 Modern binoculars allow people Bob King, "9,096 Stars in the Sky—Is That All?," SkyandTelescope.org, Sept. 17, 2014, skyandtelescope.org/astronomy-blogs/how-many-stars-night-sky-09172014/#:~:text=50%2Dmm%20binoculars%20increase%20the,can%20spy%20about%205%20million.&text=Astronomers%20use%20the%20magnitude%20scale%20to%20measure%20star%20and%20planet%20brightne.

44 "firehose of falsehood" Christopher Paul and Miriam Matthews, "The Russian 'Firehose of Falsehood' Propaganda Model: Why It Might Work and Options to Counter It," RAND Corporation, 2016, rand.org/pubs/perspectives/PE198.html.

44 One particularly fateful decision Jaron Lanier, "How We Need to Remake the Internet," TED2018, ted.com/talks/jaron_lanier_how_we_need_to_remake_the_internet?language=en.

45 "What might once have been called" *Ten Arguments for Deleting Your Social Media Accounts Right Now* (New York: Picador/Henry Holt and Co., 2018), 6.

45 He argues that social media Ibid., 20.

45 A 2022 survey found Trevor Wheelwright, "2022 Cell Phone Usage Statistics: How Obsessed Are We?," Reviews.org, Jan. 24, 2022, reviews.org/mobile/cell-phone-addiction/.

45 "distracted from distraction by distraction" T. S. Eliot, "Burnt Norton," in *Four Quartets* (New York: Harcourt Brace Jovanovich, 1971), 17.

45 **"digital amnesia"** Rebecca Seal, "Is Your Smartphone Ruining Your Memory? A Special Report on the Rise of 'Digital Amnesia,'" *Observer*, July 3, 2022, theguardian.com/global/2022/jul/03/is-your-smartphone -ruining-your-memory-the-rise-of-digital-amenesia.

45 **As Marshall McLuhan predicted** "The Playboy Interview: Marshall McLuhan," *Playboy*, Mar. 1969, redacted and edited by Phillip Rogaway, web .cs.ucdavis.edu/~rogaway/classes/188/spring07/mcluhan.pdf.

46 **"drive us down rabbit holes"** Tristan Harris, "Our Brains Are No Match for Our Technology," *The New York Times*, Dec. 5, 2019, nytimes.com/ 2019/12/05/opinion/digital-technology-brain.html.

46 **"our Paleolithic brains"** Ibid.

46 **"AI's Jurassic Park moment"** Gary Marcus, "AI's Jurassic Park Moment," *The Road to AI We Can Trust*, Dec. 10, 2022, garymarcus.substack.com/ p/ais-jurassic-park-moment.

47 **writing a biblical verse** Kevin Roose, "The Brilliance and Weirdness of ChatGPT," *The New York Times*, Dec. 5, 2022, nytimes.com/2022/12/ 05/technology/chatgpt-ai-twitter.html.

47 **only a few of the technology's possible side effects** Nico Grant and Cade Metz, "A New Chat Bot Is a 'Code Red' for Google's Search Business," *The New York Times*, Dec. 21, 2022, nytimes.com/2022/12/21/ technology/ai-chatgpt-google-search.html; Megan Cerullo, "These Jobs Are Most Likely to Be Replaced by Chatbots Like ChatGPT," CBS News, Feb. 1, 2023, cbsnews.com/news/chatgpt-artificial-intelligence -chatbot-jobs-most-likely-to-be-replaced/; Jonathan Vanian, "Why Tech Insiders Are So Excited About ChatGPT, a Chatbot That Answers Questions and Writes Essays," CNBC, Dec. 13, 2022, cnbc.com/ 2022/12/13/chatgpt-is-a-new-ai-chatbot-that-can-answer-questions -and-write-essays.html; Gary Marcus, "AI Platforms Like ChatGPT Are Easy to Use but Also Potentially Dangerous," *Scientific American*, Dec. 19, 2022, scientificamerican.com/article/ai-platforms-like-chatgpt -are-easy-to-use-but-also-potentially-dangerous/.

47 **"pocket nuclear bomb"** Connie Loizos, "Is ChatGPT a 'Virus That Has Been Released into the Wild'?," *TechCrunch*, Dec. 9, 2022, techcrunch .com/2022/12/09/is-chatgpt-a-virus-that-has-been-released-into-the -wild/?.

48 **"I no longer believe"** Kevin Roose, "A Conversation with Bing's Chatbot Left Me Deeply Unsettled," *The New York Times*, Feb. 16, 2023, nytimes.com/2023/02/16/technology/bing-chatbot-microsoft-chatgpt .html; Kevin Roose, "Bing's A.I. Chat: 'I Want to Be Alive,'" *The New York Times*, Feb. 16, 2023, nytimes.com/2023/02/16/technology/bing -chatbot-transcript.html.

49 **said he now believes** Alex Hern, "'We've Discovered the Secret of Immortality. The Bad News Is It's Not for Us': Why the Godfather of AI Fears for Humanity," *The Guardian*, May 5, 2023, theguardian.com/

technology/2023/may/05/geoffrey-hinton-godfather-of-ai-fears-for
-humanity.

49 "**If there's any way**" Manuel G. Pascual, "Geoffrey Hinton: 'We Need to
Find a Way to Control Artificial Intelligence Before It's Too Late,'" *El
País*, May 12, 2023, english.elpais.com/science-tech/2023-05-12/geoffrey
-hinton-we-need-to-find-a-way-to-control-artificial-intelligence-before
-its-too-late.html.

49 "**annotated for scientists, engineers**" Mary Shelley, *Frankenstein* (Cambridge, Mass.: MIT Press, 2017).

49 "**J. Robert Oppenheimer's sentiments**" Ibid., loc. 3053.

CHAPTER 3: CULTURE IN THE NEW MILLENNIUM

51 **The idea of "twoness"** W.E.B. Du Bois, *The Souls of Black Folk* (New York:
Gildan Media, 2019), 13.

51 "**I began to feel that dichotomy**" W.E.B. Du Bois, *The Autobiography of
W.E.B. Du Bois* (Diasporic Africa Press, Inc., 1968), 186; John P. Pett-
man, "Double Consciousness," *The Stanford Encyclopedia of Philosophy*
(Spring 2023), eds. Edward N. Zalta and Uri Nodelman, plato.stanford
.edu/entries/double-consciousness.

51 "**cultural multiplicity is no longer seen**" Henry Louis Gates Jr., "Both Sides
Now," *The New York Times*, May 4, 2003, nytimes.com/2003/05/04/
books/the-close-reader-both-sides-now.html.

52 "**in the margin is to be part**" bell hooks, "Choosing the Margin as a Space of
Radical Openness," in *Yearning: Race, Gender, and Cultural Politics* (New
York: Taylor & Francis, 2015), 149.

54 "**to document the trauma**" Marcus J. Moore, *The Butterfly Effect: How Kendrick Lamar Ignited the Soul of Black America* (New York: Atria Books,
2020), 7.

55 **increased demand for streaming content** Sara Fischer, "Americans Are Con-
suming More Foreign Content Than Ever," *Axios*, Feb. 16, 2021, axios
.com/2021/02/16/americans-consuming-foreign-entertainment
-content; Jenna Ryu, "This Is America: 'Squid Game,' K-Beauty, and
BTS—What's So Special About Korean Pop Culture?," *USA Today*,
Oct. 21, 2021, usatoday.com/story/news/2021/10/21/squid-game-bts
-k-beauty-why-korean-pop-culture-making-waves/8437852002/; Choe
Sang-Hun, "From BTS to 'Squid Game': How South Korea Became a
Cultural Juggernaut," *The New York Times*, Nov. 3, 2021, nytimes.com/
2021/11/03/world/asia/squid-game-korea-bts.html.

55 "**the hegemony of English is in decline**" "What Spotify Data Show About
the Decline of English," *Economist*, Jan. 29, 2022, economist.com/
interactive/graphic-detail/2022/01/29/what-spotify-data-show-about
-the-decline-of-english.

55 "**a growing number of the biggest pop stars**" Lucas Shaw, "The Four New

Global Capitals of Music," Bloomberg, Feb. 9, 2021, bloomberg.com/
graphics/pop-star-ranking/2021-february/the-four-new-global-capitals
-of-music.html.

55 **the most No. 1 hits** Carmen Chin, "BTS Make History with the Most Number One Hits on the Billboard Hot 100 This Decade," *NME*, Nov. 3,
2022, nme.com/news/music/bts-most-number-one-hits-billboard-hot
-100-chart-decade-3341793.

55 **Bad Bunny's album** *Un Verano Sin Ti* Keith Caulfield, "Bad Bunny's 'Un
Verano Sin Ti' Is This Year's Top Billboard 200 Album: The Year in
Charts," *Billboard*, Dec. 1, 2022, billboard.com/music/chart-beat/bad
-bunny-un-verano-sin-ti-top-billboard-200-album-year-charts-2022
-1235176756/.

56 **"probably the most advanced"** Julia Gray, "Iggy Pop Says Mitski Is the Most
Advanced American Songwriter He Knows," *Stereogum*, June 13, 2018,
stereogum.com/2001533/iggy-pop-says-mitski-is-the-most-advanced
-american-songwriter-he-knows/news/.

56 **"snapped at any subject"** Jan Kott, *Shakespeare Our Contemporary* (New
York: Doubleday, 1964), trans. Boleslaw Taborski, Kindle edition,
loc. 4168.

57 **"the broad sweep of American life"** Ralph Ellison, *The Collected Essays of
Ralph Ellison*, ed. John F. Callahan (New York: Modern Library, 1995), 93.

57 **"technique for the sake of technique"** Ibid., 91.

57 **There is "no novelist"** Tom Wolfe, "Why They Aren't Writing the Great
American Novel Anymore: A Treatise on the Varieties of Realistic Experience," *Esquire*, May 15, 2018, esquire.com/lifestyle/money/a20703846/
tom-wolfe-new-jounalism-american-novel-essay/; Tom Wolfe, "Stalking
the Billion-Footed Beast," *Harper's*, Nov. 1989, harpers.org/archive/
1989/11/stalking-the-billion-footed-beast/.

57 **"voluntary withdrawal of interest"** Philip Roth, "Writing American Fiction,"
Commentary, Mar. 1961, commentary.org/articles/philip-roth/writing
-american-fiction/.

58 **"the fury, the violence, and the desperation"** Philip Roth, *American Pastoral*
(New York: Houghton Mifflin Harcourt, 1997), 86.

58 **A similar withdrawal into the world** Carl Schorske, *Fin-de-Siècle Vienna*
(New York: Vintage Books, 1981), 15.

60 **"the true writer has nothing to say"** "Alain Robbe-Grillet," AuthorsCalendar
.info, authorscalendar.info/grillet.htm.

60 **arguments made by the influential Marxist critic** Fredric Jameson, "Postmodernism, or the Cultural Logic of Late Capitalism," web.education.wisc
.edu/halverson/wp-content/uploads/sites/33/2012/12/jameson.pdf.

62 **"So what we could do"** Tommy Orange, *There There* (New York: Knopf,
2018), 57.

63 **"the poorest, most marginal"** Robert Palmer, *Deep Blues* (New York: Penguin Books, 1982), 17.

63 "an isolated geographical pocket" Ibid., 276.

64 "I am a spy, a sleeper" Viet Thanh Nguyen, *The Sympathizer* (New York: Grove Press, 2015), 1.

64 "gives rise to compassion" "'The Refugees' Author Says We Should All Know What It Is to Be an Outsider," *All Things Considered*, NPR, Feb. 10, 2017, npr.org/2017/02/10/513694099/the-refugees-author -says-we-should-all-know-what-it-is-to-be-an-outsider.

65 the otaku—young people in Japan William M. Tsutsui, "Nerd Nation: Otaku and Youth Subcultures in Contemporary Japan," *Education About Asia* 13, no. 3 (Winter 2008), asianstudies.org/wp-content/uploads/ nerd-nation-otaku-and-youth-subcultures-in-contemporary-japan.pdf.

65 global demand for anime grew Patrick Brzeski, "How Japanese Anime Became the World's Most Bankable Genre," *Hollywood Reporter*, May 16, 2022, hollywoodreporter.com/business/business-news/japanese-anime -worlds-most-bankable-genre-1235146810/.

66 Rod Serling's *Twilight Zone* Scott D. Pierce, "Everyone Knows 'The Twilight Zone,' Which Returns Monday. Did You Know It Was Never a Hit?," *Salt Lake Tribune*, Mar. 30, 2019, sltrib.com/artsliving/2019/03/ 31/everyone-knows-twilight/.

66 the original *Star Trek* Charlie Jane Anders, "The Truth About What Went Wrong with the Third Season of *Star Trek*," *Gizmodo*, Feb. 5, 2015, gizmodo.com/the-truth-about-what-went-wrong-with-the-third-season -0-1684057419/; Dusty Stowe, "Why Star Trek: The Original Series Was Cancelled After Season 3," Screen Rant, May 21, 2019, screenrant.com/ star-trek-original-series-cancelled-season-3-reason-why/.

66 By mid-2022, the fan fiction library Archive of Our Own, archiveofourown .org.

67 "All fanwork, from fanfic to vids" Aja Romano, "The Archive of Our Own Just Won a Hugo. That's Huge for Fanfiction," Vox, Aug. 19, 2019, vox .com/2019/4/11/18292419/archive-of-our-own-wins-hugo-award -best-related-work.

67 No. 1 show in ninety-four countries Mariella Moon, "Netflix Says 142 Million Households Watched Korean Series 'Squid Game,'" *TechCrunch*, Oct. 20, 2021, techcrunch.com/2021/10/20/netflix-says-142-million -households-watched-korean-series-squid-game/.

68 "to relate to real fears" "'Get Out' Sprang from an Effort to Master Fear, Says Director Jordan Peele," NPR News, WBUR, Mar. 15, 2017, wbur .org/npr/520130162/get-out-sprung-from-an-effort-to-master-fear -says-director-jordan-peele.

68 Jacob Lawrence tackled the largest "Jacob Lawrence," Art Story, theartstory .org/artist/lawrence-jacob/.

70 In remarks made at the unveiling Smithsonian, "Obama Portrait Unveiling at the Smithsonian's National Portrait Gallery," YouTube, youtube .com/watch?v=uX8muQOfzqA; "President Obama's Speech at the

Portrait Unveiling at the Smithsonian National Portrait Gallery," Simon Says, simonsaysai.com/blog/president-obamas-speech-at-the-portrait -unveiling-at-the-smithsonian-national-portrait-gallery-ea84b191df41.

70 **someone standing slightly apart** Carol Vogel, "The Inside Story on Outsid- erness," *The New York Times,* Feb. 24, 2011, nytimes.com/2011/02/27/ arts/design/27ligon.html.

71 **"The essay is not only about race relations"** Jason Moran, "Glenn Ligon," *Interview,* May 22, 2009, interviewmagazine.com/art/glenn-ligon.

72 **"An artist must also be an activist"** Tim Lewis, "Ai Weiwei: 'An Artist Must Be an Activist,'" *The Guardian,* Mar. 22, 2020, theguardian.com/ artanddesign/2020/mar/22/ai-weiwei-an-artist-must-be-an-activist.

72 **In 2007, he and his team** Casey Schwartz, "Two Frenchmen Photograph- ing for Peace," ABC News, Mar. 8, 2006, abcnews.go.com/International/ story?id=2934696&page=1.

72 **solidarity with the Ukrainian people** Luke Harding, "'A Volatile Canvas': Banksy Bequest in Ukraine's Rubble Leaves Dilemma for Preservers," *The Guardian,* Jan. 5, 2023, theguardian.com/world/2023/jan/05/a -volatile-canvas-banksy-bequest-in-ukraines-rubble-leaves-dilemma -for-preservers.

72 **He has described street art** "Banksy Graffiti: A Book About the Thinking Street Artist," *HuffPost,* Aug. 30, 2012, huffpost.com/entry/banksy -graffiti-book_n_1827644.

73 **"Just doing a tag"** Simon Hattenstone, "Something to Spray," *The Guard- ian,* July 17, 2003, theguardian.com/artanddesign/2003/jul/17/art.arts features.

73 **$25 million in 2021** Manas Sen Gupta, "10 Most Expensive Banksy Art- works Sold at Auctions," Lifestyle Asia, Jan. 16, 2022, lifestyleasia.com/ kl/culture/art/most-expensive-banksy-art/.

73 **"We are part of the periphery"** Sebastián Vargas, "Seizing Public Space," D+C, Oct. 30, 2015, dandc.eu/en/article/politically-relevant-street-art -has-long-tradition-latin-america; Emma Freedman, "Giving a Voice to the Voiceless: Street Art as a Form of Political Protest," Panoramas, Apr. 26, 2016, panoramas.secure.pitt.edu/art-and-culture/giving-voice -voiceless-street-art-form-political-protest/.

74 **"Graffiti-Free NYC" program** Katie Honan and Coulter Jones, "New York City Businesses Fret as Graffiti-Removal Program Is Axed," *Wall Street Journal,* July 19, 2020, wsj.com/articles/new-york-city-businesses-fret -as-graffiti-removal-program-is-axed-11595178000.

74 **portrait of Breonna Taylor** Jessica Stewart, "Breonna Taylor Commemo- rated with 7,000-Square-Foot Mural," My Modern Met, July 20, 2020, mymodernmet.com/breonna-taylor-mural-future-history-now.

74 **portraits of George Floyd** Charles Passy, "George Floyd's Family Says His Iconic Selfie 'Symbolizes Who He Was'—and Helped Shape the Racial- Justice Narrative," MarketWatch, May 26, 2022, marketwatch.com/

story/george-floyds-family-says-his-iconic-selfie-symbolizes-who-he
-was-and-helped-shape-the-racial-justice-narrative-11653082948.

74 **England, Japan, Brazil, and France** Alexandra Hurtado, "30 Powerful Black
Lives Matter Murals from All Over the World You Really Need to See,"
Parade, Mar. 25, 2021, parade.com/1048964/alexandra-hurtado/black
-lives-matter-street-art-dc-berlin; Shauna Beni, "Black Lives Matter
Murals Around the World, from Kenya to Ireland," *Condé Nast Trav-
eler*, July 30, 2020, cntraveler.com/gallery/black-lives-matter-murals
-around-the-world-from-kenya-to-ireland/; Wyatte Grantham-Philips,
"Powerful Photos Show 'Black Lives Matter' Painted Across Streets
Nationwide," *USA Today*, June 19, 2020, usatoday.com/story/news/
nation/2020/06/17/black-lives-matter-painted-city-streets-see-art-nyc
-washington/3204742001/; Emily Rumball, "Murals Honoring George
Floyd Are Being Painted Around the World," *DH News*, June 8, 2020,
dailyhive.com/seattle/george-floyd-murals-around-the-world.

75 **"We have the attitude"** Jessica Stewart, "Powerful BLM Video Projections
Help Reclaim Controversial Robert E. Lee Monument," My Modern
Met, July 28, 2020, mymodernmet.com/light-projections-robert-e-lee
-memorial.

75 **most influential work** "The 25 Most Influential Works of American Protest
Art Since World War II," *The New York Times*, Oct. 15, 2020, nytimes
.com/2020/10/15/t-magazine/most-influential-protest-art.html.

CHAPTER 4: BROKEN WINDOWS AND SLIDING DOORS

77 **"the Overton window"** Maggie Astor, "How the Politically Unthinkable Can
Become Mainstream," *The New York Times*, Feb. 26, 2019, nytimes.com/
2019/02/26/us/politics/overton-window-democrats.html; "The Overton Window," Mackinac Center for Public Policy, mackinac.org/
OvertonWindow; Jason Deparle, "Right-of-Center Guru Goes Wide with
the Gospel of Small Government," *The New York Times*, Nov. 17, 2006,
nytimes.com/2006/11/17/us/politics/rightofcenter-guru-goes-wide
-with-the-gospel-of-small.html.

78 **"For anyone out there who is involved"** Francesca Willow, "What Is the
Overton Window & Why It Matters for Climate Justice Activism," Eth-
ical Unicorn, June 11, 2022, ethicalunicorn.com/2022/06/11/what-is
-the-overton-window-why-it-matters-for-climate-justice-activism.

79 **The parable, it turns out, isn't true** Whit Gibbons, "The Legend of the Boiling Frog Is Just a Legend," Savannah River Ecology Laboratory, University of Georgia, Dec. 23, 2007, archive-srel.uga.edu/outreach/
ecoviews/ecoview071223.htm.

79 **"We estimate that it takes five years"** Nick Obradovich and Frances C.
Moore, "The Data Is In. Frogs Don't Boil. But We Might," *The Washington Post*, Feb. 25, 2019, washingtonpost.com/weather/2019/02/25/

data-are-frogs-dont-boil-we-might/; Frances C. Moore et al., "Rapidly Declining Remarkability of Temperature Anomalies May Obscure Public Perception of Climate Change," *PNAS*, Feb. 25, 2019, pnas.org/doi/10.1073/pnas.1816541116.

79 **Hillary Clinton's 2,220** Wilson Andrews, Kitty Bennett, and Alicia Parlapiano, "2016 Delegate Count and Primary Results," *The New York Times*, updated July 5, 2016, nytimes.com/interactive/2016/us/elections/primary-calendar-and-results.html.

79 **A 2022 *Washington Post* study** Amelia Malpas, "Win or Lose, Progressive Challengers Have Influenced the Democrats' Agenda," *The Washington Post*, Sept. 30, 2022, washingtonpost.com/politics/2022/09/30/progressives-democrats-the-squad-socialists/.

80 **A 2019 poll** Jim Tankersley and Ben Casselman, "Wealth Tax and Free College Get Poll Support. Democrats Worry It Won't Last," *The New York Times*, July 21, 2019, nytimes.com/2019/07/21/business/wealth-tax-polling-democrats.html.

81 **"an alternative reality silo"** Elizabeth Dohms-Harter, "Wisconsin Conservative Voice Charlie Sykes Is Voting for Joe Biden," *The Morning Show*, WPR, Sept. 9, 2020, wpr.org/wisconsin-conservative-voice-charlie-sykes-voting-joe-biden/.

81 **"autocratic ruling parties"** Anna Lührmann et al., "New Global Data on Political Parties: V-Party," Briefing Paper no. 9, V-Dem Institute, Oct. 26, 2020, v-dem.net/static/website/img/refs/vparty_briefing.pdf.

81 **Sean Hannity's Fox News show** Ian Crouch, "Keurig, Papa John's, and the Politicization of American Junk," *The New Yorker*, Nov. 14, 2017, newyorker.com/culture/culture-desk/keurig-papa-johns-and-the-politicization-of-american-junk.

81 **"official shoes of white people"** Katie Mettler, "We Live in Crazy Times: Neo-Nazis Have Declared New Balance the 'Official Shoes of White People,'" *The Washington Post*, Nov. 15, 2016, washingtonpost.com/news/morning-mix/wp/2016/11/15/the-crazy-reason-neo-nazis-have-declared-new-balance-the-official-shoes-of-white-people/; Ben Popken, "New Balance Rebukes White Supremacists for Adopting Its Sneakers as Hate Symbol," NBC News, Nov. 16, 2016, nbcnews.com/business/consumer/new-balance-rebukes-white-supremacists-adopting-its-sneakers-hate-symbol-n684776; Cam Wolf, "New Balance, Under Armour, and the Year That Sneakers Got Political," *GQ*, Dec. 22, 2017, gq.com/story/new-balance-sneakers-politics-2017.

82 **a comprehensive immigration reform bill** Dan Berman, "Roll Call: Republicans Who Voted for the Bill," *Politico*, June 27, 2013, politico.com/story/2013/06/immigration-roll-call-vote-093531; Christopher Parker, "The (Real) Reason Why the House Won't Pass Comprehensive Immigration Reform," Brookings, Aug. 4, 2014, brookings.edu/blog/fixgov/2014/08/04/the-real-reason-why-the-house-wont-pass-comprehensive-immigration-reform/.

82 **A 2021 Gallup poll** Jeffrey M. Jones, "Democratic, Republican Confidence in Science Diverges," Gallup, July 16, 2021, news.gallup.com/poll/352397/democratic-republican-confidence-science-diverges.aspx.

83 **As a result, Congress has failed** Rani Molla, "Polling Is Clear: Americans Want Gun Control," Vox, June 1, 2022, vox.com/policy-and-politics/23141651/gun-control-american-approval-polling/.

83 **"following the retirements of moderate"** Neal Devins and Lawrence Baum, "Split Definitive: How Party Polarization Turned the Supreme Court into a Partisan Court," *Supreme Court Review* 2016, no. 1 (2017), journals.uchicago.edu/doi/pdf/10.1086/691096.

83 **The 2022 Supreme Court decision** "Majority of Public Disapproves of Supreme Court's Decision to Overturn Roe v. Wade," Pew Research Center, July 6, 2022, pewresearch.org/politics/2022/07/06/majority-of-public-disapproves-of-supreme-courts-decision-to-overturn-roe-v-wade/.

83 **the court limited the EPA's authority** "Supreme Court Strips Federal Government of Crucial Tool to Control Pollution," *The New York Times,* June 30, 2022, nytimes.com/live/2022/06/30/us/supreme-court-epa.

83 **reduce the effects of climate change** Alec Tyson and Brian Kennedy, "Two-Thirds of Americans Think Government Should Do More on Climate," Pew Research Center, June 23, 2020, pewresearch.org/science/2020/06/23/two-thirds-of-americans-think-government-should-do-more-on-climate/.

84 **"stems principally from attitudinal shifts"** Sandra Day O'Connor, *The Majesty of the Law* (New York: Random House, 2003), 166–67. See also Linda Greenhouse, "The Supreme Court: The Justices; Context and the Court," *The New York Times,* June 25, 2003, nytimes.com/2003/06/25/us/the-supreme-court-the-justices-context-and-the-court.html.

84 **"a new low in Gallup's nearly 50-year trend"** Jeffrey M. Jones, "Confidence in U.S. Supreme Court Sinks to Historic Low," Gallup, June 23, 2022, news.gallup.com/poll/394103/confidence-supreme-court-sinks-historic-low.aspx.

84 **This is the very thing George Washington** Washington's Farewell Address, govinfo.gov/content/pkg/GPO-CDOC-106sdoc21/pdf/GPO-CDOC-106sdoc21.pdf.

84 **In fact, scholars who study authoritarianism** "Democracy Facing Global Challenges: V-Dem Annual Democracy Report 2019," V-Dem Institute, May 2019, v-dem.net/static/website/files/dr/dr_2019.pdf.

85 **"reluctant to punish politicians"** Milan W. Svolik, "Polarization Versus Democracy," *Journal of Democracy* 30, no. 3 (July 2019): 20–32, journalofdemocracy.org/articles/polarization-versus-democracy/.

85 **"the termination" of the Constitution** Kristen Holmes, "Trump Calls for the Termination of the Constitution in Truth Social Post," CNN, Dec. 4, 2022, cnn.com/2022/12/03/politics/trump-constitution-truth-social/index.html.

86 **mandating that students be taught** Sarah Mervosh, "DeSantis Faces Swell of Criticism over Florida's New Standards for Black History," *The New York Times,* July 21, 2023, nytimes.com/2023/07/21/us/desantis-florida -black-history-standards.html; Antonio Planas, "New Florida Standards Teach Students That Some Black People Benefited from Slavery Because It Taught Useful Skills," NBC News, July 20, 2023, nbcnews.com/ news/us-news/new-florida-standards-teach-black-people-benefited -slavery-taught-usef-rcna95418.

86 **"following a trail blazed"** Zack Beauchamp, "Ron DeSantis Is Following a Trail Blazed by a Hungarian Authoritarian," Vox, Apr. 28, 2022, vox .com/policy-and-politics/2022/4/28/23037788/ron-desantis-florida -viktor-orban-hungary-right-authoritarian.

86 **members of the New Right** James Pogue, "Inside the New Right, Where Peter Thiel Is Placing His Biggest Bets," *Vanity Fair,* May 2022, vanityfair.com/news/2022/04/inside-the-new-right-where-peter-thiel -is-placing-his-biggest-bets/.

87 **"No matter what you're going to do"** Bob Woodward, "In His Debut in Washington's Power Struggles, Gingrich Threw a Bomb," *The Washington Post,* Dec. 24, 2011, washingtonpost.com/politics/in-his-debut-in -washingtons-power-struggles-gingrich-threw-a-bomb/2011/12/22/ gIQA6GKCGP_story.html.

87 **"Language: A Key Mechanism of Control"** James Salzer, "Gingrich's Language Set New Course," *The Atlanta Journal-Constitution,* July 5, 2016, ajc.com/news/local-govt--politics/gingrich-language-set-new-course/ O5bgK6lY2wQ3KwEZsYTBlO; excerpt from the Gopac pamphlet "Language: A Key Mechanism of Control," University of Houston online, uh.edu/~englin/rephandout.html.

87 **Charles and David Koch** Suzanne Goldenberg, "Tea Party Movement: Billionaire Koch Brothers Who Helped It Grow," *The Guardian,* Oct. 13, 2010, theguardian.com/world/2010/oct/13/tea-party-billionaire-koch -brothers; Tim Mak, "Koch Brothers, Behind Tea Party Wave, Face Democrats' Rising Tide in 2018," *All Things Considered,* NPR, Jan. 30, 2018, npr.org/2018/01/30/581730998/koch-brothers-behind-tea-party -wave-face-democrats-rising-tide-in-2018/.

88 **when Steve Bannon took over** Joshua Green, *Devil's Bargain: Steve Bannon, Donald Trump, and the Nationalist Uprising* (New York: Penguin Books, 2017), 146.

88 **"envisioned a great fusion"** Ibid., 146.

88 **"God Emperor," Donald Trump** Alex Krasodomski-Jones, "What Does the Alt-Right Do Now That 'God Emperor' Trump Won?," CNN, Nov. 15, 2016, cnn.com/2016/11/14/opinions/what-next-alt-right-krasodomski -jones-opinion/.

88 **"Online cultures that used to be"** Alice Marwick and Becca Lewis, "The Online Radicalization We're Not Talking About," *New York,* May 18, 2017, nymag.com/intelligencer/2017/05/the-online-radicalization-were-not

-talking-about.html; Alice Marwick and Rebecca Lewis, *Media Manipulation and Disinformation Online,* Data & Society, datasociety.net/pubs/oh/ DataAndSociety_MediaManipulationAndDisinformationOnline.pdf.

89 **Public Religion Research Institute survey** Daniel Cox and Robert P. Jones, "America's Changing Religious Identity," PRRI, Sept. 6, 2017, prri.org/ research/american-religious-landscape-christian-religiously-unaffiliated/; Ed Kilgore, "White Evangelicals Now Outnumbered by Mainline Protestants in U.S.," *New York,* July 8, 2021, nymag.com/intelligencer/2021/07/ white-mainline-protestants-outnumber-evangelicals-survey.html.

90 **"It's precisely because conservatives"** Paul Waldman, "Why Republicans Are Excited About a Culture War They Know They're Losing," *The Washington Post,* Mar. 18, 2022, washingtonpost.com/opinions/2022/ 03/18/republicans-losing-culture-war/.

90 **"The Klan is strong when its leaders"** Staff of the Klanwatch Project, "Ku Klux Klan: A History of Racism," Southern Poverty Law Center, Mar. 1, 2011, splcenter.org/20110228/ku-klux-klan-history-racism.

91 **the KKK had an estimated** Joshua D. Rothman, "When Bigotry Paraded Through the Streets," *The Atlantic,* Dec. 4, 2016, theatlantic.com/ politics/archive/2016/12/second-klan/509468/.

91 **The building of Confederate monuments** Saeed Ahmed, "There Are Certain Moments in US History When Confederate Monuments Go Up," CNN, Aug. 16, 2017, cnn.com/2017/08/16/us/confederate-monuments -backlash-chart-trnd/; Becky Little, "How the US Got So Many Confederate Monuments," History, Sept. 8, 2021, history.com/news/how-the-u-s -got-so-many-confederate-monuments; Becca Stanek, "Striking Graphic Reveals the Construction of Confederate Monuments Peaked During the Jim Crow and Civil Rights Eras," *Week,* Aug. 15, 2017, theweek.com/ speedreads/718507/striking-graphic-reveals-construction-confederate -monuments-peaked-during-jim-crow-civil-rights-eras/.

92 **Barry Goldwater led a delegation** James M. Naughton, "Nixon Slide from Power: Backers Gave Final Push," *The New York Times,* Aug. 12, 1974, nytimes.com/1974/08/12/archives/nixon-slide-from-power-backers -gave-final-push-former-defenders.html.

92 **John Birch Society** Erick Trickey, "Long Before QAnon, Ronald Reagan and the GOP Purged John Birch Extremists from the Party," *The Washington Post,* Jan. 15, 2021, washingtonpost.com/history/2021/01/15/ john-birch-society-qanon-reagan-republicans-goldwater/.

92 **grew by an estimated 55 percent** James Wilson, "White Nationalist Hate Groups Have Grown 55% in Trump Era, Report Finds," *Guardian,* Mar. 18, 2020, theguardian.com/world/2020/mar/18/white-nationalist -hate-groups-southern-poverty-law-center/; "The Year in Hate & Extremism Report 2021," Southern Poverty Law Center, Mar. 9, 2022, splcenter.org/20220309/year-hate-extremism-report-2021.

92 **by 2021 law enforcement officials** Eileen Sullivan and Katie Benner, "Top Law Enforcement Officials Say the Biggest Domestic Terror Threat Comes

from White Supremacists," *The New York Times,* May 12, 2021, nytimes
.com/2021/05/12/us/politics/domestic-terror-white-supremacists.html.

93 **"great replacement" conspiracy theory** splcenter.org/hatewatch/2022/05/
17/racist-great-replacement-conspiracy-theory-explained.

93 **Tucker Carlson repeatedly invoked** nytimes.com/2022/05/15/us/replace
ment-theory-shooting-tucker-carlson.html.

93 **At the Waco rally, Trump played a video** Stephen Neukam, "Trump
Opens Campaign Rally with Song Featuring Jan. 6 Defendants," *Hill,*
Mar. 26, 2023, thehill.com/homenews/campaign/3918877-trump-opens
-campaign-rally-with-song-featuring-jan-6-defendants/; Rob Garver,
"Trump Celebrates Jan. 6 Attack in Large Campaign Rally," VOA,
Mar. 27, 2023, voanews.com/a/trump-celebrates-jan-6-attack-in-large
-campaign-rally/7024839.html.

93 **"For those who have been wronged"** Elaine Godfrey, "Trump Begins the 'Retribution' Tour," *The Atlantic,* Mar. 26, 2023, theatlantic.com/politics/
archive/2023/03/donald-trump-rally-waco-2024-campaign/673526/.

93 **Voter intimidation surged** Gram Slattery, "North Carolina Reports Possible Voter Intimidation, Threats Ahead of Midterm Elections," Reuters,
Nov. 4, 2022, reuters.com/world/us/north-carolina-reports-possible
-voter-intimidation-threats-ahead-midterms-2022-11-04/.

93 **"threats of hanging, firing squads"** Linda So, "Trump-Inspired Death
Threats Are Terrorizing Election Workers," Reuters, June 11, 2021,
reuters.com/investigates/special-report/usa-trump-georgia-threats/.

93 **"one in six election officials"** Ruby Edlin and Turquoise Baker, "Poll of
Local Election Officials Finds Safety Fears for Colleagues—and Themselves," Brennan Center for Justice, Mar. 10, 2022, brennancenter.org/
our-work/analysis-opinion/poll-local-election-officials-finds-safety
-fears-colleagues-and.

94 **"if elected leaders will not protect"** Blake Hounshell and Leah Askarinam,
"How Many Americans Support Political Violence?," *The New York
Times,* Jan. 5, 2022, nytimes.com/2022/01/05/us/politics/americans
-political-violence-capitol-riot.html; Daniel A. Cox, "After the Ballots
Are Counted: Conspiracies, Political Violence, and American Excep-
tionalism," Survey Center on American Life, Feb. 11, 2021, american
surveycenter.org/research/after-the-ballots-are-counted-conspiracies
-political-violence-and-american-exceptionalism/.

94 **"not Americans in any meaningful sense"** Elisabeth Zerofsky, "How the
Claremont Institute Became a Nerve Center of the American Right," *The
New York Times Magazine,* Aug. 3, 2022, nytimes.com/2022/08/03/
magazine/claremont-institute-conservative.html.

94 **Curtis Yarvin, a software engineer** Jacob Siegel, "The Red-Pill Prince,"
Tablet, Mar. 30, 2022, tabletmag.com/sections/news/articles/red-pill
-prince-curtis-yarvin.

94 **Viktor Orbán** Shaun Walker, "Viktor Orbán Sparks Outrage with Attack
on 'Race Mixing' in Europe," *The Guardian,* July 24, 2022, theguardian

.com/world/2022/jul/24/viktor-orban-against-race-mixing-europe
-hungary/; Patrick Smith, "Why Trump and the GOP Love Hungary's
Authoritarian Leader," NBC News, Aug. 4, 2022, nbcnews.com/news/
world/viktor-orban-cpac-trump-gop-hungary-leader-rcna40199/;
David Smith, "Viktor Orbán Turns Texas Conference into Transatlantic
Far-Right Love-In," *The Guardian*, Aug. 6, 2022, theguardian.com/us
-news/2022/aug/06/viktor-orban-cpac-far-right-us-trump/.

94 **In a 2022 *Vanity Fair* article** James Pogue, "Inside the New Right, Where
Peter Thiel Is Placing His Biggest Bets," *Vanity Fair*, Apr. 20, 2022,
vanityfair.com/news/2022/04/inside-the-new-right-where-peter-thiel
-is-placing-his-biggest-bets.

95 **nihilism of political leaders** Donald B. Ayer and Alan Charles Raul, "Naked
Republican Hypocrisy Is Destroying Trust in Supreme Court: Reagan,
Bush Lawyers," *USA Today*, Oct. 12, 2020, usatoday.com/story/
opinion/2020/10/12/republican-mcconnell-hypocrisy-destroying
-supreme-court-column/5966069002/.

95 **It's also a sign that "owning the libs"** Derek Robertson, "How 'Owning the
Libs' Became the GOP's Core Belief," *Politico Magazine*, Mar. 21, 2021,
politico.com/news/magazine/2021/03/21/owning-the-libs-history
-trump-politics-pop-culture-477203.

96 **a wave of unprecedented grassroots activism** Erica Chenoweth, "The Trump
Years Launched the Biggest Sustained Protest Movement in U.S. History.
It's Not Over," *The Washington Post*, Feb. 8, 2021, washingtonpost.com/
politics/2021/02/08/trump-years-launched-biggest-sustained-protest
-movement-us-history-its-not-over/; Crowd Counting Consortium,
sites.google.com/view/crowdcountingconsortium/home.

CHAPTER 5: THE RESISTANCE STRIKES BACK

99 **"movement moment"** Simon Black, "The Importance of Making Trouble:
In Conversation with Frances Fox Piven," *Canadian Dimension*, July 26,
2016, canadiandimension.com/articles/view/the-importance-of-making
-trouble-in-conversation-with-frances-fox-piven/; Mie Inouye, "Frances
Fox Piven on Why Protesters Must 'Defend Their Ability to Exercise Disruptive Power,'" *Jacobin*, June 17, 2020, jacobin.com/2020/06/frances
-fox-piven-protests-movement-racial-justice/.

100 **a "legitimation crisis"** Inouye, "Frances Fox Piven on Why Protesters
Must 'Defend Their Ability to Exercise Disruptive Power.'"

100 **had died of COVID** National Data: Deaths, COVID Tracking Project at
The Atlantic, covidtracking.com/data/national/deaths/.

100 **U.S. unemployment had jumped** Heather Long and Andrew Van Dam,
"U.S. Unemployment Rate Soars to 14.7 Percent, the Worst Since the
Depression Era," *The Washington Post*, May 8, 2020, washingtonpost
.com/business/2020/05/08/april-2020-jobs-report/.

100 **"more than one every other day"** Alex Altman, "Why the Killing of George

Floyd Sparked an American Uprising," *Time*, June 4, 2020, time.com/ 5847967/george-floyd-protests-trump/.

100 Those protests were the largest Larry Buchanan, Quoctrung Bui, and Jugal K. Patel, "Black Lives Matter May Be the Largest Movement in U.S. History," *The New York Times*, July 3, 2020, nytimes.com/interactive/ 2020/07/03/us/george-floyd-protests-crowd-size.html.

101 Between 2015 and 2020, a survey Giovanni Russonello, "Why Most Americans Support the Protests," *The New York Times*, June 5, 2020, nytimes .com/2020/06/05/us/politics/polling-george-floyd-protests-racism .html; Zeynep Tufekci, "Do Protests Even Work?," *The Atlantic*, June 24, 2020, theatlantic.com/technology/archive/2020/06/why -protests-work/613420/.

101 "the white moderate" Martin Luther King Jr., "Letter from Birmingham Jail," Apr. 16, 1963, Bill of Rights Institute, billofrightsinstitute.org/ primary-sources/letter-from-birmingham-jail.

101 "masses of people coming together" Angela Davis, interview, Channel 4 News, YouTube, youtube.com/watch?v=peyv1-a48qk.

102 More than four million people Erica Chenoweth and Jeremy Pressman, "This Is What We Learned by Counting the Women's Marches," *The Washington Post*, Feb. 7, 2017, washingtonpost.com/news/monkey-cage/wp/2017/ 02/07/this-is-what-we-learned-by-counting-the-womens-marches/.

102 At least 1.2 million people turned out German Lopez, "It's Official: March for Our Lives Was One of the Biggest Youth Protests Since the Vietnam War," Vox, Mar. 26, 2018, vox.com/policy-and-politics/2018/3/26/ 17160646/march-for-our-lives-crowd-size-count/.

103 A 2018 *Washington Post* poll Mary Jordan and Scott Clement, "Rallying Nation," *The Washington Post*, Apr. 6, 2018, washingtonpost.com/news/ national/wp/2018/04/06/feature/in-reaction-to-trump-millions-of -americans-are-joining-protests-and-getting-political/.

103 According to *Politico*, there was a wave Susannah Savage, "Protests over Food and Fuel Surged in 2022—the Biggest Were in Europe," *Politico*, Jan. 17, 2023, politico.eu/article/energy-crisis-food-and-fuel-protests -surged-in-2022-the-biggest-were-in-europe/.

104 Trump's presidency turned the gender gap Michael Hais and Morley Winograd, "The Future Is Female: How the Growing Political Power of Women Will Remake American Politics," Brookings, Feb. 19, 2020, brookings.edu/blog/fixgov/2020/02/19/the-future-is-female-how -the-growing-political-power-of-women-will-remake-american -politics/.

105 Enraged by Trump's shameless misogyny Leah Gose and Theda Skocpol, "Resist, Persist, and Transform: The Emergence and Impact of Grassroots Resistance Groups Opposing the Trump Presidency," Harvard University, scholar.harvard.edu/files/thedaskocpol/files/resist_persist _and_transform_3-21-19_.ap_.pdf.

105 And in 2018, with a record number Li Zhou, "A Historic New Congress

Will Be Sworn in Today," Vox, Jan. 3, 2019, vox.com/2018/12/6/18119733/congress-diversity-women-election-good-news/; Samantha Cooney, "Here Are Some of the Women Who Made History in the Midterm Elections," *Time*, Nov. 19, 2018, time.com/5323592/2018-elections-women-history-records/; Leslie Shapiro et al., "125 Women Won Their Elections," *The Washington Post*, Nov. 6, 2018, washingtonpost.com/graphics/2018/politics/women-congress-governor/?noredirect=on&utm_term=.0f83e54ccb69/.

105 **In Iran, the death in custody** Peter Kenyon, "Iran Demonstrators Vow to Continue Protests Despite Ongoing Crackdowns," NPR, Jan. 6, 2023, npr.org/2023/01/06/1147376644/iran-protests-crackdown-mahsa-amini/; Nilo Tabrizy, Atthar Mirza, and Babak Dehghanpisheh, "Videos Show Evidence of Escalating Crackdown on Iranian Protests," *The Washington Post*, Feb. 2, 2023, washingtonpost.com/world/2023/02/02/iran-protests-government/; Farnaz Fassihi and Cora Engelbrecht, "Three More Executed in Iran over Protests," *The New York Times*, May 22, 2023, nytimes.com/article/iran-protests-death-sentences-executions.html.

106 **The demonstrations were a testament** Vivian Yee and Farnaz Fassihi, "'They Have Nothing to Lose': Why Young Iranians Are Rising Up Once Again," *The New York Times*, Sept. 24, 2022, nytimes.com/2022/09/24/world/middleeast/iran-protests-raisi-khamenei-hijab.html; Jessie Yeung et al., "Iranian Women Burn Their Hijabs as Hundreds Protest Death of Mahsa Amini," CNN, Sept. 21, 2022, cnn.com/2022/09/21/middleeast/iran-mahsa-amini-death-widespread-protests-intl-hnk.

106 **In a 2022 study** Erica Chenoweth and Zoe Marks, "Revenge of the Patriarchs: Why Autocrats Fear Women," *Foreign Affairs*, Feb. 8, 2022, foreignaffairs.com/articles/china/2022-02-08/women-rights-revenge-patriarchs.

107 **Critics were quick to write** Andrew Ross Sorkin, "Occupy Wall Street: A Frenzy That Fizzled," *The New York Times*, Sept. 17, 2012, archive.nytimes.com/dealbook.nytimes.com/2012/09/17/occupy-wall-street-a-frenzy-that-fizzled/.

107 **Even liberals who applauded** Nina Mandell, "Occupy Atlanta Offshoot of Wall Street Protest Denies Rep. John Lewis Chance to Speak at Gathering," *Daily News*, Oct. 10, 2011, protect-us.mimecast.com/s/Z9Y-CrkY5gI8QV011h3Di9-J?domain=nydailynews.com; Andrew Anthony, "'We Showed It Was Possible to Create a Movement from Almost Nothing': Occupy Wall Street 10 Years On," *The Guardian*, Sept. 12, 2021, theguardian.com/us-news/2021/sep/12/occupy-wall-street-10-years-on/; Joan Walsh, "The Man Who Blocked John Lewis Speaks," *Salon*, Oct. 13, 2011, salon.com/2011/10/13/the_man_who_blocked_john_lewis_speaks/.

108 **"For everything that Occupy got wrong"** Michael Levitin, *Generation Occupy: Reawakening American Democracy* (Berkeley, California: Counterpoint, 2021), Kindle edition, pp. 212–13.

108 **Levitin also argues that today's** Ibid., 126–27.

108 **In a 1982 essay** Irving Howe, "The Decade That Failed," *The New York Times*, Sept. 19, 1982, nytimes.com/1982/09/19/magazine/the-decade -that-failed.html.

109 **the win column for Joe Biden** Maya King, "How Stacey Abrams and Her Band of Believers Turned Georgia Blue," *Politico*, Nov. 8, 2020, politico .com/news/2020/11/08/stacey-abrams-believers-georgia-blue-434985.

109 **The group created** Maya King, "Black Lives Matter Launches a Political Action Committee," *Politico*, Oct. 9, 2020, politico.com/news/2020/ 10/09/black-lives-matter-pac-428403; Erin Aubry Kaplan, "Black Lives Matter as Electoral Powerhouse," *American Prospect*, Nov. 17, 2020, prospect.org/politics/black-lives-matter-as-electoral-powerhouse/.

109 **"hashtags don't build movements"** Alicia Garza, *The Purpose of Power: How We Come Together When We Fall Apart* (New York: One World, 2021), 137.

109 **"take seriously the task"** Ibid., 216.

110 **Occupy activists helped Walmart employees** Michael Levitin, "Occupy Wall Street Did More Than You Think," *The Atlantic*, Sept. 14, 2021, theatlantic .com/ideas/archive/2021/09/how-occupy-wall-street-reshaped -america/620064/; Susan Berfield, "Wal-Mart's Black Friday Strikes: Are the Workers Already Winning?," Bloomberg, Nov. 28, 2014, bloomberg .com/news/articles/2014-11-28/wal-mart-black-friday-strikes-are-the -workers-already-winning#xj4y7vzkg?leadSource=uverify%20wall; Mi- chael Sainato, "US Retail Employees Call Out Working Conditions with Black Friday Protests," *The Guardian*, Nov. 29, 2019, theguardian.com/ business/2019/nov/29/black-friday-protests-working-conditions-labor -issues/.

110 **tumbling from some 35 percent** Steven Greenhouse, "Young Workers Are Organizing. Can Their Fervor Save Unions?," *The Washington Post*, Sept. 2, 2022, washingtonpost.com/outlook/2022/09/02/young -workers-unions-starbucks-amazon/.

110 **10.7 percent in 2017** Bureau of Labor Statistics, "Union Members—2017," press release, Jan. 19, 2018, bls.gov/news.release/archives/union2 _01192018.pdf.

110 **The West Virginia walkout** Caroline O'Donovan, "Facebook Played a Piv- otal Role in the West Virginia Teacher Strike," *BuzzFeed News*, Mar. 7, 2018, buzzfeednews.com/article/carolineodonovan/facebook-group-west -virginia-teachers-strike/; Gregory Krieg, "Is the West Virginia Teach- ers' Strike the Future of American Labor?," CNN, Mar. 5, 2018, cnn.com/ 2018/03/05/politics/west-virginia-teachers-strike-future-unions/index .html; Andrew Van Dam, "Teacher Strikes Made 2018 the Biggest Year for Worker Protest in a Generation," *The Washington Post*, Feb. 14, 2019, washingtonpost.com/us-policy/2019/02/14/with-teachers-lead-more -workers-went-strike-than-any-year-since/; Dana Goldstein, "Teachers in Oklahoma and Kentucky Walk Out: 'It Really Is a Wildfire,'" *The New*

York Times, Apr. 2, 2018, nytimes.com/2018/04/02/us/teacher-strikes -oklahoma-kentucky.html.

111 **"a wave of workers' strikes"** Laura Spinney, *Pale Rider: The Spanish Flu of 1918 and How It Changed the World* (New York: PublicAffairs, 2017), Kindle edition, pp. 253, 255.

111 **"To find similar excitement"** Steven Greenhouse, "Op-Ed: A New Generation Is Reviving Unions. The Old Guard Could Help," *Los Angeles Times,* May 23, 2022, latimes.com/opinion/story/2022-05-23/starbucks -amazon-apple-union-campaigns-history/.

111 **By 2021, a Gallup poll** Abigail Higgins, "More Starbucks Stores Want to Unionize. These Women and Nonbinary Workers Are Leading the Push," *The Washington Post,* Mar. 4, 2022, washingtonpost.com/lifestyle/2022/ 03/04/starbucks-employees-unionizing/; Megan Brenan, "Approval of Labor Unions at Highest Point Since 1965," Gallup, Sept. 2, 2021, news .gallup.com/poll/354455/approval-labor-unions-highest-point-1965 .aspx.

111 **"the most pro-union president"** Ahiza García-Hodges, "Biden's Vow to Be 'Most Pro-union President' Tested in First Year," NBC News, Jan. 20, 2022, nbcnews.com/business/economy/bidens-vow-union -president-tested-first-year-rcna12791.

112 **outsourced to artificial intelligence** Simmone Shah, "The Writers Strike Is Taking a Stand on AI," *Time,* May 4, 2023, time.com/6277158/writers -strike-ai-wga-screenwriting/; Mia Galuppo, "All the Actors Strike Questions You Were Afraid to Ask," *The Hollywood Reporter,* July 20, 2023, hollywoodreporter.com/business/business-news/sag-actors-strike-faq -questions-1235538870/.

112 **As for unionization at Amazon** Charlotte Alter, "He Came Out of Nowhere and Humbled Amazon. Is Chris Smalls the Future of Labor?," *Time,* Apr. 25, 2022, time.com/6169185/chris-smalls-amazon-labor -union/; "We're Organizing Unions at Amazon and Starbucks. We Won't Back Down," interview with Christian Smalls and Jaz Brisack, *Jacobin,* May 26, 2022, jacobin.com/2022/05/amazon-starbucks-labor -union-busting-nlrb; Jodi Kantor and Karen Weise, "How Two Best Friends Beat Amazon," *The New York Times,* Apr. 2, 2022, nytimes.com/ 2022/04/02/business/amazon-union-christian-smalls.html.

112 **In the case of Starbucks** Amelia Lucas, "Here's a Map of Starbucks Stores That Voted to Unionize," CNBC, Dec. 9, 2022, cnbc.com/2022/12/09/ map-of-starbucks-stores-that-voted-to-unionize.html; "These Baristas Take You Inside the Union Fight Against the US's Largest Coffee Chain," CNN Business, cnn.com/videos/business/2022/11/01/starbucks-union -buffalo-memphis-store-vote-risk-takers-orig.cnn-business.

112 **much of the actual organizing** Walter Orechwa, "What Can We Learn from TikTok, Free Weed, and an Amazon Union Campaign?," Projections, projectionsinc.com/what-we-learn-from-amazons-union-campaign/;

Rani Molla, "How a Bunch of Starbucks Baristas Built a Labor Movement," *Vox*, Apr. 8, 2022, vox.com/recode/22993509/starbucks -successful-union-drive/.

113 **In the 2020 election, exit polls** Abigail Johnson Hess, "The 2020 Election Shows Gen Z's Voting Power for Years to Come," CNBC, Nov. 18, 2020, cnbc.com/2020/11/18/the-2020-election-shows-gen-zs-voting-power -for-years-to-come.html.

113 **"a progressive youthquake"** Charlotte Alter, "How Millennial Leaders Will Change America," *Time*, Jan. 23, 2020, time.com/magazine/us/ 5770116/february-3rd-2020-vol-195-no-3-u-s/.

113 **Surveys indicate that members** Kim Parker, Nikki Graf, and Ruth Igielnik, "Generation Z Looks a Lot Like Millennials on Key Social and Political Issues," Pew Research Center, Jan. 17, 2019, pewresearch.org/social -trends/2019/01/17/generation-z-looks-a-lot-like-millennials-on-key -social-and-political-issues/; "On the Cusp of Adulthood and Facing an Uncertain Future: What We Know About Gen Z So Far," Pew Research Center, May 14, 2020, pewresearch.org/social-trends/2020/05/14/on -the-cusp-of-adulthood-and-facing-an-uncertain-future-what-we-know -about-gen-z-so-far-2/.

114 **"most profound generational transition"** Ronald Brownstein, "The GOP's Demographic Doom," *The Atlantic*, Oct. 23, 2020, theatlantic.com/ politics/archive/2020/10/millennials-and-gen-z-will-soon-dominate -us-elections/616818/; Rob Griffin, William H. Frey, and Ruy Teixeira, "America's Electoral Future: The Coming Generational Transforma- tion," Center for American Progress, Oct. 19, 2020, americanprogress .org/article/americas-electoral-future-3/.

114 **"were perfectly positioned to take"** Andrew B. Lewis, *The Shadows of Youth: The Remarkable Journey of the Civil Rights Generation* (New York: Hill and Wang, 2009), 301–2.

115 **"Second Reconstruction"** Ibid., 305.

115 **"the sunlit path of racial justice"** Martin Luther King Jr., "I Have a Dream," Aug. 28, 1963, American Rhetoric, americanrhetoric.com/speeches/ mlkihaveadream.htm.

115 **"Dissent and dissidence are overwhelmingly"** Tony Judt, *Ill Fares the Land* (New York: Penguin Press, 2010), 163.

115 **"the unfinished work"** Abraham Lincoln, Gettysburg Address, Nov. 19, 1863, abrahamlincolnonline.org/lincoln/speeches/gettysburg.htm.

115 **"not an end, but a beginning"** King, "I Have a Dream."

115 **"perfecting our union"** Ron Fournier, "Obama's New American Exception- alism," *The Atlantic*, July 28, 2016, theatlantic.com/politics/archive/ 2016/07/obamas-new-american-exceptionalism/493415/.

115 **"relay race"** Ruth Umoh, "Barack Obama on Success: Not a Marathon or Sprint, but a 'Relay Race,'" CNBC, Dec. 27, 2017, cnbc.com/2017/12/ 27/barack-obama-to-prince-harry-leadership-success-is-a-relay-race .html.

116 "the principles of equality" Barack Obama, "Remarks at the Selma Voting Rights March Commemoration in Selma, Alabama," Mar. 4, 2007, presidency.ucsb.edu/documents/remarks-the-selma-voting-rights-march-commemoration-selma-alabama.

116 "Freedom is not a state" John Lewis, *Across That Bridge: Life Lessons and a Vision for Change* (New York: Grand Central Publishing, 2012), Kindle edition, p. 15.

CHAPTER 6: OUTLAW NATION

121 "things are trending downward" Alessandra Stanley, "This Thing of Ours, It's Over," *The New York Times*, Apr. 8, 2007, nytimes.com/2007/04/08/arts/television/08stan.html.

121 "we used to make shit" "Frank Sobotka," IMDb, imdb.com/title/tt0749423/characters/nm0061777.

122 "the hottest show of 2020" Andrew Unterberger, "*The Sopranos* Is the Hottest Show of 2020," *GQ*, May 8, 2020, gq.com/story/the-sopranos-is-the-hottest-show-of-2020.

122 "It's good to be in something" *The Sopranos*, "Pilot," season 1, episode 1, aired Jan. 10, 1999, on HBO.

122 "This is still where people" *The Sopranos*, "Made in America," season 6, episode 21, aired June 10, 2007, on HBO.

122 "everything is in constant motion" Alexis de Tocqueville, *Democracy in America*, trans. Henry Reeve, vol. 2 (New York: Penguin Books, 2014); Kindle edition: Digireads.com Publishing, 2016, p. 5.

123 the first generation in the nation's history Tami Luhby, "Many Millennials Are Worse Off Than Their Parents—a First in American History," CNN, Jan. 11, 2020, cnn.com/2020/01/11/politics/millennials-income-stalled-upward-mobility-us/index.html.

123 "no genre suited the baby boomers' dueling impulses" Brett Martin, *Difficult Men: Behind the Scenes of a Creative Revolution: From "The Sopranos" and "The Wire" to "Mad Men" and "Breaking Bad"* (New York: Penguin Books, 2014), 84.

124 he needs to make $737,000 *Breaking Bad*, "Seven Thirty-Seven," season 2, episode 1, aired Mar. 8, 2009, on AMC.

124 "I am not in danger" "'Breaking Bad': 25 Most Badass Quotes," *Hollywood Reporter*, hollywoodreporter.com/gallery/breaking-bad-quotes-20-badass-612801/10-i-am-the-one-who-knocks/.

124 "shows about the end" Alan Sepinwall, *The Revolution Was Televised: The Cops, Crooks, Slingers, and Slayers Who Changed TV Drama Forever* (self-published edition, 2012), 112.

124 "The America of *The Wire* is broken" Ibid., 80.

125 "all the pieces matter" *The Wire*, season 1, episode 6, aired July 7, 2002, on HBO.

125 "left in the shallows" David Simon, introduction to *"The Wire": Truth Be Told*, by Rafael Alvarez (New York: Pocket Books, 2009), 7.

125 "the romantic version" Matt Zoller Seitz and Alan Sepinwall, *The Sopranos Sessions* (New York: Abrams Press, 2019), 417.

126 James Fenimore Cooper's *Leatherstocking Tales* "Happy 220th Birthday to James Fenimore Cooper," *Face-to-Face* (blog), National Portrait Gallery, npg.si.edu/blog/happy-220th-birthday-james-fenimore-cooper.

127 "A man has to be" "Shane: A Man Has to Be What He Is, Joey: 1953," YouTube, youtube.com/watch?v=oeqR625n2LQ.

127 "not acknowledging the common continent of men" Herman Melville, *Moby-Dick*, Project Gutenberg, gutenberg.org/files/2701/2701-h/2701 -h.htm.

127 In a 1980 essay Richard E. Meyer, "The Outlaw: A Distinctive American Folktype," *Journal of the Folklore Institute* 17, nos. 2/3 (May–Dec. 1980): 94–124, jstor.org/stable/3813890.

129 with the decline of tradition-directed societies David Riesman, *The Lonely Crowd: A Study of the Changing American Character*, with Nathan Glazer and Reuel Denney (New Haven: Yale University Press, 2000).

130 the counterculture could be commodified Michiko Kakutani, "Jeans Now Need Their Own Specialist Scholars: Call It Jeanitics," *The New York Times*, Aug. 8, 2006, nytimes.com/2006/08/08/books/08kaku.html; David Skinner, "The Graying of the 'Greening of America,'" *Washington Examiner*, Dec. 19, 2005, washingtonexaminer.com/weekly-standard/the -graying-of-the-greening-of-america.

131 rare, early vintage Levi's David Sharp, "Don't Toss Those Old Jeans: 125-Year-Old Levi's Sell for Nearly $100K," *Mercury News*, May 26, 2018, mercurynews.com/2018/05/26/dont-toss-those-old-jeans-125-year -old-levis-sell-for-nearly-100k/.

131 a two-piece meditation pillow set "The Ritual Sit Set," Goop, goop.com/b -yoga-the-ritual-sit-set/one-size/p/?variant_id=99542.

131 pyramid-shaped mahogany cabinet Food & Wine, "Goop Opened a Ghost Kitchen to Deliver You a 'Clean' Lunch," Mar. 8, 2021, Yahoo Finance; finance.yahoo.com/news/goop-opened-ghost-kitchen-deliver-153628264 .html.

131 At the same time, a growing number of designers Colleen Kratofil, "Luxury Fashion Brands That Are Anti-fur," *People*, June 30, 2021, people.com/ style/fur-free-luxury-fashion-brands/.

132 In 2020, PETA announced "Victory! 'I'd Rather Go Naked Than Wear Fur' Goes Out with a Bang," PETA, peta.org/features/id-rather-go -naked-than-wear-fur-campaign-ends/; Oscar Holland, "PETA Ends 'I'd Rather Go Naked' Anti-fur Campaign After Three Decades," CNN, Feb. 5, 2020, cnn.com/style/article/peta-naked-fur-campaign -ends/index.html.

132 As of early 2022, a survey found Taylor Rogers, "Companies Urged to Hon-

our Racial Justice Pledges," *Financial Times,* Jan. 18, 2022, ft.com/
content/f29449c1-aa80-40b3-9794-5b02bb557019.

CHAPTER 7: THE CENTRIFUGAL REPUBLIC

135 **Its central precepts, he wrote** Steven Levy, *Hackers: Heroes of the Computer
Revolution* (Sebastopol, California: O'Reilly Media, 2010), 23–25.

136 **the development of "packet switching"** "The Origins of the Internet," in "A
Short History of the Internet," Science and Media Museum, Dec. 3, 2020,
scienceandmediamuseum.org.uk/objects-and-stories/short-history
-internet#what-is-packet-switching.

136 **an array of egalitarian protocols** "History of the Web," World Wide Web
Foundation, webfoundation.org/about/vision/history-of-the-web/.

137 **"has evolved into an engine of inequity"** Tim Berners-Lee, "One Small Step
for the Web . . . ," Medium, Sept. 29, 2018, medium.com/@timberners
_lee/one-small-step-for-the-web-87f92217d085.

137 **Berners-Lee has proposed a new platform** Solid, solidproject.org; Thomas
Macaulay, "Web Inventor Tim Berners-Lee: Screw Web3—My Decentralized Internet Doesn't Need Blockchain," TNW, June 23, 2022,
thenextweb.com/news/web-inventor-tim-berners-lee-screw-web3-my
-decentralized-internet-doesnt-need-blockchain; Peter Verdegem, "Tim
Berners-Lee's Plan to Save the Internet: Give Us Back Control of Our
Data," *Conversation,* Feb. 5, 2021, theconversation.com/tim-berners-lees
-plan-to-save-the-internet-give-us-back-control-of-our-data-154130;
Greg Noone, "What Is Web 3.0? Three Visions for the Internet's Future," *Tech Monitor,* Aug. 13, 2021, techmonitor.ai/technology/emerging
-technology/how-will-the-web-future-evolve.

138 **In 2014, Gavin Wood** Gavin Wood, "What Is Web 3? Here's How Future
Polkadot Founder Gavin Wood Explained It in 2014," Yahoo, Jan. 4, 2022,
yahoo.com/video/3-future-polkadot-founder-gavin-155942673.html.

138 **Bitcoin was released** Joshua Davis, "The Crypto-currency," *The New
Yorker,* Oct. 3, 2011, newyorker.com/magazine/2011/10/10/the-crypto
-currency.

138 **spectacular crash of the cryptocurrency exchange** Paul R. La Monica, "Crypto
Crash and Gold Sell-Off Show There's No Place for Investors to Hide,"
CNN Business, Nov. 10, 2022, cnn.com/2022/11/10/investing/bitcoin
-crypto-ftx-gold.

139 **"associations of a thousand" kinds** Alexis de Tocqueville, *Democracy in
America,* trans. Arthur Goldhammer (New York: The Library of America, 2012), 595.

140 **"belonged to 'pluribus,' not 'unum'"** Joseph Ellis, *The Cause: The American
Revolution and Its Discontents, 1773–1783* (New York: W. W. Norton),
Epilogue.

140 "arduous work" Hamilton to Washington, Mar. 24, 1783, Founders Online, founders.archives.gov/documents/Hamilton/01-03-02-0191.

141 "to be a Disunited People" Ellis, *Cause,* Kindle edition, p. 322.

141 As of January 2023 "State Partisan Composition," National Conference of State Legislatures, Feb. 28, 2023, ncsl.org/about-state-legislatures/state -partisan-composition.

142 The American Library Association reported Hillel Italie, "Book Ban Attempts Reach Record High in 2022, American Library Association Report Says," Canvas, *PBS NewsHour,* Mar. 23, 2023, pbs.org/newshour/arts/book -ban-attempts-reach-record-high-in-2022-american-library-association -report-says; American Library Association, "American Library Association Reports Record Number of Demands to Censor Library Books and Materials in 2022," press release, Mar. 22, 2023, ala.org/news/press -releases/2023/03/record-book-bans-2022; Eesha Pendharkar, "A School Librarian Pushes Back on Censorship and Gets Death Threats and Online Harassment," *Education Week,* Sept. 22, 2022, edweek.org/policy -politics/a-school-librarian-pushes-back-on-censorship-and-gets-death -threats-and-online-harassment/2022/09.

143 critical race theory as a hot-button topic Theodoric Meyer, Maggie Severns, and Meridith McGraw, "'The Tea Party to the 10th Power': Trumpworld Bets Big on Critical Race Theory," *Politico,* June 23, 2021, politico .com/news/2021/06/23/trumpworld-critical-race-theory-495712; Terry Gross, "Uncovering Who Is Driving the Fight Against Critical Race Theory in Schools," *Fresh Air,* NPR, June 24, 2021, npr.org/ 2021/06/24/1009839021/uncovering-who-is-driving-the-fight-against -critical-race-theory-in-schools; Sarah Schwartz, "Who's Really Driving Critical Race Theory Legislation? An Investigation," *Education Week,* July 19, 2021, edweek.org/policy-politics/whos-really-driving -critical-race-theory-legislation-an-investigation/2021/07.

143 In attempts to counter Republican policy-making Kelsey Butler, "Blue States Vow to Be Abortion Havens if Roe v. Wade Overturned," Bloomberg Law, May 3, 2022, news.bloomberglaw.com/health-law-and-business/ blue-states-vow-to-be-abortion-havens-if-roe-v-wade-overturned; Lisa Kashinsky, Shia Kapos, and Victoria Colliver, "Blue States Want to Become Abortion Safe Havens. It Will Cost Them," *Politico,* May 11, 2022, politico.com/news/2022/05/11/blue-states-abortion-safe-havens -00031526.

143 the AP reported apnews.com/article/abortion-ohio-ballot-e3db04beec5c 1edd860df5d648adfd60.

144 After the Supreme Court struck Myah Ward, "Blue State Gun Laws on the Chopping Block with Supreme Court Ruling," *Politico,* June 23, 2022, politico.com/news/2022/06/23/blue-state-gun-laws-scotus-00041934; Jeremy B. White and Katelyn Cordero, "The Supreme Court Knocked Back Blue States on Gun Restrictions. They're Seeing How Far They

Can Step Forward," *Politico*, July 8, 2022, politico.com/news/2022/07/08/blue-states-test-limits-of-gun-laws-after-supreme-court-raises-the-bar-00044486; Ali Watkins, "After Another Mass Shooting, New Jersey Tightens Gun Laws," *The New York Times*, July 5, 2022, nytimes.com/2022/07/05/nyregion/new-jersey-gun-law-murphy.html.

144 **In 2017, when President Trump announced** Elizabeth Shogren, "As Trump Retreats, States Are Joining Forces on Climate Action," *Yale Environment 360*, Oct. 9, 2017, e360.yale.edu/features/as-trump-retreats-states-are-stepping-up-on-climate-action; Sam Ricketts, Rita Cliffton, and Lola Oduyeru, "States Are Laying a Road Map for Climate Leadership," Center for American Progress, Apr. 30, 2020, americanprogress.org/article/states-laying-road-map-climate-leadership/; Sophie Quinton, "Trump's Environmental Actions Spark Resistance in Many States," Pew Charitable Trusts, Jan. 22, 2018, pewtrusts.org/en/research-and-analysis/blogs/stateline/2018/01/22/trumps-environmental-actions-spark-resistance-in-many-states/.

144 **"As the primary drivers of climate change"** Michael Bloomberg and Carl Pope, *Climate of Hope* (New York: St. Martin's Press, 2017), 21.

144 **C40 network** C40, c40.org/about-c40/.

144 **the "fifteen-minute city" concept** Linda Poon, Laura Millan Lombraña, and Sam Dodge, "Cities Are Our Best Hope for Surviving Climate Change," Bloomberg, Apr. 21, 2021, bloomberg.com/graphics/2021-cities-climate-solutions/?leadSource=uverify%20wall.

145 **In their 2006 book** Ori Brafman and Rod A. Beckstrom, *The Starfish and the Spider: The Unstoppable Power of Leaderless Organizations* (New York: Penguin Books), 17–21.

146 **A 2020 report** Gregor Jost et al., "How COVID-19 Is Redefining the Next-Normal Operating Model," *McKinsey Quarterly*, Dec. 10, 2020, mckinsey.com/capabilities/people-and-organizational-performance/our-insights/how-covid-19-is-redefining-the-next-normal-operating-model.

147 **"many of the dreary aspects"** Zeynep Tufekci, *Twitter and Tear Gas: The Power and Fragility of Networked Protest* loc. 94.

147 **"shared experience and tribulation"** Ibid., loc. 257.

147 **lack the institutional depth** Ibid., loc. 319–20.

147 **"In the twenty-first century"** Moisés Naím, *The End of Power: From Boardrooms to Battlefields and Churches to States, Why Being in Charge Isn't What It Used to Be* (New York: Basic Books, 2014), 1.

147 **In 2019, the anti-Semitic invective** Tracy McNicoll, "Yellow Vests at Crossroads as Anti-Semitic Incidents Cloud Message," France 24, Feb. 19, 2019, france24.com/en/20190219-france-yellow-vest-protests-crossroads-anti-semitic-insults-cloud-message-finkielkraut; Adam Nossiter, "Anti-Semitic Taunts by Yellow Vests Prompt French Soul-Searching," *The New York Times*, Feb. 18, 2019, nytimes.com/2019/02/18/world/europe/france-antisemitism-yellow-vests-alain-finkielkraut.html;

Alexander Hurst, "The Ugly, Illiberal, Anti-Semitic Heart of the Yellow Vest Movement," *New Republic*, Jan. 7, 2019, newrepublic.com/article/ 152853/ugly-illiberal-anti-semitic-heart-yellow-vest-movement.

148 **In fact the idea of "leaderless resistance"** Linda Pattillo, "Shadowy Threat of Extremist Hate Groups Quietly Growing," CNN, Apr. 24, 1998, cnn .com/SPECIALS/views/y/9804/pattillo.unholywar/.

148 **much the way that al-Qaeda and ISIS** Christine Abizaid (director, National Counterterrorism Center), statement for the record, U.S. Senate Committee on Homeland Security and Government Affairs, Annual Threat Assessment to the Homeland, Nov. 17, 2022, dni.gov/index.php/ newsroom/congressional-testimonies/congressional-testimonies -2022/item/2342-2022-ata-d-nctc-opening-statement-of-record-to -the-hsgac; J. M. Berger, "The Strategy of Violent White Supremacy Is Evolving," *The Atlantic*, Aug. 7, 2019, theatlantic.com/ideas/archive/ 2019/08/the-new-strategy-of-violent-white-supremacy/595648/.

148 **A paper published** Liam Collins, "Rapid and Radical Adaptation in Counterinsurgency: Task Force 714 in Iraq," Modern War Institute, Sept. 28, 2021, mwi.usma.edu/rapid-and-radical-adaptation-in-counterinsurgency -task-force-714-in-iraq/.

149 **"a new generation of Ukrainian leaders"** Simon Shuster and Vera Bergengruen, "Inside the Ukrainian Counterstrike That Turned the Tide of the War," *Time*, Sept. 26, 2022, time.com/6216213/ukraine-military-valeriy -zaluzhny/; Kris Osborn, "Ukraine's Decentralized Command Puts Russia on the Defensive," *National Interest*, Sept. 10, 2022, national interest.org/blog/buzz/ukraines-decentralized-command-puts-russia -defensive-204714.

149 **The high casualty rate** Meredith Deliso, "Why Russia Has Suffered the Loss of an 'Extraordinary' Number of Generals," ABC News, May 8, 2022, abcnews.go.com/International/russia-suffered-loss-extraordinary -number-generals/story?id=84545931.

149 **this archaic, top-down model** Max Boot, "Russia Keeps Losing Wars Because of Its Dysfunctional Military Culture," *The Washington Post*, Apr. 12, 2022, washingtonpost.com/opinions/2022/04/12/ukraine -military-culture-advantage-over-russia/.

150 **That agency's many initiatives** "State of Resilience: How Ukraine's Digital Government Is Supporting Its Citizens During the War," Tony Blair Institute for Global Change, Mar. 18, 2022, institute.global/insights/tech -and-digitalisation/state-resilience-how-ukraines-digital-government -supporting-its-citizens-during-war; Elise Labott, "'We Are the First in the World to Introduce This New Warfare': Ukraine's Digital Battle Against Russia," *Politico Magazine*, Mar. 8, 2022, politico.com/news/ magazine/2022/03/08/ukraine-digital-minister-crypto-cyber-social -media-00014880.

150 **The open-source investigative group Bellingcat** Ben Smith, "How Investigative Journalism Flourished in Hostile Russia," *The New York*

Times, Feb. 21, 2021, nytimes.com/2021/02/21/business/media/
probiv-investigative-reporting-russia.html; Scott Pelley, "Bellingcat:
The Online Investigators Tracking Alleged Russian War Crimes in
Ukraine," CBS News, May 15, 2022, cbsnews.com/news/bellingcat
-russia-putin-ukraine-60-minutes-2022-05-15/.

151 **"We don't have a chain of command"** Labott, " 'We Are the First in the
World to Introduce This New Warfare.' "

CHAPTER 8: OPTIMIZING MARGINALITY

153 **In a 1980 speech** Daniel J. Boorstin, "The Fertile Verge: Creativity in
the United States," scribd.com/document/117696334/Fertile-Verge
-by-Daniel-Boorstin#.

154 **Trump's immigration policies** Britta Glennon, "Why the Trump Administration's Anti-immigration Policies Are the United States' Loss and the
Rest of the World's Gain," Brookings, July 20, 2020, brookings.edu/
blog/up-front/2020/07/20/why-the-trump-administrations-anti
-immigration-policies-are-the-united-states-loss-and-the-rest-of-the
-worlds-gain/; Sonia Paul, "The Trump Administration Is Driving
Away Immigrant Entrepreneurs," *Defense One,* June 9, 2018, defenseone
.com/ideas/2018/06/trump-administration-driving-away-immigrant
-entrepreneurs/148829/.

154 **more than half of top U.S. tech companies** Maya Kosoff, "12 Immigrants Behind Some of Silicon Valley's Biggest Companies," *Vanity Fair,* Feb. 3, 2017,
vanityfair.com/news/photos/2017/02/12-immigrants-behind-some
-of-silicon-valleys-biggest-companies; Sara Salinas, "More Than Half
of the Top American Tech Companies Were Founded by Immigrants or
the Children of Immigrants," CNBC, May 30, 2018, cnbc.com/2018/
05/30/us-tech-companies-founded-by-immigrants-or-the-children-of
-immigrants.html; Tina Huang, Zachary Arnold, and Remco Zwetsloot,
"Most of America's 'Most Promising' AI Startups Have Immigrant Founders," Center for Security and Emerging Technology, Oct. 2020, cset
.georgetown.edu/wp-content/uploads/CSET-Most-of-Americas-Most
-Promising-AI-Startups-Have-Immigrant-Founders.pdf.

154 **A 2019 Stanford University paper** Shai Bernstein, Rebecca Diamond, Ab-
hisit Jiranaphawiboon, Timothy McQuade, and Beatriz Pousada, "The
Contribution of High-Skilled Immigrants to Innovation in the United
States" (Dec. 17, 2022), 2, stanford.edu/~diamondr/BDMP.pdf.

155 **a 2021 Cato Institute study** Robert Krol, "Effects of Immigration on Entrepreneurship and Innovation," *Cato Journal* (Fall 2021), cato.org/cato
-journal/fall-2021/effects-immigration-entrepreneurship-innovation.

155 **"as immigrants themselves"** Neal Gabler, *An Empire of Their Own: How the
Jews Invented Hollywood* (New York: Knopf Doubleday, 2010), 5.

156 **"America represented freedom"** David Lehman, *A Fine Romance: Jewish
Songwriters, American Songs* (New York: Schocken Books, 2009), 20.

156   "to compose the music and words" Ibid., 10.

156   When I interviewed the writer and actor Michiko Kakutani, "Myths, Dreams, Realities—Sam Shepard's America," *The New York Times,* Jan. 29, 1984, nytimes.com/1984/01/29/theater/myths-dreams-realities-sam-shepard -s-america.html.

157   Noubar Afeyan, describes innovation Joel Rose, "If COVID-19 Vaccines Bring an End to the Pandemic, America Has Immigrants to Thank," *All Things Considered,* NPR, Dec. 18, 2020, npr.org/2020/ 12/18/947638959/if-covid-19-vaccines-bring-an-end-to-the-pandemic -america-has-immigrants-to-than.

157   Afeyan is not the only immigrant Andreas Kluth, "Here's to the Immigrant Heroes Behind the BioNTech Vaccine," Bloomberg, Nov. 13, 2020, bloomberg.com/opinion/articles/2020-11-13/here-s-to-the-immigrant -heroes-behind-the-biontech-pfizer-vaccine?leadSource=uverify %20wall.

157   Katalin Karikó, who began studying mRNA "Katalin Kariko, Ph.D," Penn Medicine, pennmedicine.org/providers/profile/katalin-kariko.

158   It was a pioneering breakthrough Gina Kolata and Benjamin Mueller, "Halting Progress and Happy Accidents: How mRNA Vaccines Were Made," *The New York Times,* Jan. 15, 2022, nytimes.com/2022/01/15/health/ mrna-vaccine.html; Gina Kolata, "Kati Kariko Helped Shield the World from the Coronavirus," *The New York Times,* Apr. 8, 2021, nytimes.com/ 2021/04/08/health/coronavirus-mrna-kariko.html; Carolyn Y. Johnson, "A One-Way Ticket. A Cash-Stuffed Teddy Bear. A Dream Decades in the Making," *The Washington Post,* Oct. 1, 2021, washingtonpost .com/health/2021/10/01/katalin-kariko-covid-vaccines/; David Cox, "How mRNA Went from a Scientific Backwater to a Pandemic Crusher," *Wired,* Dec. 2, 2020, wired.co.uk/article/mrna-coronavirus-vaccine -pfizer-biontech.

159   "the fastest any vaccine" Philip Ball, "The Lightning-Fast Quest for COVID Vaccines—and What It Means for Other Diseases," *Nature,* Dec. 18, 2020, nature.com/articles/d41586-020-03626-1.

159   In this case, a decision was made "Novel 2019 Coronavirus Genome," Virological.org, virological.org/t/novel-2019-coronavirus-genome/319; Jon Cohen, "Chinese Researchers Reveal Draft Genome of Virus Implicated in Wuhan Pneumonia Outbreak," *Science,* Jan. 11, 2020, science .org/content/article/chinese-researchers-reveal-draft-genome-virus -implicated-wuhan-pneumonia-outbreak.

159   immediately started working Jon Gertner, "Un-locking the Covid Code," *The New York Times Magazine,* Mar. 25, 2021, nytimes.com/interactive/ 2021/03/25/magazine/genome-sequencing-covid-variants.html.

159   Moderna reported it had used Susie Neilson, Andrew Dunn, and Aria Bendix, "Moderna's Groundbreaking Coronavirus Vaccine Was Designed in Just 2 Days," *Insider,* Dec. 19, 2020, businessinsider.com/moderna -designed-coronavirus-vaccine-in-2-days-2020-11.

159 **by the end of 2020** Claire Klobucista, "A Guide to Global COVID-19 Vaccine Efforts," Center on Foreign Relations, Dec. 5, 2022, cfr.org/backgrounder/guide-global-covid-19-vaccine-efforts; World Health Organization, "COVAX Announces Additional Deals to Access Promising COVID-19 Vaccine Candidates; Plans Global Rollout Starting Q1 2021," news release, Dec. 18, 2020, who.int/news/item/18-12-2020-covax-announces-additional-deals-to-access-promising-covid-19-vaccine-candidates-plans-global-rollout-starting-q1-2021.

159 **The public posting of the COVID-19 genome** Charlie Campbell, "Exclusive: The Chinese Scientist Who Sequenced the First COVID-19 Genome Speaks Out About the Controversies Surrounding His Work," *Time*, Aug. 24, 2020, time.com/5882918/zhang-yongzhen-interview-china-coronavirus-genome/; Victoria Gill, "Coronavirus: Virus Provides Leaps in Scientific Understanding," BBC News, Jan. 10, 2021, bbc.com/news/science-environment-55565284; Jon Gertner, "Unlocking the Covid Code," *The New York Times Magazine*, Mar. 25, 2021, nytimes.com/interactive/2021/03/25/magazine/genome-sequencing-covid-variants.html; Mark Zastrow, "Open Science Takes on the Coronavirus Pandemic," *Nature*, Apr. 24, 2020, nature.com/articles/d41586-020-01246-3.

159 **Meanwhile, open sourcing during the pandemic** "Open Source Project Hubs for COVID-19," New America, newamerica.org/digital-impact-governance-initiative/reports/building-and-reusing-open-source-tools-government/open-source-project-hubs-for-covid-19/.

160 **Taiwan, for instance, made some** Erin Hale, "How Taiwan Used Simple Tech to Help Contain Covid-19," BBC News, Feb. 25, 2022, bbc.com/news/business-60461732; Eric Jaffe, "How Open Data and Civic Participation Helped Taiwan Slow Covid," *Sidewalk Talk* (blog), Mar. 27, 2020, medium.com/sidewalk-talk/how-open-data-and-civic-participation-helped-taiwan-slow-covid-b1449bab5841.

160 **A growing number of organizations** U.S. General Services Administration, About CitizenScience.gov, citizenscience.gov/about/#; Citizen Science, *Scientific American*, scientificamerican.com/citizen-science/.

160 **As businesses have increasingly come** Luc Rinaldi, "A Kickstarter Approach to Science," *Maclean's*, Aug. 11, 2015, macleans.ca/economy/business/a-kickstarter-approach-to-science/; About Us, Wazoku, wazoku.com/about-us/; What Challenge Will You Solve Today?, Wazoku, wazoku.com/challenges/.

161 **"The more they teach you"** "Innovation Through Co-creation: Engaging Customers and Other Stakeholders," Mack Center for Technological Innovation, Wharton School, University of Pennsylvania, Nov. 18, 2011, mackinstitute.wharton.upenn.edu/wp-content/uploads/2012/12/Innovation-through-Co-Creation_Full-Conference-Summary.pdf.

161 **3M has long had a 15 percent rule** "Richard Gurley Drew," National Inventors Hall of Fame, invent.org/inductees/richard-gurley-drew; Emily

Matchar, "How the Invention of Scotch Tape Led to a Revolution in
How Companies Managed Employees," *Smithsonian Magazine*, June 20,
2019, smithsonianmag.com/innovation/how-invention-scotch-tape-led
-revolution-how-companies-managed-employees-180972437.

161 Decades later, Post-it notes "History Timeline: Post-it Notes," Post-it, post
-it.com/3M/en_US/post-it/contact-us/about-us/; "A Mishap with a
Bookmark Changed How We Communicate, Forever," 3M, 3m.com.au/
3M/en_AU/company-au/news-releases/full-story/?storyid=c2e52b7a
-c422-4383-84a7-9c3f883ebdad.

162 Crash the Super Bowl contest Paul R. La Monica, "Doritos: You Create
Our Super Bowl Commercial," CNN Money, Sept. 14, 2006, money
.cnn.com/2006/09/14/news/funny/doritos_superbowl/index.htm;
Chris Plante, "Doritos and the Decade-Long Scam for Free Super Bowl
Commercials," *Verge*, Feb. 3, 2016, theverge.com/2016/2/3/10898942/
doritos-super-bowl-commercial-contest.

162 Lego reported a $238 million loss Daryl Austin, "The Inside Story of
How a 'Band of Misfits' Saved Lego," *National Geographic*, July 21,
2021, nationalgeographic.com/culture/article/adult-legos; Johnny
Davis, "How Lego Clicked: The Super Brand That Reinvented Itself,"
Observer, June 4, 2017, theguardian.com/lifeandstyle/2017/jun/04/
how-lego-clicked-the-super-brand-that-reinvented-itself.

162 revenue of $3.62 billion "Lego Towers over Competition with Record
2021 Profit," Motley Fool, Sept. 28, 2021, fool.com/investing/2021/
09/28/lego-towers-over-competition-with-record-2021-prof/; Associated Press, "Lego Profit Surges as Revenue Jumps 46%," MarketWatch,
Sept. 28, 2021, marketwatch.com/story/lego-profit-surges-as-revenue
-jumps-46-01632815116.

162 Winning ideas, the Lego website says Product Idea Guidelines, Lego, ideas
.lego.com/guidelines.

162 Popular fan-designed products Austin, "Inside Story of How a 'Band of
Misfits' Saved Lego"; Davis, "How Lego Clicked."

163 When they first published a paper Ronak Gupta, "What Wiped Out the Dinosaurs?," *Wire*, May 10, 2016, thewire.in/environment/what-wiped-out
-the-dinosaurs; Yarris, "Alvarez Theory on Dinosaur Die-Out Upheld,"
newscenter.lbl.gov/2010/03/09/alvarez-theory-on-dinosaur/#:~:
text=An%20international%20panel%20of%20experts,the%20extinction
%20of%20the%20dinosaurs; Diana Crow, "A Catastrophic Hypothesis," *Lateral*, Aug. 23, 2018, lateralmag.com/columns/paradigms/a
-catastrophic-hypothesis.

163 Their theory was validated by the discovery Geoff Brumfiel, "Geologists
Find Clues in Crater Left by Dinosaur-Killing Asteroid," *All Things
Considered*, NPR, May 6, 2016, npr.org/sections/thetwo-way/2016/
05/06/476871766/geologists-find-clues-in-crater-left-by-dinosaur
-killing-asteroid; Riley Black, "What Happened the Day a Giant,
Dinosaur-Killing Asteroid Hit the Earth," *Smithsonian Magazine*,

Sept. 9, 2019, smithsonianmag.com/science-nature/dinosaur-killing
-asteroid-impact-chicxulub-crater-timeline-destruction-180973075/;
Douglas Preston, "The Day the Dinosaurs Died," *The New Yorker*,
Mar. 29, 2019, newyorker.com/magazine/2019/04/08/the-day-the
-dinosaurs-died.

164 **Together, Penfield and Hildebrand located** Charles Q. Choi, "Chicxulub
Asteroid Impact: The Dino-Killer That Scientists Laughed At," Space
.com, Feb. 7, 2013, space.com/19681-dinosaur-killing-asteroid-chicxulub
-crater.html; Michael J. Benton, "How Does an Invisible Underwater Crater Prove an Asteroid Killed the Dinosaurs?," *Conversation*, Apr. 14, 2016,
theconversation.com/how-does-an-invisible-underwater-crater-prove
-an-asteroid-killed-the-dinosaurs-57711; Sean B. Carroll, "The Day the
Mesozoic Died," *Nautilus*, Jan. 13, 2016, nautil.us/the-day-the-mesozoic
-died-235760/.

164 **the Alvarezes' theory was ratified in 2010** Yarris, "Alvarez Theory on Dinosaur Die-Out Upheld"; Paul Rincon, "Dinosaur Extinction Link to Crater Confirmed," BBC News, Mar. 4, 2010, news.bbc.co.uk/2/hi/8550
504.stm.

164 **In his 1997 book** Walter Alvarez, T. rex *and the Crater of Doom* (Princeton,
NJ: Princeton University Press, 2013), 83–84.

165 **Steve Jobs liked to describe creativity** Gary Wolf, "Steve Jobs: The Next In-
sanely Great Thing," *Wired*, Feb. 1, 1996, wired.com/1996/02/jobs-2/;
Steve Jobs, commencement address, Stanford University, June 12, 2005,
news.stanford.edu/2005/06/12/youve-got-find-love-jobs-says/.

165 **"in the beginner's mind"** Shunryu Suzuki, *Zen Mind, Beginner's Mind*
(Boulder, Colorado: Shambhala Publications, 2020), 1.

CHAPTER 9: RESILIENCE IN THE VUCA-VERSE

167 **"a time of crisis"** Desmond Tutu, *Crying in the Wilderness* (London: Mow-
bray, 1990), 15.

168 **Trump signed a law watering down** David Enrich, "Back-to-Back Bank Col-
lapses Came After Deregulatory Push," *The New York Times*, Mar. 13,
2023, nytimes.com/2023/03/13/business/signature-silicon-valley-bank
-dodd-frank-regulation.html.

169 **"only a crisis—actual or perceived"** Naomi Klein, *Shock Doctrine: The Rise of
Disaster Capitalism* (New York: Picador, 2011), 174.

169 **"foreign investors and international lenders"** Ibid., 9.

169 **"malleable moments when we are psychologically unmoored"** Ibid., 25–26.

170 **when Mitch Landrieu took office** Klint Finley, "How New Orleans Built a
Bustling Tech Hub in Katrina's Wake," *Wired*, Aug. 28, 2015, wired
.com/2015/08/new-orleans-built-bustling-tech-hub-katrinas-wake/;
Jaquetta White, "Mitch Landrieu Says Hurricane Katrina, While Tragic,
Spurred Positive Change for New Orleans," NOLA.com, Apr. 29, 2015,
nola.com/news/politics/mitch-landrieu-says-hurricane-katrina-while

-tragic-spurred-positive-change-for-new-orleans/article_398e4077-efc3
-54e1-80be-c52701abac4c.html; Tom Dart, "New Orleans Launches Resilience Roadmap to Tackle Climate and Social Challenges," *The Guardian*, Aug. 26, 2015, theguardian.com/cities/2015/aug/26/new-orleans
-resilience-roadmap-climate-social-issues; Amy Liu, "Building a Better
New Orleans: A Review of and Plan for Progress One Year After Hurricane Katrina," Brookings Institution, Aug. 2006, brookings.edu/wp
-content/uploads/2016/06/200608_katrinareview.pdf; "Hurricane Katrina Statistics Fast Facts," CNN, Jan. 16, 2023, cnn.com/2013/08/23/
us/hurricane-katrina-statistics-fast-facts/index.html.

170 **The terrorist attacks of 9/11** "September 11 Attacks," History, updated
Mar. 27, 2023, history.com/topics/21st-century/9-11-attacks#section_6;
nytimes.com/2021/09/06/nyregion/9-11-ground-zero-victims-remains
.html.

170 **Under the direction of Mayor Michael Bloomberg** Alina Selyukh, "How
New York City Rebuilt Anew After Its Darkest Day," *15 Years Later: The
Sept. 11 Terrorist Attacks*, NPR, Sept. 8, 2016, npr.org/2016/09/08/
492960193/how-new-york-city-rebuilt-anew-after-its-darkest-day.

170 **A key component in New York City's comeback** Annie Correal, "How
N.Y.C.'s Population Expert Says the City Will Bounce Back," *The New
York Times*, Apr. 1, 2021, nytimes.com/2021/04/01/nyregion/nyc
-population-pandemic-recovery.html.

171 **By the end of World War II, an estimated fifty-three million** "World War II,"
Defense Casualty Analysis System, Defense Manpower Data Center,
Office of the Secretary of Defense, U.S. Department of Defense, dcas
.dmdc.osd.mil/dcas/app/conflictCasualties/ww2.

171 **another sixty million had been uprooted** "The Blast of World War II," *Britannica*, britannica.com/topic/history-of-Europe/The-blast-of-World
-War-II.

171 **In Hiroshima, an estimated 140,000 people** Seren Morris, "How Many People
Died in Hiroshima and Nagasaki?," *Newsweek*, Aug. 3, 2020, newsweek
.com/how-many-people-died-hiroshima-nagasaki-japan-second-world
-war-1522276.

171 **The U.S. firebombing of Tokyo** "Legacy of the Great Tokyo Air Raid,"
Japan Times, Mar. 15, 2015, japantimes.co.jp/opinion/2015/03/15/
editorials/legacy-great-tokyo-air-raid.

171 **1945 was called "Year Zero"** Neal Ascherson, "Year Zero: A History of 1945
by Ian Buruma—Review," Oct. 11, 2013, book review, *The Guardian*,
theguardian.com/books/2013/oct/11/year-zero-1945-ian-buruma
-review.

172 **"head off a return of the old demons"** Tony Judt, *Postwar: A History of Europe Since 1945* (New York: Penguin Books, 2006), 6.

173 **"So many of our advances"** Margaret MacMillan, *War: How Conflict Shaped
Us* (New York: Random House, 2020), 25.

173 **mass-produced by the drugmaker Pfizer** Judah Ginsberg, "Pfizer's Work

on Penicillin for World War II Becomes a National Historic Chemical Landmark," ACS, news release, June 12, 2008, acs.org/pressroom/newsreleases/2008/june/pfizers-work-on-penicillin-for-world-war-ii-becomes-a-national-historic-chemical-landmark.html.

173 **Penicillin and other antibiotics** "Find Out What Medical Development Helped World War II Soldiers," *Britannica,* britannica.com/video/222824/medical-inventions-World-War-II; Ellen Hampton, "How World War I Revolutionized Medicine," *The Atlantic,* Feb. 24, 2017, theatlantic.com/health/archive/2017/02/world-war-i-medicine/517656/.

173 **"To say that war brings benefits"** MacMillan, *War,* 28.

173 **It's an argument that echoes ideas** Barry Eichengreen, "Schumpeter's Virus: How 'Creative Destruction' Could Save the Coronavirus Economy," *Prospect,* May 26, 2020, prospectmagazine.co.uk/ideas/economics/40254/schumpeters-virus-how-creative-destruction-could-save-the-coronavirus-economy; Sharon Reier, "Half a Century Later, Economist's 'Creative Destruction' Theory Is Apt for the Internet Age: Schumpeter: The Prophet of Bust and Boom," *The New York Times,* June 10, 2000, nytimes.com/2000/06/10/your-money/IHT-half-a-century-later-economists-creative-destruction-theory-is.html; Richard Florida, "Innovation and Economic Crises," *The Atlantic,* July 17, 2009, theatlantic.com/national/archive/2009/07/innovation-and-economic-crises/20576/.

174 **DuPont introduced neoprene** Tom Nicholas, "Innovation Lessons from the 1930s," *McKinsey Quarterly,* Dec. 2008, hbs.edu/ris/Publication%20Files/Tom_McKinsey_Quarterly_8421a1a0-0104-4cf1-843d-fc32fa51ddoa.pdf.

174 **the handheld cellphone** *Britannica,* "Martin Cooper," britannica.com/biography/Martin-Cooper.

174 **Airbnb, which was valued** "How Airbnb Was Built: It Started as Air Beds on the Floor for a Conference," *NZ Herald,* Oct. 9, 2020, nzherald.co.nz/business/how-airbnb-was-built-it-started-as-air-beds-on-the-floor-for-a-conference/MRDCZ3E6VBGNU4CVSTJ5PXJOTE/; Knowledge at Wharton, "The Inside Story Behind the Unlikely Rise of Airbnb," *Knowledge at Wharton,* Apr. 26, 2017, knowledge.wharton.upenn.edu/podcast/knowledge-at-wharton-podcast/the-inside-story-behind-the-unlikely-rise-of-airbnb/.

175 **"the new mRNA technology"** Zeynep Tufekci, "3 Ways the Pandemic Has Made the World Better," *The Atlantic,* Mar. 18, 2021, theatlantic.com/health/archive/2021/03/three-ways-pandemic-has-bettered-world/618320/.

175 **"tidal wave of death"** Laura Spinney, "The World Changed Its Approach to Health After the 1918 Flu. Will It After the COVID-19 Outbreak?," *Time,* Mar. 7, 2020, time.com/5797629/health-1918-flu-epidemic/.

176 **the science writer John Kelly argues** John Kelly, *The Great Mortality: An Intimate History of the Black Death, the Most Devastating Plague of All Time* (New York: HarperCollins, 2005), Kindle edition, pp. 325–26.

176 "Someone figured out that one easy" Ibid., 62.

177 **Marine Le Pen** Paul Kirby, "French Election: Far-Right Le Pen's Long Quest for Power in France," BBC News, Apr. 22, 2022, bbc.com/news/world-europe-61147709.

177 **still won 41.5 percent of the vote** Rick Noack, Michael Birnbaum, and Elie Petit, "France's Macron Wins Presidency, Holding Off Le Pen's Far-Right Threat to Upend Europe and Relations with Russia," *The Washington Post*, Apr. 24, 2022, washingtonpost.com/world/2022/04/24/french-election-2022-results/.

177 **Months later, Giorgia Meloni** Associated Press, "Italy's Far-Right Leader Giorgia Meloni Forms New Government," NBC News, Oct. 21, 2022, nbcnews.com/news/world/italy-far-right-leader-giorgia-meloni-new-government-fascist-roots-rcna53453/.

177 **And in Sweden, a party with neo-Nazi roots** Steven Erlanger and Christina Anderson, "How the Far Right Bagged Election Success in Sweden," *The New York Times*, Sept. 17, 2022, nytimes.com/2022/09/17/world/europe/sweden-far-right-election.html.

177 **A 2021 survey found that 78 percent** Fredrik Carlsson et al., "The Climate Decade: Changing Attitudes on Three Continents," Resources for the Future, Jan. 2021, rff.org/publications/working-papers/the-climate-decade-changing-attitudes-on-three-continents/.

178 **The army plans to cut emissions** Michael Birnbaum and Tik Root, "The U.S. Army Has Released Its First-Ever Climate Strategy. Here's What That Means," *The Washington Post*, Feb. 10, 2022, washingtonpost.com/climate-solutions/2022/02/10/army-military-green-climate-strategy/.

178 **the navy launched its "Great Green Fleet"** "The Great Green Fleet," *All Hands,* allhands.navy.mil/Features/GGF/.

179 **for thousands of years** "Ar6 Synthesis Report: Summary for Policymakers Headline Statements," Intergovernmental Panel on Climate Change, 2023, ipcc.ch/report/ar6/syr/resources/spm-headline-statements/.

EPILOGUE

182 **One of his lesser-known prints** "Rare Hokusai Woodblock Is Themed on 1707 Mt. Fuji Eruption," *Asahi Shimbun*, May 6, 2019, asahi.com/ajw/articles/13063386; "Hokusai, a Master of the Elements," *Elemental Japan*, Aug. 15, 2020, elementaljapan.com/2020/08/15/hokusai-a-master-of-the-elements/.

182 **which occurred in 1707** Naomichi Miyaji et al., "High-Resolution Reconstruction of the Hoei Eruption (AD 1707) of Fuji Volcano, Japan," *Journal of Volcanology and Geothermal Research* 207, nos. 3–4 (2011): 113–29, sciencedirect.com/science/article/abs/pii/S0377027311001879.

183 **an average of fifteen hundred earthquakes a year** Brett Israel, "Japan's Explosive Geology Explained," Live Science, Sept. 15, 2022, livescience.com/30226-japan-tectonics-explosive-geology-ring-of-fire-110314.html.

183 **Disaster Prevention Day** J. Charles Schencking, "The Great Kantō Earth-quake of 1923 and the Japanese Nation," *Education About Asia* 12, no. 2 (Fall 2007), asianstudies.org/wp-content/uploads/the-great-kanto-earth quake-of-1923-and-the-japanese-nation.pdf; Yuko Tamura, "Take Some Time to Refresh Your Emergency Vocabulary on Disaster Prevention Day," *Japan Times*, Sept. 1, 2022, japantimes.co.jp/life/2022/09/01/language/take-time-refresh-emergency-vocabulary-disaster-prevention -day.

183 **It has also implemented** Bob Yirka, "Japanese Companies Develop Quake Damping Pendulums for Tall Buildings," Phys.org, Aug. 2, 2013, phys .org/news/2013-08-japanese-companies-quake-damping-pendulums .html; "Construction Expertise from Japan: Earthquake Proof Build-ings," PlanRadar, May 27, 2022, planradar.com/gb/japan-earthquake -proof-buildings; Martha Henriques, "How Japan's Skyscrapers Are Built to Survive Earthquakes," BBC Future, Jan. 16, 2019, bbc.com/ future/article/20190114-how-japans-skyscrapers-are-built-to-survive -earthquakes.

183 **Still, nothing could prepare Japan** Kevin Voigt, "Quake Moved Japan Coast 8 Feet, Shifted Earth's Axis," CNN, Apr. 20, 2011, cnn.com/2011/ WORLD/asiapcf/03/12/japan.earthquake.tsunami.earth/index.html.

183 **Together, these three disasters** Mari Yamaguchi, "Still Recovering, Japan Marks 10 Years Since Tsunami Hit," AP News, Mar. 11, 2021, apnews .com/article/world-news-yoshihide-suga-tsunamis-japan-earthquakes -9779f932f8205815c0b217aab6b6a42b; Elizabeth Ferris and Mireya Solís, "Earthquake, Tsunami, Meltdown—the Triple Disaster's Impact on Japan, Impact on the World," Brookings, Mar. 11, 2013, brookings.edu/ blog/up-front/2013/03/11/earthquake-tsunami-meltdown-the-triple -disasters-impact-on-japan-impact-on-the-world/.

184 **The plans experts devised** Michael Carlowicz, "Ten Years After the Tsu-nami," Earth Observatory, earthobservatory.nasa.gov/images/148036/ ten-years-after-the-tsunami.

184 **one step toward fighting the multiplying dangers** European Commis-sion, "Digital Services Act: EU's Landmark Rules for Online Plat-forms Enter into Force," press release, Nov. 16, 2022, ec.europa.eu/ commission/presscorner/detail/en/IP_22_6906; Adam Satariano, "E.U. Takes Aim at Social Media's Harms with Landmark New Law," *The New York Times*, Apr. 22, 2022, nytimes.com/2022/04/22/technology/ european-union-social-media-law.html.

185 **Finland launched a national curriculum** Jon Henley, "How Finland Starts Its Fight Against Fake News in Primary Schools," *The Guardian*, Jan. 29, 2020, theguardian.com/world/2020/jan/28/fact-from-fiction-finlands -new-lessons-in-combating-fake-news; Eliza Mackintosh, "Finland Is Winning the War on Fake News. What It's Learned May Be Crucial to Western Democracy," CNN, edition.cnn.com/interactive/2019/05/ europe/finland-fake-news-intl/; Jenny Gross, "How Finland Is Teach-

ing a Generation to Spot Misinformation," *The New York Times,* Jan. 10, 2023, nytimes.com/2023/01/10/world/europe/finland-misinformation -classes.html.

185 **alarming drop in student test scores** ipcc.ch/report/ar6/syr/resources/ spm-headline-statements.

186 **The updated Electoral Count Act** Clare Foran, "Congress Passes First Legislative Response to January 6 Capitol Attack," CNN, Dec. 23, 2022, cnn.com/2022/12/23/politics/congress-legislation-january-6-capitol -attack/index.html; Amy B. Wang and Liz Goodwin, "House Joins Senate in Passing Electoral Count Act Overhaul in Response to Jan. 6 Attack," *The Washington Post,* Dec. 23, 2022, washingtonpost.com/ politics/2022/12/19/electoral-count-reform-omnibus/.

187 **demolishing vital checks and balances** Jonathan Swan, Charlie Savage, and Maggie Haberman, "Trump and Allies Forge Plans to Increase Presidential Power in 2025," *The New York Times,* updated July 18, 2023, nytimes .com/2023/07/17/us/politics/trump-plans-2025.html.

187 **"built on a basic assumption"** David Montgomery, "The Abnormal Presidency," *The Washington Post,* Nov. 10, 2020, washingtonpost.com/ graphics/2020/lifestyle/magazine/trump-presidential-norm-breaking -list/.

187 **"the Yeats Test"** Fintan O'Toole, " 'Yeats Test' Criteria Reveal We Are Doomed," *Irish Times,* July 28, 2018, irishtimes.com/opinion/fintan-o -toole-yeats-test-criteria-reveal-we-are-doomed-1.3576078.

188 **Indeed, phrases from that poem** William Butler Yeats, "The Second Coming," Poetry Foundation, poetryfoundation.org/poems/43290/the-second -coming.

188 **another burst of "Second Coming" citations** Scott Simon, "Opinion: Reading William Butler Yeats 100 Years Later," *Weekend Edition Saturday,* NPR, Nov. 28, 2020, npr.org/2020/11/28/939561949/opinion-reading -william-butler-yeats-100-years-later; Dorian Lynskey, " 'Things Fall Apart': The Apocalyptic Appeal of WB Yeats's the Second Coming," *The Guardian,* May 30, 2020, theguardian.com/books/2020/may/30/ things-fall-apart-the-apocalyptic-appeal-of-wb-yeats-the-second -coming.

188 **His favorite poet, however** Chloe Foussianes, "Joe Biden's Love of Irish Poet Seamus Heaney Dates Back to His Teenage Years," *Town & Country,* Jan. 19, 2021, townandcountrymag.com/society/politics/a35253095/joe -biden-seamus-heaney-irish-poet/; Jonathan Jones, "Joe Biden's Love for Seamus Heaney Reveals a Soul You Can Trust," Books Blog, *The Guardian,* Nov. 9, 2020, theguardian.com/books/booksblog/2020/ nov/09/joe-biden-love-for-seamus-heaney-poetry.

188 **Biden's favorite Heaney lines** Paul Corcoran, "Why Joe Biden Keeps Quoting Seamus Heaney on When 'Hope and History Rhyme,' " *America: The Jesuit Review,* Mar. 17, 2021, americamagazine.org/arts-culture/ 2021/03/17/joe-biden-seamus-heaney-240256.

189 "hope for a great sea-change" Seamus Heaney, *The Cure at Troy* (New York: Farrar, Straus and Giroux, 1991), 77.

189 "the extraordinary events" Mark Ringer, "THEATER; Ancient Troy Meets Modern Troubles in a Poet's Drama," *The New York Times*, Mar. 29, 1998, nytimes.com/1998/03/29/theater/theater-ancient-troy-meets-modern-troubles-in-a-poet-s-drama.html.

189 the Good Friday Agreement "Good Friday Agreement: What is it?," BBC News, Apr. 3, 2023, bbc.com/news/uk-northern-ireland-61968177.

189 "It opened the door" "The Guardian View on the Good Friday Agreement: Still a Shared Achievement," *The Guardian*, Apr. 9, 2018, the guardian.com/commentisfree/2018/apr/09/the-guardian-view-on-the-good-friday-agreement-still-a-shared-achievement.

189 In a 1996 letter to a friend Heaney to Marianne McDonald, quoted in Marianne McDonald, "Seamus Heaney: An Irish Poet Mines the Classics," in *Seamus Heaney and the Classics: Bann Valley Muses*, ed. Stephen Harrison, Fiona Macintosh, and Helen Eastman (Oxford: Oxford University Press, 2019), 133–34.

ADDITIONAL SOURCES

Azhar, Azeem, *The Exponential Age: How Accelerating Technology Is Trans-forming Business, Politics and Society* (New York: Diversion Books, 2021).

Balfour, Amelie, *Hokusai: Thirty-Six Views of Mount Fuji* (New York: Prestel, 2019).

Beard, Mary, *S.P.Q.R.: A History of Ancient Rome* (New York: W.W. Norton & Company, 2016).

Bishop, Bill, *The Big Sort: Why the Clustering of Like-Minded America Is Tearing Us Apart* (New York: Mariner Books, 2009).

Boorstin, Daniel J., *The Daniel J. Boorstin Reader* (New York: The Modern Library, 1995).

Bremmer, Ian, *The Power of Crisis: How Three Threats—and Our Response—Will Change the World* (New York: Simon & Schuster, 2022).

Bridgeman, Tess, and Brianna Rosen, "National Security Implications of Trump's Indictment: A Damage Assessment," *Just Security,* June 10, 2023, justsecurity.org/86887/national-security-implications-of-trumps -indictment-a-damage-assessment/.

Brockman, John, ed., *Culture: Leading Scientists Explore Societies, Art, Power, and Technology* (New York: Edge Foundation, Inc., 2011).

Brownstein, Ronald, *The Second Civil War: How Extreme Partisanship Has Paralyzed Washington and Polarized America* (New York: Penguin Books, 2008).

Cantor, Norman F., *In the Wake of the Plague: The Black Death & the World It Made* (New York: Simon & Schuster, 2015).

Carney, Timothy P., *Alienated America: Why Some Places Thrive While Others Collapse* (New York: Harper Paperbacks, 2020).

Chenoweth, Erica, *Civil Resistance: What Everyone Needs to Know* (New York: Oxford University Press, 2021).

Christensen, Clayton M., *The Innovator's Dilemma: When New Technologies Cause Great Firms to Fail* (Boston: Harvard Business Review Press, 2015).

Diamond, Jared, *Upheaval: Turning Points for Nations in Crisis* (New York: Little, Brown and Company, 2019).

Foner, Eric, *The Second Founding: How the Civil War and Reconstruction Remade the Constitution* (New York: W.W. Norton & Company, 2019).

Forrer, Matthi, ed., *Hokusai: Prints and Drawings* (New York: Prestel, 2019).

Fukuyama, Francis, *The End of History and the Last Man* (New York: Free Press, 2006).

Fussell, Paul, *The Great War and Modern Memory* (New York: Oxford University Press, 2013).

Gerstle, Gary, *The Rise and Fall of the Neoliberal Order: America and the World in the Free Market Era* (New York: Oxford University Press, 2022).

Gitlin, Todd, *Occupy Nation: The Roots, the Spirit, and the Promise of Occupy Wall Street* (New York: It Books/HarperCollins, 2012).

Glaude, Eddie S., Jr., *Begin Again: James Baldwin's America and Its Urgent Lessons for Today* (New York: Chatto & Windus, 2021).

Gleick, James, *The Information: A History, a Theory, a Flood* (New York: Vintage, 2011).

Goldberg, Jeffrey, "Trump: Americans Who Died in War Are 'Losers' and 'Suckers,'" *The Atlantic*, Sept. 3, 2020, theatlantic.com/politics/archive/2020/09/trump-americans-who-died-at-war-are-losers-and-suckers/615997/?utm_source=twitter&utm_medium=social&utm_campaign=share.

Grandin, Greg, *The End of the Myth: From the Frontier to the Border Wall in the Mind of America* (New York: Metropolitan Books, 2020).

Guth, Christine M. E., *Hokusai's Great Wave* (Honolulu: University of Hawaii Press, 2015).

Hale, Grace Elizabeth, *A Nation of Outsiders: How the White Middle Class Fell in Love with Rebellion in Postwar America* (New York: Oxford University Press, 2011).

Hamilton, Alexander, James Madison, and John Jay, *The Federalist Papers* (Dublin, OH: Coventry House Publishing, 2015).

Herbst, Susan, *Politics at the Margin: Historical Studies of Public Expression Outside the Mainstream* (New York: Cambridge University Press, 1994).

Herlihy, David, and Samuel K. Cohn, Jr., eds., *The Black Death and the Transformation of the West* (Cambridge, MA: Harvard University Press, 1997).

Hirschman, Charles, "Contributions of Immigrants to American Culture," *Daedalus* 142, no. 3, Summer 2013.

Hofstadter, Richard, *Anti-intellectualism in American Life* (New York: Vintage, 1963).

———, *The Age of Reform: From Bryan to FDR* (New York: Vintage Books, 2011).

hooks, bell, *Feminist Theory: From Margin to Center* (New York: Routledge, 2015).

Huizinga, Johan, *The Waning of the Middle Ages* (Chicago: Steppenwolf Press, 2019).

Isaacson, Walter, *Steve Jobs* (New York: Simon & Schuster, 2011).

Jones, Steve, *Antonio Gramsci* (New York: Routledge, 2006).

Kakutani, Michiko, "Democracies Around the World Are Under Threat. Ours Is No Exception," *Los Angeles Times*, Oct. 31, 2020, latimes.com/opinion/story/2020-10-31/op-ed-democracies-around-the-world-are-under-threat.

Klein, Ezra, *Why We're Polarized* (New York: Simon & Schuster, 2020).

Lanier, Jaron, *You Are Not a Gadget* (New York: Vintage Books, 2011).

Lipset, Seymour Martin, and Earl Raab, *The Politics of Unreason: Right-Wing Extremism in America, 1790–1970* (New York: Harper & Row, 1970).

Luce, Edward, *The Retreat of Western Liberalism* (New York: Atlantic Monthly Press, 2017).

MacMillan, Margaret, *The Rhyme of History: Lessons of the Great War* (Washington, D.C.: Brookings Institution Press, 2013).

Marantz, Andrew, "Does Hungary Offer a Glimpse of Our Authoritarian Future?," *The New Yorker*, July 4, 2022, newyorker.com/magazine/2022/07/04/does-hungary-offer-a-glimpse-of-our-authoritarian-future.

Markoff, John, *What the Dormouse Said: How the Sixties Counterculture Shaped the Personal Computer Industry* (New York: Penguin Books, 2006).

McLuhan, Marshall, Quentin Fiore, and Shepard Fairey (illustrator), *The Medium Is the Massage: An Inventory of Effects* (Berkeley: Gingko Press, 2001).

Mishra, Pankaj, *Age of Anger: A History of the Present* (New York: Farrar, Straus and Giroux, 2017).

Monbiot, George, *How Did We Get into This Mess?: Politics, Equality, Nature* (Brooklyn: Verso, 2017).

Muller, Jan-Werner, *What Is Populism?* (Philadelphia: University of Pennsylvania Press, 2016).

Nisbet, Robert A., *The Sociology of Emile Durkheim* (New York: Oxford University Press, 1974).

Orwell, George, *Nineteen Eighty-Four* (New York: Mariner Books, 2013).

Osnos, Evan, *Wildland: The Making of America's Fury* (New York: Farrar, Straus and Giroux, 2021).

Palmer, Robert, *Blues & Chaos: The Music Writing of Robert Palmer*, edited by Anthony DeCurtis (New York: Scribner, 2009).

Parker, Ashley, and Josh Dawsey, "Constraints on Presidency Being Redefined in Trump Era, Report Fallout Shows," *The Washington Post*, Apr. 22, 2019, washingtonpost.com/politics/constraints-on-presidency

-being-redefined-in-trump-era-report-fallout-shows/2019/04/22/
6ebed060-6510-11e9-a1b6-b29b90efa879_story.html.

Piven, Frances Fox, *Challenging Authority: How Ordinary People Change America* (Washington, D.C.: Rowman & Littlefield, 2006).

Pomerantsev, Peter, *Nothing Is True and Everything Is Possible* (New York: PublicAffairs, 2015).

Potter, David, *Disruption: Why Things Change* (New York: Oxford University Press, 2021).

Raymond, Eric S., *The Cathedral & the Bazaar: Musings on Linux and Open Source by an Accidental Revolutionary* (Sebastopol, CA: O'Reilly Media, Inc., 2001).

Ross, Carne, *The Leaderless Revolution: How Ordinary People Will Take Power and Change Politics in the 21st Century* (New York: Plume, 2013).

Rubin, Jennifer, *Resistance: How Women Saved Democracy from Donald Trump* (New York: William Morrow, 2021).

Schama, Simon, *The American Future: A History* (New York: Ecco Press, 2009).

Schmidt, Michael S., Alan Feuer, Maggie Haberman, and Adam Goldman, "Trump Supporters' Violent Rhetoric in His Defense Disturbs Experts," *The New York Times,* June 10, 2023, nytimes.com/2023/06/10/us/politics/trump-supporter-violent-rhetoric.html.

Scott, James C., *Seeing Like a State: How Certain Schemes to Improve the Human Condition Have Failed* (New Haven: Yale University Press, 1998), Kindle edition.

Snyder, Timothy, *The Road to Unfreedom: Russia, Europe, America* (New York: Crown, 2018).

Stiglitz, Joseph E., "The End of Neoliberalism and the Rebirth of History," Project Syndicate, Nov. 4, 2019, project-syndicate.org/commentary/end-of-neoliberalism-unfettered-markets-fail-by-joseph-e-stiglitz-2019-11?barrier=accesspaylog.

Thompson, Helen, *Disorder: Hard Times in the 21st Century* (New York: Oxford University Press, 2022).

Tooze, Adam, *Crashed: How a Decade of Financial Crises Changed the World* (New York: Penguin Books, 2018).

Wilson, Colin, *The Outsider* (New York: Jeremy P. Tarcher/Putnam, 1982).

Wolfe, Tom, ed., *The New Journalism* (New York: Picador Books, 1975).

Wu, Tim, *The Master Switch: The Rise and Fall of Information Empires* (New York: Vintage Books, 2010).

MICHIKO KAKUTANI is a
Pulitzer Prize–winning literary critic
and the former chief book critic of
The New York Times. She is also the
author of the *New York Times* bestseller
The Death of Truth, and *Ex Libris.*

Twitter: @michikokakutani

Instagram: @michi_kakutani